The Mexican War

DAVID S. HEIDLER AND
JEANNE T. HEIDLER

Greenwood Guides to Historic Events, 1500–1900
Linda S. Frey and Marsha L. Frey, Series Editors

GREENWOOD PRESS
Westport, Connecticut • London

Library of Congress Cataloging-in-Publication Data

Heidler, David Stephen, 1955–
   The Mexican War / David S. Heidler and Jeanne T. Heidler.
      p.   cm.—(Greenwood guides to historic events, 1500–1900, ISSN 1538–442X)
   Includes bibliographical references and index.
   ISBN 0–313–32792–0 (alk. paper)
   1. Mexican War, 1846–1848.   I. Heidler, Jeanne T.   II. Title.   III. Series.
E404.H44   2006
973.6'2—dc22   2005018724

British Library Cataloguing in Publication Data is available.

Library of Congress Catalog Card Number: 2005018724
ISBN: 0–313–32792–0
ISSN: 1538–442X

First published in 2006

Greenwood Press, 88 Post Road West, Westport, CT 06881
An imprint of Greenwood Publishing Group, Inc.
www.greenwood.com

Printed in the United States of America

∞™

The paper used in this book complies with the
Permanent Paper Standard issued by the National
Information Standards Organization (Z39.48–1984).

10 9 8 7 6 5 4 3 2 1

To
Joseph L. Twiggs and Sarah D. Twiggs
Simply splendid. . . .

CONTENTS

Photo essay follows page 78.

SERIES FOREWORD

American statesman Adlai Stevenson stated that "We can chart our future clearly and wisely only when we know the path which has led to the present." This series, *Greenwood Guides to Historic Events, 1500–1900*, is designed to illuminate that path by focusing on events from 1500 to 1900 that have shaped the world. The years 1500 to 1900 include what historians call the Early Modern Period (1500 to 1789, the onset of the French Revolution) and part of the modern period (1789 to 1900).

In 1500, an acceleration of key trends marked the beginnings of an interdependent world and the posing of seminal questions that changed the nature and terms of intellectual debate. The series closes with 1900, the inauguration of the twentieth century. This period witnessed profound economic, social, political, cultural, religious, and military changes. An industrial and technological revolution transformed the modes of production, marked the transition from a rural to an urban economy, and ultimately raised the standard of living. Social classes and distinctions shifted. The emergence of the territorial and later the national state altered man's relations with and view of political authority. The shattering of the religious unity of the Roman Catholic world in Europe marked the rise of a new pluralism. Military revolutions changed the nature of warfare. The books in this series emphasize the complexity and diversity of the human tapestry and include political, economic, social, intellectual, military, and cultural topics. Some of the authors focus on events in U.S. history such as the Salem Witchcraft Trials, the American Revolution, the abolitionist movement, and the Civil War. Others analyze European topics, such as the Reformation and Counter Reformation and the French Revolution. Still others bridge cultures and continents by examining the voyages of discovery, the Atlantic slave trade, and the Age of Imperialism. Some focus on intellectual questions that have shaped the modern world, such as Darwin's *Origin of Species* or on turning points such as the Age of Romanticism. Others examine defining economic, religious, or legal events or issues such as the building of the railroads, the Second Great Awakening, and abolitionism. Heroes (e.g., Lewis and Clark), scientists (e.g., Darwin), military leaders (e.g., Napoleon), poets (e.g., Byron), stride across its pages. Many of these events were seminal in that they marked profound changes or turning points. The Scientific Revolution, for example, changed the way individuals viewed themselves and their world.

The authors, acknowledged experts in their fields, synthesize key events, set developments within the larger historical context, and, most important, present a well-balanced, well-written account that integrates the most recent scholarship in the field.

The topics were chosen by an advisory board composed of historians, high school history teachers, and school librarians to support the curriculum and meet student research needs. The volumes are designed to serve as resources for student research and to provide clearly written interpretations of topics central to the secondary school and lower-level undergraduate history curriculum. Each author outlines a basic chronology to guide the reader through often confusing events and a historical overview to set those events within a narrative framework. Three to five topical chapters underscore critical aspects of the event. In the final chapter the author examines the impact and consequences of the event. Biographical sketches furnish background on the lives and contributions of the players who strut across this stage. Ten to fifteen primary documents ranging from letters to diary entries, song lyrics, proclamations, and posters, cast light on the event, provide material for student essays, and stimulate a critical engagement with the sources. Introductions identify the authors of the documents and the main issues. In some cases a glossary of selected terms is provided as a guide to the reader. Each work contains an annotated bibliography of recommended books, articles, CD-ROMs, Internet sites, videos, and films that set the materials within the historical debate.

These works will lead to a more sophisticated understanding of the events and debates that have shaped the modern world and will stimulate a more active engagement with the issues that still affect us. It has been a particularly enriching experience to work closely with such dedicated professionals. We have come to know and value even more highly the authors in this series and our editors at Greenwood, particularly Kevin Ohe. In many cases they have become more than colleagues; they have become friends. To them and to future historians we dedicate this series.

Linda S. Frey
University of Montana

Marsha L. Frey
Kansas State University

INTRODUCTION

The United States went to war with Mexico in the spring of 1846 and by the fall of 1847 American soldiers were walking the streets of the Mexican capital. The following February, Mexico was forced to sign the Treaty of Guadalupe Hidalgo, which ceded to the United States a huge expanse of territory encompassing the Southwest and the Pacific Coast. Rather than an isolated episode, the war was the culmination of a series of events that began before Mexican independence and included treaty arrangements with Spain, the revolt of Mexico's northern province of Texas, and the growing discord over American reactions to Texan independence. The legacy of the Mexican War was dire for both countries. The victorious United States commenced a bitter argument over the fate of slavery in territories acquired from Mexico, an argument that eventually led to the secession crisis of 1860–1861 and caused the Civil War. Defeated Mexico coped for decades with a ruined economy and a broken political system while nursing a grudge against the Colossus of the North.

This book examines these events from both the American and Mexican perspectives. Chapter 1 compares and contrasts the history of the two republics from their origins as colonial appendages of European powers to their achieving independence. Understanding the different paths that each took during their formative years is important to understanding why they found themselves in serious disagreement during the 1840s.

Their principal dispute stemmed from problems over Texas, the subject of chapter 2. Always sparsely populated, the region was the site of an innovative immigration experiment undertaken by American pro-

moters and consented to by Mexican authorities. The result was a burgeoning Anglo population that gradually alarmed the Mexican government because of both its size and its attitude, which was steadfastly
American and increasingly quarrelsome. The revolution that achieved
Texan independence initiated an uneasy period of debate and distrust
between the United States, which wanted to and eventually did annex
Texas, and Mexico, which claimed that Texas still belonged to the Mexican nation. Chapter 3 traces the diplomatic crisis that resulted from
American annexation of Texas. It also describes the crossed purposes
of American expansionist aims with American domestic concerns over
slavery. In the end, Mexico's unraveling political situation contributed
to the adoption of inflexible positions by both sides, and the subsequent American military presence on what Mexico felt was its territory
made war apparently inevitable. The concluding sections of chapter 3
describe the opening of the conflict, further related in chapter 4, which
follows the course of northern campaigns that won the United States
New Mexico and California. Chapter 5 describes Winfield Scott's amphibious landing and siege at Veracruz and his epic march to Mexico
City, where American victory was finally sealed. It also charts the collapse of the Mexican government, which fell victim to political intrigue,
radical reform, and the resistance that reform provoked. The chapter
concludes with the difficulties of crafting a peace with a shattered Mexican government. Chapter 6 explains the peace settlement and examines the legacies of the conflict for both countries as well as some of
the prominent people who fought in it.

    In addition to this narrative, we have provided a detailed chronol-
ogy that begins with the significant events of the Mexican independence movement and concludes with the Treaty of Guadalupe Hidalgo
that ended the war. There are also thumbnail sketches of important
people in a section that follows the book's narrative, and these are in
turn followed by primary documents that shed light on the course of
events stretching from Texas independence to the end of the war. An
annotated bibliography arranged by category includes a wide array of
sources for further, more detailed reading on both general and particular aspects of the war and events surrounding it. Finally, an index
makes it easy to find specific items and people throughout the book.

    We are grateful to Linda and Marsha Frey for inviting us to con-
tribute this volume to their fine series. They are ideal editors and good

friends, which combination any author knows is a pearl beyond price. Senior editor Michael Hermann at Greenwood has been patient, supportive, and consistently pleasant. Several colleagues and fellow scholars have read parts of this book and a few have tackled the whole of it, all to make suggestions that in every instance have made it better. Especially valuable were the insightful remarks and suggestions by Robert Carriedo, to whom we are considerably indebted. Any errors that remain are ours alone.

CHRONOLOGY OF EVENTS

1810

September 16   *Grito de Dolores*

1811

July 31   Execution of Miguel Hidalgo y Costilla

1813

August 18   Revolutionary Army of the North crushed

1820

December 26   Moses Austin seeks permission to settle 300 American families in Texas

1821

January 17   Moses Austin receives permission to settle 300 American families in the form of a significant land grant from Mexico

February 14   Plan of Iguala

February 22   Adams-Onís Treaty is ratified by both the United States and Spain

February 24   Mexico declares independence from Spain

June 10   Moses Austin dies and his son Stephen F. Austin takes over the administration of the land grant

September 27   Treaty of Córdoba

1822

December 12   United States recognizes Mexico as a sovereign nation

1823

February 1   Plan of Casa Mata

February 18   Mexican emperor Agustín de Iturbide revalidates the Austin land grant

1824

May 7   Mexico's new constitution organizes Texas and Coahuila into states

1825

March 24   Texas and Coahuila officially open to American settlement

1826

December   Fredonia Rebellion begins

1828

January 12   United States and Mexico sign treaty confirming their common border as the Sabine River

April 28   Senate ratifies treaty establishing the Sabine River boundary

1829

July   Failed Spanish attempt to invade at Tampico

September 15   Mexico abolishes slavery

1834

January 3   Stephen Austin is arrested by the Mexican government after presenting a resolution from Americans in Texas requesting greater autonomy

April   Santa Anna declares dictatorship

1835

June 30   William Travis leaves Americans in an attempt to seize a Mexican post at Anáhuac

July	Andrew Jackson is rebuffed in his offer to purchase Texas from Mexico
October	Skirmish between Texans and Mexican military at Gonzales
November	Texans besiege San Antonio de Bexar
December 10	Mexicans surrender the Alamo

1836

February 23	Santa Anna's army begins a siege of the Alamo
March 2	Convention of Tejanos and Americans at Washington-on-the-Brazos declares Texas independence
March 4	Sam Houston is appointed commander of Texan army
March 6	The Alamo falls
March 17	Texas adopts a constitution
March 20	James Fannin surrenders at Coleto Creek
March 27	Goliad massacre
April 21	Battle of San Jacinto
May 14	Treaty of Velasco
May 25	John Quincy Adams formally opposes Texas annexation in the House of Representatives
July 1	U.S. Senate resolves to recognize Texas
July 4	House of Representatives resolves to recognize Texas
September 2	Referendum in Texas registers desire for U.S. annexation
October 22	Sam Houston becomes the first president of the Texas Republic

1837

| March 3 | Andrew Jackson recognizes Texas and nominates Alceé La Branche as chargé d'affaires to the republic |

1838

| October 12 | Texas reacts to U.S. rebuff regarding annexation by withdrawing its offer to submit |

November	France invades at Veracruz starting the Pastry War
December	Mirabeau B. Lamar becomes president of Texas and adopts policies to assert republic's independence

1839

April 11	United States–Mexico arbitration treaty to settle claims by American citizens
September 25	France signs a treaty with the Republic of Texas

1840

November 13	Great Britain signs a commercial treaty with Texas

1842

September 11	Mexican military crosses the Rio Grande and captures San Antonio

1843

August 23	Santa Anna warns that U.S. annexation of Texas would mean war with Mexico
October 16	Secretary of State Abel P. Upshur renews annexation talks with Texas' Minister to the United States, Isaac Van Zant (Houston later declines because of fears that sectional concerns would kill the agreement and would alienate Great Britain)

1844

January 16	Upshur seeks to assure Houston that annexation will secure the required two-thirds vote in the Senate
February 28	Abel Upshur killed aboard the *Princeton*
March 6	John C. Calhoun becomes secretary of state
April 12	Treaty signed authorizing annexation of Texas
April 22	President John Tyler submits treaty of annexation to the Senate
April 27	Henry Clay and Martin Van Buren publicly oppose Texas annexation
May 27–29	Democratic National Convention in Baltimore nominates James K. Polk over Martin Van Buren on a pro-annexation platform

June 8	Senate rejects Texas annexation treaty
December 4	Polk defeats Clay for the presidency
December 6	Joaquín Herrera comes to power as a result of a coup that overthrows Santa Anna
December 12	Anson Jones becomes president of Texas

1845

January 25	House passes joint resolution to annex Texas
February 27	Senate passes joint resolution to annex Texas
February 28	Congress adopts a joint resolution to annex Texas
March	Negotiations between Texas and Mexico to establish Texan independence break down after the receipt of news of the congressional resolution
March 1	President Tyler signs joint resolution to annex Texas
March 4	Polk refers to Texas annexation in his Inaugural Address
March 6	Mexican minister asks for his passports
March 28	Mexico breaks diplomatic relations with the United States
May 28	Polk dispatches Zachary Taylor and an "Army of Observation" to Texas
June 23	Special session of Texas Congress votes to accept annexation
July	John L. O'Sullivan coins the phrase "Manifest Destiny" to justify American expansion as providential
July 4	Texas convention accepts immediate statehood
October 17	Polk instructs American consul in Monterey, California, to encourage annexation
November 10	Polk sends envoy John Slidell to Mexico to settle all disputes with that country and purchase New Mexico and California
December	John C. Frémont enters California
December 16	Mexican president Herrera refuses to meet with Slidell

December 29	Texas becomes twenty-eighth state of the Union; Maj. Gen. Mariano Paredes y Arrillaga leads coup that overthrows President Herrera

1846

January 13	Polk reacts to the rebuff of Slidell by ordering Taylor to the Rio Grande
April 23	Paredes y Arrillaga declares defensive war against the United States
April 24	Maj. Gen. Mariano Arista arrives to take command of Mexican Army at Matamoros
May 3	Mexican soldiers attack a detachment of Taylor's troops
May 8	Battle of Palo Alto
May 9	Battle of Resaca de la Palma
May 13	Congress declares war on Mexico
May 17	Arista evacuates Matamoros
May 18	Taylor occupies Matamoros
May–June	U.S. Navy blockades Mexico's Gulf and Pacific ports
June 3	Col. Stephen Watts Kearny is ordered to take Santa Fe and proceed to California
June	Stephen Watts Kearny leads Army of the West from Fort Leavenworth
June 14	California Republic is proclaimed
June 15	Oregon Treaty is ratified ending the potential for a serious dispute with Great Britain over the Pacific Northwest
June 17	Opposition to the war with Mexico finds voice in James Russell Lowell's *Biglow Papers*
July	Taylor establishes base at Camargo
July 4	Bear Flag Republic declared
July 5	John C. Frémont takes command of forces in California
July 7	Commodore John Sloat claims California for the United States, hoisting the American flag at Monterey

July 15	Commodore Robert Stockton arrives in California
July 18	Oregon Treaty ratified
August 2	Army of the West leaves Bent's Fort
August 4	Paredes y Arrillaga's government is overthrown
August 8	Democratic congressman David Wilmot of Pennsylvania proposes an amendment to an appropriation bill that would abolish slavery in any territory gained from Mexico
August 13	Ships under Commodore Robert Stockton assist Frémont in capturing Los Angeles
August 15	After occupying Las Vegas, Kearny announces annexation of New Mexico to United States
August 16	Santa Anna returns to Mexico
August 17	Commodore Robert Stockton announces annexation of California
August 18	Kearny establishes an American government at Santa Fe
September 14	Santa Anna enters Mexico City and takes command of the Mexican Army
September 20–24	Battle of Monterrey
September 22	José María Flores leads a revolt against U.S. forces in California
September 25	Kearny leaves for California
November 5	Kearny becomes official U.S. governor of California
November 16	Taylor captures Saltillo
November 19	Scott given command of Mexico City campaign
December	Mexican legislature convenes and elects Santa Anna president; Alexander Doniphan's march to Chihuahua begins
December 6	Kearny fights Mexican insurgents at San Pascual, California
December 12	Kearny enters San Diego
December 25	Battle of El Brazito
December 29	Taylor occupies Tamaulipas

1847

January	Indian revolt in New Mexico
January 3	Winfield Scott requisitions the bulk of Taylor's force to attack Veracruz
January 8	Battle of Bartolo Ford
January 10	Stockton and Kearny retake Los Angeles
January 16	Stockton names Frémont governor of California
February 10	Agua Nueva Massacre
February 22–23	Zachary Taylor defeats Santa Anna at Buena Vista
February 27	*Polkos* Revolt
February 28	Battle of Rio Sacramento
March 2	Doniphan enters Chihuahua
March 9	Winfield Scott's army lands south of Veracruz
March 29	Veracruz surrenders to Winfield Scott
April 8	Scott's army begins march to Mexico City
April 17–18	Battle of Cerro Gordo
August 7	Scott's army begins leaving Puebla
August 19–20	Battle of Padierna
August 20	Battle of Churubusco
September 7	Armistice ends
September 8	Battle of Molino del Rey
September 11	Council of Piedad
September 12	Bombardment of Chapultepec begins
September 13	U.S. forces take Chapultepec and begin movement toward Mexico City
September 13–14	During the night, Santa Anna pulls army out of Mexico City
September 14	Scott enters Mexico City
November 11	Pedro María Anaya elected interim Mexican president

1848

January 8	Manuel de la Peña y Peña becomes Mexican president
February 2	Treaty of Guadalupe Hidalgo signed
March 10	U.S. Senate ratifies Treaty of Guadalupe Hidalgo

CHAPTER 1

THE TWO REPUBLICS

In the spring of 1846, war broke out between the United States and Mexico and ended twenty-one months later with Mexico losing an enormous amount of its territory. The result seemed inevitable because the antagonists were so unevenly matched on the battlefield, in part a reflection of the dissimilar paths taken by their governments, one seeking stability and the other courting chaos. In their beginnings, however, the two countries evolved from similar origins and pursued comparable dreams. Both had been colonial extensions of Old World powers, and both had rebelled against colonial rule to establish independent nations. In fact, Mexico's independence held promises of success as abundant as they were likely. The colony of New Spain had been the most valued of His Most Catholic Majesty's colonial possessions. Its rich silver mines financed Spain's imperial mission all over the world and made Spaniards leading participants in European diplomatic, religious, and military affairs. During the opening years of the nineteenth century, the colony became a vital player in the international economy as Mexican silver helped to finance the European war between France and Britain and their allies. After achieving independence from Spain in 1821, the most obvious evidence indicated that Mexico could become a great nation, perhaps the most powerful in the Western Hemisphere. Geographically vast and governed by sophisticated, erudite Creoles, Mexico eliminated official class distinctions, adopted a progressive constitution, and abolished slavery during its first decade of independence.

The thirteen British colonies in North America were another story. They were rustic outposts rooted in agriculture, dependent on Britain for most manufactured goods, and lacking any obvious mineral wealth to boost their economies and increase their worth. The colony of Virginia had stumbled on tobacco as a lucrative cash crop, but it was hardly the match of Mexican silver. The British colonies were administratively divided by imperial design and culturally dissimilar by the accident of settlements occurring variously in different regions. New England Puritans in Massachusetts had little in common with Scots-Irish yeomen in North Carolina, and citizens of New York and Charleston felt more kinship with Londoners than to each other. When this motley collection of colonists rebelled against Britain in the 1770s, nothing suggested that the revolt would become a revolution, let alone that it would succeed. After the colonies achieved independence, odds were heavily against the United States even remaining united, let alone that the new country would become a vigorous engine of extensive economic growth. Nobody would have suggested that the weak and querulous republic would in only decades become an aggressive agent of expansion, convinced of a grand destiny to extend its reach to the Pacific Ocean.

The story of the Mexican War does not begin with the firing of first shots or even the angry exchanges of impatient diplomats. The story begins with the origins of these two antagonists, the two republics that held such different prospects of success at their outsets and incredibly, by the time of their clash, had experienced a complex reversal of fortunes that all but predetermined the outcome of the contest. The close of that contest also settled a strange curse on both victor and vanquished. Mexico in defeat would attempt significant reforms and discard discredited Creole rulers, but the country staggered and reeled under a broken economy and created enormous social inequities under one-party rule; the United States in victory courted calamity by reanimating slumbering arguments over the extension of slavery that ultimately caused its terrible Civil War.

New Spain

Beginning with their epic voyages of exploration in the late fifteenth century and continuing with the rapid conquest of the Indian empires of Mesoamerica, Catholic Spain established itself as the dominant colonial power in the New World for more than a hundred years. The extent of Spain's wealth and power was seemingly limitless as treasure ships ferried precious metals from Central and South American mines to the coffers of imperial Madrid. Spaniards carried both sword and cross to establish settlements and expand their influence in the Americas, an enormous domain they called New Spain. Its capital city was raised up on the ruins of the old Aztec citadel of Tenochtitlán and was named Mexico City after the Mexica Indians. Spaniards rapidly established towns, excavated mines, and marked off huge estates called haciendas, and in only fifty years transformed Montezuma's grand empire into a Spanish colony. The cost for indigenous peoples was incalculable because Spaniards not only seized lands and compelled their former owners to labor on them, they also inadvertently brought diseases that ravaged the native population, obliging a shrinking number of survivors to shoulder even more work. Meanwhile, new processes that used mercury for extracting silver from ore encouraged a burgeoning mining industry whose output enriched Spain and brought substantial material comfort to its New World colony. Food grown on farms was for domestic consumption while a huge labor force in the mines hauled out silver for shipment to Spain. The economy settled into a two-dimensional system of haciendas in the valley and southern regions and of silver mines in the central regions and northern frontier. Both Spain and Europe's hunger for precious metals was insatiable, and silver mining dominated the Mexican economy for the entire colonial period.

Colonial society was stratified by race and wealth into three main groups. Whites sat atop the social pyramid and were themselves divided into *peninsulares* (natives of Spain who occupied all the important administrative posts) and *criollos* or Creoles (whites native to Mexico who only occasionally enjoyed a prestigious government office). *Criollos* eventually developed deep resentments over such exclusion. Mestizos, people of mixed race, were the result of intermarriage between Spaniards, natives, and blacks, the last of these imported as slaves during the early years of colonization. Mestizos eventually came to dominate and direct the course of Mexican history, but many years would pass before that occurred. White colonial society ranked them as inferior. Even more inferior as a caste were the Indians and black slaves who formed the broad underside of this society. The Spanish crown and the Catholic Church, ubiquitous and culturally dominant, were the principal sources of unity for this diverse set of cultures and classes.

Exploration and expansive acquisitions augmented this diversity. In the late 1600s, New Spain began establishing settlements in the empty reaches of its northern frontiers. These meager communities and the native people they encountered received spiritual guidance from Catholic missions and physical protection from lightly manned military garrisons (presidios). Hostile Indians as well as French and British interlopers were the principal threat, but isolation and hardship were almost as daunting, and the number of settlers remained few with even fewer coming in subsequent years. Nevertheless, the outposts endured, and Spaniards continued to press outward. In the late 1690s, they were establishing missions and presidios in Baja (lower) California and in the next century founded towns in Alta (upper) California. At the end of the eighteenth century, Spaniards gazed upon the Atlantic from St. Augustine in Florida, upon the Gulf of Mexico from Veracruz in Mexico, upon the Pacific from Monterey in Alta California, and could claim all the land that lay between. New Spain, the core of a vast global empire, was the brightest jewel in His Most Catholic Majesty's crown.

The Shifting Colonial Relationship

Despite New Spain's indispensable importance for the Spanish Empire, during the seventeenth and eighteenth centuries the colony became a distant and steadily diminishing concern for Iberian Spaniards as they coped with dramatic changes in Europe. The rising colonial ambitions of Britain and France were one cause for alarm, and rapacious pirates working for Spain's jealous rivals menaced the treasure fleets. In a series of costly European wars, Spanish armies suffered military setbacks as a prelude to Spain's shrinking status in the continent's affairs. The broad Spanish Empire likewise began a transformation, especially the most prized part of it in New Spain, which became a curiously remote appendage increasingly independent from the mother country in deeds if not by formal separation. Socially stable, well administered, and prosperous, New Spain boasted a growing population and a developing provincial network of commercial, social, and political interests. Flush with silver and blessed with appreciable agricultural potential, New Spain could buy what it wanted and produce what it needed. The king in Spain remained a source of stability during these years, but actual control of the colony was in the hands of his resident agent, the viceroy.

With the help of the church, Spanish colonial officials generally governed the colony with reasonable laws rather than coercion, and their involvement in local associations, sometimes by marriage, made them part of the communities they governed, increasing their understanding of the colony's welfare and how to balance it with Spain's interests.

Extraordinary events meanwhile worked to erode New Spain's ties to its mother country. At the start of the 1700s, a great power shift occurred in Europe when the childless and mentally deficient Hapsburg king of Spain died and his will named the grandson of the French king Louis XIV, a Bourbon, heir to the Spanish throne. The joining of France and Spain under the same monarchical family instantly altered Europe's balance of power and shocked Britain and Austria. The War of the Spanish Succession (1702–1714) resulted and ended in an uneasy peace that recognized the Bourbons as legitimate heirs to the Spanish throne, a change in monarchy that had unexpected consequences for New Spain. Colonial reorganization under the Bourbons streamlined New Spain's administration to revitalize royal authority and to strengthen the colony's reliance on the mother country. Both goals were unpopular. Bourbon economic reforms undertaken between 1756 and 1804 were also harmful by upsetting the local arrangements that had accounted for New Spain's economic stability. Likewise, secular reforms that raided the church's coffers to enrich royal ones not only impaired the Catholic Church's ability to exert social control but also radicalized certain segments of the priesthood whose ranks produced Mexico's first revolutionary leaders. Along with spreading resentment against Spain and her colonial representatives, the examples of the American and French revolutions in the late eighteenth century fueled a general desire for autonomy that eventually matured into a full-blown drive for independence.

Jealousy and suspicion kept arrogant *peninsulares* and resentful *criollos* divided, however, even as their shared, inherent conservatism eschewed revolution and revered king and church as the twin bulwarks of stable society and responsible government. Whites agreed that mestizos could not be trusted with power, but *peninsulares* regarded anyone without a European pedigree as inferior, and *criollos* reacted by developing a heightened sense of Mexican nationalism. Such was the situation when France's aggressive militarism gravely shook New Spain's faith in their king. Napoleon invaded Spain in 1808, forced the

abdication of Carlos IV and his son Ferdinand, to install Joseph Bonaparte, Napoleon's brother, on the Spanish throne. Spaniards never accepted the change, and only those under French bayonets grudgingly
resigned themselves to it. When Spanish royalists proclaimed Ferdinand the true king of Spain, they created a rallying point for opposition to the unpopular Joseph Bonaparte. This puzzling situation
perplexed New Spain about the identity of its true ruler, and the
colony's viceroy José de Iturrigaray opportunistically plotted to exploit
the confusion for his own advantage. Scheming to become king of an
independent Mexico, Iturrigaray encouraged *criollos'* fervent nationalism, stoked their revulsion to the turmoil in Spain, and backed their
idea of establishing a Mexican junta. *Peninsulares* were alarmed at the
growing power of *criollos* and deposed Iturrigaray in 1808, installed a
doddering puppet, and reasserted their authority as well as the colony's
allegiance to Spain. Angry and frustrated, some *criollos* plotted small,
stillborn conspiracies that hardly threatened the entrenched powers.
Yet, the fact gradually emerged that both the monarchy and viceroyalty's legitimacy had been profoundly shaken by these events. A Bonaparte on the throne in Madrid and the dismantling of Iturrigaray's
government forced *criollos* to reassess their habitual loyalty to the
crown and their traditional association with the *peninsulares*. Some
criollos and mestizos drifted into a wary alliance against arrogant
peninsulares, increasingly perceived as a common enemy. These bud-
ding Mexican nationalists contemptuously called Spanish-born
colonists *gachupines* (settlers) to turn what for centuries had been a
badge of honor into a mark of disgrace.

The Struggle for Independence

Father Miguel Hidalgo y Costilla was the parish priest in the village of Dolores north of Mexico City. A *criollo*, Hidalgo had become increasingly radical under the press of events in Spain and Mexico, and
he became prominent in the growing discontent that bridged traditional class divisions to include progressive *peninsulares*, angry *criollos*,
displaced mestizos, and even Indians. Just as the church had once been
a unifying force for stability under the crown, this militant cleric represented a new radicalism in the priesthood, a unifying force for op-

position to the usurpers in Madrid and the self-anointed and repressive *peninsulares* in Mexico City.

By 1810, seething anger was verging on open rebellion. Government spies betrayed an uprising scheduled to begin on December 8, 1810, and Hidalgo, with his conspirators unmasked and their arrest imminent, set the rebellion in motion early. On September 16, 1810, he instructed his villagers to strike down the *peninsulares* and the corrupt Spanish administration, an exhortation that became famous as the *Grito de Dolores* (Cry of Dolores). An enraged mob descended on Guanajuato, the regional capital, where locals also joined the revolt. Years of pent-up class resentment turned into blood lust in Guanajuato as *peninsulares* were brutally massacred. The violence was so vicious, in fact, that it appalled many *criollos*. Although Hidalgo's uprising had a few subsequent successes, *criollo* resistance against its ferocity mounted, and rebel forces did not take Mexico City. Instead, Hidalgo headed north to join another uprising in the province of Coahuila-Texas. The government shattered his rebel force near Monclava where Hidalgo fell to capture in March 1811 and was tried by the Catholic Church's Inquisition on charges of heresy and treason. He was executed on July 31, 1811.

Hidalgo's death and the dispersal of his forces transformed the revolutionary movement rather than killed it. Under the leadership of another priest, José María Morelos y Pavón, overt elements of violent social antagonisms that had marred Hidalgo's uprising were all but eliminated. Hidalgo had called for a class war; Morelos called for a congress. Accordingly, revolutionary delegates met in Chilpancingo to draw up a document calling for an independent Mexico. Leaders envisioned a new state based on universal male suffrage and the elimination of all forced labor, especially slavery. Roman Catholicism would remain the official state religion, but government monopolies in other areas would be abolished. Meanwhile, Morelos laid siege to Mexico City hoping to starve it into submission, but Spanish forces broke out of the city and marched on Chilpancingo. By 1815, the rebellion was in tatters. Morales died before a firing squad and only small, uncoordinated bands remained in the wake of thorough government suppression. When Spanish viceroy Juan Ruiz de Apodaca shrewdly offered a general pardon to all rebels who pledged allegiance to the crown, the gesture fractured the revolutionary movement. In fact, Apodaca's pardons in conjunction with the defeat of Napoleon and the restoration of the Spanish throne to Ferdinand VII seemingly secured Spanish dominion over New Spain permanently. Even the charismatic leadership of men like Manuel Félix Fernández (who took the revolutionary moniker Guadalupe Victoria) and Vicente Guerrero could not maintain let alone revive declining enthusiasm for revolution.

Yet additional events unexpectedly broke Spain's hold on its chief mainland American colony. Planning to destroy the few rebel holdouts who had rebuffed his conciliatory pardon, Apodaca dispatched an army under Gen. Agustín de Iturbide to crush Vicente Guerrero's forces. Iturbide seemed a good choice for the mission. An old school *criollo*, he appeared reliably loyal to both church and crown, an allegiance confirmed by his zealous participation in putting down the Hidalgo and Morelos uprisings. Iturbide, however, concealed deep resentments. Aside from secretly brooding over the inferior status of *criollos* to *peninsulares*, he chaffed at being punished by superiors irritated by his penchant for corruption. After committing his forces to some indecisive skirmishes with Guerrero's rebels, Iturbide abruptly ceased hostilities and arranged a fateful meeting with Guerrero himself in which they forged an alliance to overthrow Spanish authority. The Plan of Iguala, named for the town where it was announced on February 14, 1821, fused the bargain by pledging independence, equality, of *criollos* and *peninsulares* and Catholicism as the official religion as the aims of a new Mexican government. These "Three Guarantees" blended reform and traditionalism to address *criollos* grievances while allaying fears about a chaotic and violent revolution dominated by mestizos outside of Catholic control. Guerrero accepted the plan, but most importantly Iturbide's soldiers did so as well. His erstwhile royalist force joined Guerrero's rebels to form the Trigarante Army (Army of the Three Guarantees), which quickly grew as rebels from all regions of Mexico flocked to its ranks.[1]

Iturbide at the head of the impressive Trigarante Army quickly brought down Spanish rule. Apodaca had fled, and his successor, Juan O'Donoju, glumly concluded that reestablishing Spanish authority in the rebellious colony was unlikely.[2] Moreover, he judged a wiser policy was to placate Mexico and preserve cultural and commercial ties between the new nation and Spain. On September 27, 1821, the last viceroy of New Spain consented to the Treaty of Córdoba, recognizing Mexican Independence and endorsing the Plan of Iguala.

It appeared that a long and bloody struggle had at last ended in revolutionary triumph. Yet as far as Madrid was concerned, O'Donoju had overstepped his bounds. Spain disowned his actions, rejected the Treaty of Córdoba, and insisted that Mexico was still a part of the Spanish Empire. In 1821, Spain lacked the ability to act on the assertion, but the refusal to make a clean break meant that Mexico had to maintain a costly military vigilance against a possible Spanish invasion. Indeed, a Spanish garrison remained in place in San Juan de Ulúa, the fortress at Veracruz, until Spain finally surrendered in 1825.

Iturbide's ambition was a more immediate and dangerous threat to the revolution's success. Having emerged as the most popular figure in the independence movement, he maneuvered to secure its fruits for himself. The Plan of Iguala had envisioned a constitutional monarchy headed by a European prince imported for the job. At Iturbide's urging, however, the Treaty of Córdoba gave the Mexican Congress the option of selecting a Mexican *criollo* to be the king. With that provision in place, the revolution was unavoidably destined to make Agustín de Iturbide Mexico's ruler.

From Empire to Republic

The provisional Congress working to establish a permanent Mexican government under the Plan of Iguala wisely voted to reduce the Trigarante Army, and that action forced Iturbide's hand. It also provided him with an army, suddenly anxious over its fate at the hands of the provisional legislature, to impose his will. He ordered the army to march through Mexico City on May 18, 1822, in a seemingly popular demonstration, but the display was actually a naked show of force aimed at influencing both the Congress and the city. Gathering outside Iturbide's quarters, the army's numbers were swelled by citizens awed by and swept up in the excitement. Shouted chants implored Iturbide to become emperor, and after feigning reluctance, he agreed. Congress, bowing to the popular will, confirmed his ascension on May 19 by declaring Iturbide Agustín I, emperor of Mexico.

His reign was brief and troubled. Mexico was broke, its government bloated, and its army, to which Iturbide was imprudently indebted, large and expensive. When congressional criticism mounted against him, Iturbide reacted with a heavy hand in August 1822 by dissolving the legislature and arresting his opponents. Revolutionary leaders who had only recently been Iturbide's allies now became his enemies. Among their ranks they counted a fascinating compatriot, the dashing Antonio López de Santa Anna Pérez de Lebrón, commander of the military garrison at Veracruz and until the advent of Iturbide, a fervent royalist officer. On December 1, 1822, Santa Anna reacted to Iturbide's repressions by proclaiming a republic with Vicente Guerrero and Guadalupe Victoria's endorsement. Briefly besieged at Veracruz, Santa Anna successfully appealed to Iturbide's forces with the Plan of Casa Mata on February 1, 1823, that denounced centralized authority and called for a federal republic. Mexico's provinces found it appealing as well and openly opposed Iturbide's rule. Just two weeks after the announcement of Casa Mata, Iturbide abdicated, and Santa Anna's forces entered Mexico City unopposed. The bloodless event was misleading, though. Despite Santa Anna's popularity, Iturbide's disrepute, and the ostensible decency of the movement that removed him from power, the affair was still a coup and set a regrettable precedent. Mexico was less than two years old, and its first government had been unseated by the threat of force.

Nevertheless, for the next twelve years Mexico was a republic, albeit a troubled one. The constitutional convention that met in November 1823 immediately divided into the two factions that would compete for Mexico's future during the next twenty-five years. Federalists, composed of progressive *criollos* and mestizos, wanted a decentralized government with significant power in the hands of states. Centralists, as their name implied, wanted power vested in Mexico City. Although Centralists were composed of traditionalist *criollos* and had the support of the church, the army, and the *peninsulares,* the Federalists were the stronger of the factions. Centralists nonetheless could hold their own because of the influential, traditional sources of support they enjoyed. In drafting the Constitution of 1824, all parties agreed to emulate the best available model for the document, which was the U.S. Constitution. Accordingly, Centralists won at least the point that Mexico's central government would be strong and meaningful. The Constitution of 1824 established the Estados Unidas Mexicanos (United Mexican States), a republic of nineteen states and four territories. (See Map 1.1.) The central government consisted of an ex-

Map 1.1

ecutive, a bicameral legislature, and a judiciary, with the president and
vice president elected by state assemblies for four-year terms. Although an apparent replica of the U.S. document, important differences marked the Mexican Constitution of 1824. Centralists won a
crucial victory with clauses that preserved Catholicism as the state religion and sustained military and church privileges (*fueros*).[3] The president was also empowered to assume extraordinary powers in
emergencies.

Mexico nearly always found itself in an emergency. Writing a constitution and installing a government were one thing, but governing an
impoverished and fractious nation whose population was divided along
ethnic and class lines was quite another. The first president was the
revolutionary Guadalupe Victoria, who would have the distinction of
being the only president of the republic to serve his full four-year term.
Although he governed with mainly good intentions, a pure heart was
a pale substitute for economic solvency and social stability. By trying
to assume and fund all national and state debts to restore confidence

in Mexico's credit and stabilize its economy, Victoria's government took on a staggering burden and became aware of the stark reality that honest *criollos* could pay bills no better with an empty treasury than could corrupt *gachupines*. In addition to this already tall order, Mexico felt obliged to keep its enormous standing army intact because a Spanish invasion remained a real possibility.

Mexico had an abundance of resources, as the German traveler Alexander von Humboldt had recorded years earlier, but there was a troubling problem connected to them. They were not where most people lived. Maps of the country were old and unreliable, and the country's population was small and fragmented. In a domain comprising more than 2.5 million square miles there lived only about 7 million people, most of them Indians living in small villages. Deserts spanned the northern regions while fetid woodlands flanked the tropical shores of the gulf. Steep mountain ranges ran the length of much of the country from north to south inland from both eastern and western coasts, creating a valley and fecund Central Plateau. The haciendas marked the sprawling land holdings of the landed upper class, but they were notoriously inefficient. The once productive silver mines of the midlands had gone to ruin during the wars of independence with most flooded and many stripped of shoring timbers for firewood, which made them deathtraps. Even hefty amounts of British capital could not completely reclaim them, and without this crucial source of revenue, the sum of Mexico's financial burdens was too much to handle. Similarly, Mexico had no industry to speak of and lacked even the natural transportation routes navigable rivers would have provided, let alone a sensible system of roads. Consequently, Victoria was obliged to take out foreign loans, usually under usurious terms. Mexico's penury was the bane of its search for stable government, and the loans seriously undermined its quest for complete independence from outside forces.

Inside the government, ambitious officials who joined secret societies made the Mexican polity extremely fragile. Gradually spreading from urban settings to smaller towns throughout the country, Masonic lodges divided along different rites to provide a handy organization for factions. Traditionalists and royalists who wanted to reconstruct a centralist regime resembling the old viceroyalty banded together under the older Scottish rite to become *escoses*, while proponents of federal decentralization and radicals who loathed anything Spanish and exalted everything Mexican joined York-rite lodges (*yorquinos*). Their time of significant influence was relatively brief, but it occurred at a crucial point in the life of the new nation. The rival Masonic lodges with their penchant for secrecy and paranoid plotting were a symptom of a cancer at the core of the republic's political establishment.

Convinced that Victoria had become an ineffectual pawn of special interests, Vice President Nicolás Bravo led an unsuccessful revolt against the government in 1827. Under the shadow of that event, the 1828 elections resulted in a messy dispute that eroded confidence in the legitimacy of presidential succession. Centralist Manuel Gómez Pedraza won the election by taking ten of the nineteen states, but Federalist Vicente Guerrero and his supporters accused the army of intimidating the states to stage a bloodless electoral coup. (It did not help appearances that Gómez Pedraza had been secretary of war in Victoria's bipartisan cabinet.) After the election, Mexico briefly had two governments, Gómez Pedraza's holed up in the presidential residence and Guerrero's in the field. When Santa Anna threw his support to Guerrero and the liberal Federalists, Gómez Pedraza had no choice but to vacate the presidency. Yet Guerrero had become president under dubious circumstances and consequently would labor under doubts about his legitimacy in office.

The Caudillo State

In July 1829, Spain finally acted on its rejection of the Treaty of Córdoba and tardily sought to suppress the Mexican rebellion by landing Gen. Isidro Barradas and three thousand soldiers at Tampico. President Guerrero invoked his emergency powers and sent Santa Anna to fight the invading Spaniards. The Mexican Army, maintained for years at great expense, was actually more formidable on paper than in the field, and when Santa Anna sallied forth, he did so with only a small fraction of its roster. The army that existed in these years was a product of the revolutionary struggle for independence. Apodaca's amnesty program had brought a number of rebels into the service, for instance, but Spaniards departed throughout the 1820s and were eliminated by their official expulsion from Mexico in 1827. Thereafter the army was commanded by *criollos* and manned by mestizos and Indians. In any case, the regular army was only part of the picture, for the active militia formed the bulk of forces charged with the duty of guarding the coastline and disciplining hostile Indians. As noted, the entire force was sizable on paper, boasting a roster in the later 1820s of almost sixty thousand, but more than half of that number was the active militia of which less then a third were actually under arms.

The Spaniards proved stubborn, but their numbers were small and Tampico's citizens did not embrace them as liberators. In the end, starvation and yellow fever did more than Santa Anna's army to force Barradas's surrender, but Santa Anna's indirect success at Tampico established him as the country's savior, the first of many odd events that repeatedly bound together his and Mexico's fate for the next quarter-century.

The emergence of the caudillo was not unique to Mexico, for as the influence of Spanish colonial rule faded away, strongmen emerged in the vacuum. They patterned themselves on the deeply ingrained military tradition that had been part of Spanish culture since feudal times and was reinvigorated by the Reconquista, that reclamation of Iberia from Muslim conquerors from North Africa called the Moors. In Mexico, military chieftains at first were Catholic priests such as Hidalgo and Morelos, but the achievement of independence, especially the great struggles that were part of that achievement, transformed the leading elite as *criollos* assumed a dominant role. Their most infamous example was Santa Anna, and his time in power would exemplify the failure of his class, only writ large. In failure, as in everything else, Santa Anna did nothing small.

The world would judge him as complex, but he was less complicated than clever, a collection of appetites and ambitions that found expression in one overarching trait, which was a capacity for survival. Santa Anna was born into privilege, a *criollo* whose heritage was *peninsular*, the inheritor of a large estate in the high country of Jalapa, which he continuously added to and improved. He was also the inheritor of the caudillo tradition, the exaltation of the gentleman warrior who was born to rule through power, whose legitimate right to rule in fact derived from his wielding power, the distillation of the concept that might makes right. It was only natural for him to follow the path of the army, his lieutenancy secured in 1812 and his spurs won (as well as his first wound suffered) during the suppression of the Hidalgo and Morelos rebellions. Some writers claim that he learned cruelty during these campaigns, which is perhaps true, but it is not so easy to determine the reason for his habitual duplicity. Santa Anna climbed the officer ranks to become a lieutenant colonel through a combination of obsequious service and bona fide bravery, but he never cultivated loyalty as a habit. He instead remained vigilant for opportunities and rarely saw one he did not grasp. Betraying a cause that had earlier claimed his devotion was easy for him, and every single person who trusted him eventually regretted doing so. Strangely, however, Santa Anna's betrayals never more than temporarily estranged his victims. He enchanted and alienated the Mexican people no less than eleven times, seizing power with their blessing and falling from grace in an astonishing cycle of recrimination and reconciliation. The only constant in his character was his artful talent to foist off transparent lies as obvious truths, for he was a chameleon who could be generous and then stingy, brutal and then kind, wise and then foolish, affectionate and then cruel. His pursuit of power was, like his seduction of women, more important than the attainment of it or the conquest of them. He never completed one of his eleven terms as leader of Mexico, and he proved remarkably indifferent to exercising power in any deliberate, diligent, or thoughtful way. Instead, he ruled in fits and starts, reacting with bursts of energy to circumstances or threats, otherwise retreating into languor and self-indulgence, all the while looting the treasury for costly personal pleasures. This was the man to whom Mexico fell victim in its crucial formative years.

Guerrero's unraveling presidency excited Santa Anna's ambitions. Watching these events unfold, Simón Bolívar noted the influence of Santa Anna, whom he described as "the most perverse of mortals."[4] Guerrero kept the emergency powers he had invoked during the Spanish invasion, using them to make sweeping reforms by fiat, the last straw for Centralists still angry about the 1828 election. Their champion was Guerrero's vice president, Anastasio Bustamante, who staged a military coup in early 1830 to become Mexico's third president in as many years. Although Bustamante himself was a cultured man, he presided over a government that was more a regime than an administration, for it ruled with intimidation and brutality. The deposed Guerrero became a refugee whose attempt to leave Mexico in early 1831 ended with his capture and execution, a warning to those who dared to oppose Bustamante.[5] In 1832, however, Santa Anna had his loyal sol-

diers occupy Veracruz and take over its customs house. This provocative bit of bravado paid off, and soon all of Mexico was in rebellion.
Bustamante's regime collapsed and, ironically, Gómez Pedraza was recalled to serve out what was left of his term.

From this chaos, Santa Anna emerged as a seemingly resolute vi-
sionary, and his extraordinary popularity made him the certain victor
in the 1833 presidential election. He easily won under the liberal Federalist banner but proved coy when presented the prize. Possibly he realized that Mexico's factions, mounting debt, and deep class resentments
made the country ungovernable and shrewdly chose to retreat to his
estate in the pleasant high country of Jalapa. Some have suggested that
Santa Anna's inherent laziness and distaste for the daily routines required of the president caused the mysterious lapses in health that he
repeatedly claimed compelled his semiretirement. In any case, he left
his vice president, the *puro*-Federalist Valentín Gómez Farías, in charge
as acting president at lengthy intervals and either deliberately or un-
wittingly saddled him with the responsibility for unpleasant events and
unpopular measures. *Puros* were advocates of a "pure" federalism and
wanted to confer significant autonomy to local authorities to cope with
Mexico's dynamic economic, social, and racial diversity. Committed to
the Constitution of 1824, *puros* believed that the states should be empowered to superintend their own affairs unencumbered by national
interference. They lamented the strong hold the Catholic Church had
over the government, the centralizing tendencies of the army, and the
apparent incompetence of strutting Creole military officers, who had
been the principal political leaders since independence. All these forces
were obstructing the true federalism that would solve Mexico's problems, they said, and Mexico's problems would only grow until both
church and military were broken like a willful horse. In the *puros'* ideal
world, poverty could be eradicated, a well-organized and trained militia could provide adequate defense, and Mexico's rich natural resources
could promote economic dynamism and national greatness. *Puros* believed that as long as the upper classes conspired with the church and
the army to hoard those resources for their own benefit there would be
grinding poverty.

Working from such tenets, Gómez Farías as acting president was
heedless of the political perils Santa Anna had avoided. With the ar-

dency of a true believer, Gómez Farías vigorously began to eliminate all vestiges of Centralist political influence, especially as wielded by the Catholic Church. He ended the church's *fueros* and cut off its independent revenue by eliminating compulsory tithes and hobbled its administrative independence by empowering the government to make church appointments. In addition, he abolished the military's *fueros* and reduced the army. Such dramatic gestures eliminated virtually all the concessions awarded to Centralists in the Constitution of 1824 and naturally roused a legion of powerful enemies. Perhaps Mexico, insolvent and fractious, was incapable of sustaining democratic government at that time, but by so completely marginalizing his opponents, Gómez Farías compelled them to become inflexible, unyielding, and prone to intrigue. Worse, the degenerating political climate completely extinguished an already frail fidelity to regular electoral processes.

By April 1834, Mexico was in the throes of yet another rebellion, although of a quite different sort. Its leader was none other than President Santa Anna. Stirring himself from semiretirement, he acted the part of his hero Napoleon Bonaparte to displace his own government. After removing Gómez Farías, Santa Anna dissolved the legislature and declared a national emergency to justify his dictatorship. Santa Anna repealed the reforms enacted by Gómez Farías, and nullified the Constitution of 1824, paving the way for the adoption of a new constitution in 1836, the Siete Leyes (Seven Laws). The new constitution transformed Mexico into a centralized regime controlled by Mexico City. Former states became military districts under the governance of vice-caudillos. Universal male suffrage, the jewel in the crown of the old revolutionary movement, was replaced by property requirements for both voters and officeholders.

On the face of it, a charlatan and his cronies had engineered a crude power grab, but Santa Anna possessed neither the magnetism nor his henchmen the influence to transform the democratic republic to a centralized caudillo state. Instead, sincere alarm that the country was out of control and on the verge of disintegration helped to bring about the Constitution of 1836. Decentralization during lax colonial administration had raised worries among traditionalists who predicted that anarchy would result when federalism was institutionalized in the Constitution of 1824. Events seemed to vindicate their concerns. The unrelenting cycle of coups was bad enough, but universal male suffrage, the autonomy of states, and the insolence of local caudillos threatened to fragment the country into a random collection of disparate provinces, each vulnerable to indigenous rebellion or foreign occupation. The conservatives who assisted Santa Anna in reshaping the government in the 1830s did not do it for Santa Anna; they did it for Mexico. They genuinely believed that to leave the government unaltered would soon leave them with no country to govern.[6]

These changes were exceedingly unpopular, however, which meant they were also perilous, because state autonomy had grown muscular while the central government was preoccupied with sorting out leaders and weathering military uprisings. States confronted with the prospect of being transformed into military districts controlled by the central government grumbled, and some openly rebelled. Santa Anna suppressed an uprising in Zacatecas just north of Mexico City in 1835 with such brutality he surprised even those familiar with his appetite for cruelty. Farther to the north, Coahuila-Texas also raised vehement objections to the new Constitution. The most vocal protests came from touchy American transplants in Texas who took up arms. Santa Anna marched north to suppress this revolt as well, and his northern campaign would be marked by cruelties rivaling those in Zacatecas, but its conclusion would be entirely different.

The United States

As Mexico embarked on its journey from colony to Republic, its neighbor to the north had already followed a similar path but to a markedly different destination. The United States had waged a revolution against its mother country, fighting a war almost as long and in some cases as internally divisive as Mexico's struggle for its independence, and just as in Mexico, colonial habits of regionalism persisted after the United States achieved its independence.

Yet fundamental differences also marked the formative years of the other North American republic. The thirteen British colonies in North America were accustomed to the responsibility of self-government because the British colonial establishment had encouraged political self-sufficiency and local control of affairs. When the staggering debt built up in the Seven Years' War (1756–1763) compelled Britain, like Spain, to tighten its lax imperial policies, the impact on American self-rule in the 1760s caused the American Revolution in the 1770s. The British colonies, unlike New Spain, though, revolted at a time when circumstances favored their undertaking. The averred American ideal of liberty within a body of natural rights appealed to Enlightenment thinkers and stirred the hearts of European intellectuals, even in Britain. On a practical level, Britain's victory in the Seven Years' War gave rise to misgivings among many European nations and fueled an enduring malice in defeated France. Many of those nations implicitly supported the American Revolution because it hurt Britain, and France openly aided the American cause by officially recognizing the United States, entering a military alliance with it, and sending armies, naval squadrons, and money to help in the fight. Mexico's fight for independence, more an internal civil war between royalists and Mexican nationalists, occurred during the maelstrom of the Napoleonic Wars and their aftermath. European governments, weary of ceaselessly fighting Revolutionary France, were tending toward monarchy after defeating Napoleon and were alarmed rather than sympathetic when revolutions broke out anywhere. Britain's judgment to accept American independence at the close of the Revolution was also in sharp contrast to Spain's rejection of Mexican independence as established in the Treaty of Córdoba. The United States began its postwar years with alliances, official recognition from its former owner, and the end of an overt threat to its independence.

This did not mean, however, that the United States was without problems. Bitter disagreements over the role of the central government complicated domestic affairs throughout the years of the early Republic. These arguments and disputes over perceived threats from abroad helped to create factions and harden them into political parties. Through it all, though, Americans held fast to the notion that opposition to the government was not the same as threatening its function, for menacing the government would have been regarded as disloyal to the country. Even the most contentious arguments did not impinge on the results after the ballots were cast and counted. Overarching the sharpest disagreements was a sense that elections were regulated by rules, that their results were protected from the caprice of defeated candidates, and that their decisions were never to be overturned by force of arms. Thomas

Jefferson and his Republican Party won in 1800—a significant shift from the dominant political party, the Federalists—without a political revolt or barracks rebellion. Avoiding a reference to the contentious nature of political parties, Jefferson appealed to a broader embrace of citizens by insisting in his First Inaugural, "We are all republicans, we are all federalists."[7] Other elections such as the 1824 presidential contest were equally as unsettling and even troubled by charges of corruption, but they did not disrupt the political establishment. No equivalent exists in American political history to the Mexican military *pronunciamento* and the usurpation of a sitting government. On the few occasions when discontent grew to noticeable rancor, such as when moonshining farmers challenged federal authority over the Whiskey Tax or New England Federalists flirted with secession to resist unpopular national policies, the rest of the country looked upon the episodes as aberrations and their authors as rogues. The Hartford Convention in late 1814, New England's culminating protest against the War of 1812, left the Federalist Party discredited and in shambles, never again to be consequential in national councils.

Two basic differences distinguished the young American Republic from its Mexican neighbor. One difference was evident in the type of people who became political leaders in the United States. George Washington is an ideal example. Although he rose to prominence because of his military exploits in the American Revolution, Washington sensibly established and sustained a tradition of military subordination to civil authority. At the close of the Revolution, when disgruntled officers began plotting to dissolve Congress and set up a military dictatorship, Washington used his considerable influence to quash the plan and shame its promoters. As the country's first president, he behaved as a chief executive rather than a martial autocrat, and more importantly, he retired from office after serving two terms, a move that surprised friends and opponents alike. Everyone had expected him to remain president for the rest of his life, and a lesser man likely would have. Washington's example of a self-imposed two-term limit would guide presidents for more than a century. Neither the popularity of a president nor the perceived need under emergency for his continuance in office overrode the tradition. America would not become a dictatorship or even a de facto constitutional monarchy, and nobody seriously aspired to make it one.

American distrust of the military was the other major difference. From their British origins, Americans inherited an abiding suspicion of standing armies. Events that preceded the American Revolution reinforced those suspicions, especially Britain's clumsy plan of enforcing imperial policy with garrisons quartered in the colonies. After the Revolution, Americans refused to maintain a large military establishment for both economic and philosophical reasons. In 1784, the U.S. Army consisted of a paltry eighty men, even though foreign threats and internal dangers from hostile Indians could have easily justified a larger force.[8] Instead, the country relied on local militias composed of part-time citizen soldiers, confident that they would protect American liberty without menacing it. Militias frequently proved unreliable in emergencies, but they at least did not threaten the government.

In this relatively stable political environment, Americans conducted their affairs under a solid system of fundamental law defined by the Constitution. After the addition of the first ten amendments (the Bill of Rights) as a package in 1791, the document was amended only two times in the next seventy-five years, and the Eleventh and Twelfth Amendments marked procedural rather than significant changes.[9] Steadiness fostered a growing political maturity that could tolerate dissent, hold regular elections, and entertain innovative ideas that occasionally roused partisan resentments but never provoked rebellions. The election of 1860, conducted in the clamor of increasingly violent arguments over slavery, proved the axiom that democracy can only succeed when opponents disagree about things that do not matter. Even then, however, the objective of southern secession was to leave the American Union, not to overthrow its government.

Ironically, the crisis of 1860 that plunged the United States into its terrible Civil War occurred just twelve years after the Mexican War and was in many ways a direct result of that conflict. Without the land acquired from Mexico, the slavery question would not have emerged in the 1850s as a fractious moral and political issue, one that ultimately proved irresolvable short of war. In that respect, nobody won the Mexican War, for just as losing half its territory grievously injured Mexico, acquiring the territory gravely imperiled the United States as arguments raged over its potential for free or slave status. The Civil War was, first and last, about the land: the owning, settling, taming, and using of it.

Those same questions caused the war between the United States and Mexico. It was always, first and last, about the land.

The Adams-Onís Treaty

In 1815, the United States was a union of eighteen states with a population of some 7.5 million people. That population was growing as it was spreading, and five additional states had come into the Union by 1820. The War of 1812, fought from 1812–1815 with Great Britain over American trading rights and the protection of American honor, had been a near disaster for the young Republic, with shattering military defeats along the Canadian border, the destruction of Washington, D.C., and ruinous raids on the American coast from Maine to the Mississippi River. Yet there had been American successes on Lake Erie, at Baltimore, at Plattsburgh, and most famously at New Orleans. Significantly, American forces during the war virtually eliminated organized Indian resistance to white settlement on the western frontier. The country thus emerged from the war invigorated by a new sense of patriotism and purpose. Its people, impatient with old machines and restless in familiar locales, invented new gadgets and struck out for new places. A sizable number of them headed for that part of Mexico called Texas.

These were turbulent years throughout the Western Hemisphere as Spain's Latin American colonies rebelled and established republics. The United States served as both inspiration and example for these new nations, but these new governments did not always exactly follow the American model, and the inspiration faded in the face of America's official response to Latin American revolutions. On a popular level, Latin American rebels invited comparison to American patriots struggling against Britain and correspondingly raised the sympathy of the American people. Some Americans went so far as to mount filibustering expeditions to aid insurrectionaries and to finance privateers that sailed from American ports to attack Spanish shipping. There were prominent voices in the government offering support as well. Henry Clay was an eloquent champion of Latin American rebellions against Spain's despotism. But the government's official response was complicated by a number of factors, especially the desire to acquire Florida, which Spain owned. When Secretary of State John Quincy Adams entered into prolonged negotiations with Spanish minister Don Luis de Onís about

Florida, Onís made clear that the wrong American response to Latin American uprisings would earn only Spain's displeasure. The stance of Clay and others therefore embarrassed the State Department, eager to placate Spain and ease the acquisition of Florida. The U.S. government tried to stop filibusters and privateering with a sweeping neutrality act in 1818, but after Latin American countries secured independence and established republics, the problem became more snarled. Many Americans regarded the recognition of these new sister republics as not only logical but also morally imperative. After all, were they not inheritors of the American appetite for freedom from European colonialism? Meanwhile, recognition was sure to alienate Spain at the very moment Adams was on the verge of successfully buying Florida. Worse, an angry Spain might take up arms and seek allies in Europe eager to punish the American upstart while reasserting monarchical rule in the rebellious colonies.[10] On the other hand, a prolonged refusal to recognize the Latin American republics was sure to risk their resentment, making enemies of neighbors whose lucrative trade would flow to friendlier countries, such as Britain. For the time being, Adams regarded Spanish amity as more important than Latin American trade, and he staunchly opposed all attempts to have the United States open diplomatic relations with the republics. As far as the U.S. government was concerned, the republics were still part of Spain, a posture that remained policy until the Florida matter was resolved.

The Florida matter was resolved more by force than diplomacy, however. In 1818, Andrew Jackson led an army into Spanish Florida, ostensibly to punish marauding Seminole Indians, but the campaign at last convinced Spain to sell Florida to the United States. Unable to protect its distant province from American incursions and uneasy about losing face with the outright loss of Florida, Spain consented to the Adams-Onís Treaty. Signed in early 1819, it was to have an important impact on events in the Southwest for the next quarter-century, for in addition to transferring Florida to the United States, the treaty defined the western boundary of the Louisiana Purchase. Because Spain had owned Louisiana from 1783 until ceding it to France in 1803, and because Napoleon refused to delineate precisely the extent of Louisiana when he sold it to the United States, the boundary had been in dispute. Many Americans had insisted that Louisiana included the part of New Spain known as Texas. Spain, already angry over France's sale of

Louisiana to the Americans, vehemently disagreed. In 1819, the Adams-Onís Treaty endorsed the Spanish position by setting the border at the mouth of the Sabine River up to the Red River and then extending northward to the 42nd parallel and to the Pacific Coast. The United States relinquished any claim to Texas by agreeing to this border, but the gesture was unpopular and became a political sore spot as the years wore on and Americans focused increasingly on expanding their borders in the Southwest. Many saw Texas as the great missed opportunity of Adams' otherwise brilliant diplomatic triumph, and they almost immediately began thinking of ways to retrieve that opportunity and correct the blunder. The task, as it happened, was made much easier by the fact that Texas, with Mexico's consent, was filling up with Americans.

Conclusion

When Mexico commenced its struggle for independence in 1810, the United States had been functioning under its Constitution for more than twenty years, had held four presidential elections without serious incident, and had with the Louisiana Purchase doubled its territory through diplomacy rather than warfare. During the eleven years it took for Mexico to achieve independence, the United States survived a war against Great Britain and emerged from it energized with renewed national purpose and unity.

Meanwhile, Mexico's winning of independence in 1821 featured an uncertain future, a ruined economy, an empty treasury, and ambitious politicians. By 1823, the country had already discarded one government (Iturbide's empire) and with difficulty established a constitutional republic that labored under bitter disputes between Federalists who insisted upon decentralization and Centralists nostalgic for the days of royalist stability. The Constitution of 1824 established an anemic national government and encouraged a heightened political and economic autonomy among the states. While the Mexican Republic was able to obtain British recognition in 1824, the diplomatic achievement was tempered by Mexico's need to negotiate high-interest loans with Britain to stave off bankruptcy, incurring in the process a crippling indebtedness. The broad suffrage among an illiterate and impoverished population made elections vulnerable to demagogues who plotted in secret societies and often staged outright coups. The system embodied in the Constitution of 1824 survived the fiasco of its first presidential election in 1828, but only because inertia allowed it to remain in place. Politicians, erstwhile revolutionaries, and caudillos plotted, maneuvered, and sometimes took the government by force of arms. By 1836, only thirteen years after achieving independence, Mexico had had one emperor, eleven presidents, and five coups. The barracks rebellion, in fact, had become a routine event that the populace treated as an occasion for festivals. By 1836, the system was in such disrepute that most in the government welcomed its dismantlement as "reform." Nevertheless, the inauguration of the centralist state opened a disastrous period for Mexico. In the ensuing years, the country suffered dire calamities. Losing Texas and fighting a ruinous war with the United States were the most stunning.

Notes

1. The Trigarante Army was to leave its stamp forever on Mexico for the three colors of the Mexican flag symbolize the Three Guarantees in the Plan of Iguala.

2. Francisco Novello was briefly viceroy between the departure of Apodaca and the arrival of O'Donoju.

3. *Fueros* were a relic of old Spanish practice that had been translated to the colony of New Spain. These privileges essentially exempted the military and the church from taxation and having to stand trial in civil courts, and their maintenance by Mexico would become a great source of controversy throughout the period of the republic and afterward.

4. Quoted in Enrique Krauze, *Mexico: Biography of Power, A History of Modern Mexico, 1810–1996*, trans. Hank Heifetz (New York: HarperCollins, 1997), 130.

5. Vicente Guerrero was a *casta*, and some writers have concluded that his execution was a message to the lower classes to keep in their place.

6. For an interpretation that the proponents of central authority, not the advocates of federalism, were the actual cause of chaos in Mexico see Timothy E. Anna, *Forging Mexico: 1821–1835* (Lincoln, NE: University of Nebraska Press, 1998).

7. John Ferling has pointed out that Jefferson's remark is often misrepresented by erroneously capitalizing "Federalists" and "Republicans," thus inferring that he was talking about political parties. Yet, Jefferson's draft lowercased these words, indicating that he was instead describing a common agreement among citizens who all believed in both the Constitution and the

limits of government power. See Ferling, *Adams vs. Jefferson: The Tumultuous Election of 1800* (Oxford: Oxford University Press, 2004), 205.

8. The need to patrol the frontier led to an increase in the army during the 1790s, but the country continued to rely heavily on militia during the period.

9. The Eleventh Amendment addressed the judicial reach of federal and state authorities as sovereign entities. The Twelfth Amendment adjusted the method of selecting the president and vice president to prevent the recurrence of the awkward tie that had occurred in the 1800 election.

10. The close of the Napoleonic Wars saw the formation of the so-called Holy Alliance. Led by autocratic Russia, war-weary European powers sought to preserve monarchy against future revolutions by pledging military assistance to any king threatened by radical domestic uprisings. Britain protested the scheme as costly and meddlesome and consequently never joined the Holy Alliance, but Americans feared that it could nevertheless be invoked to restore to the king of Spain his splintering Latin American empire.

CHAPTER 2

THE TEXAS PROBLEM

While Hernán Cortés and his conquistadors conquered Mexico in 1521, Spanish voyagers in the Caribbean were mapping the coastline of what would become Texas. Shortly afterward a party of shipwreck survivors, including the intrepid Álvar Núñez Cabeza de Vaca, trudged through the southern part of the region. Purposeful exploratory expeditions followed during the next hundred and fifty years. Spaniards who ranged into the region found its inhabitants peaceful, so much so that one group, the Hasanai, labeled the visitors with the fair skins *techas*, a term that loosely translated into "allies" or "friends." Spanish pronunciation corrupted the Hasanai word to *tejas*, and they soon were using it for both the land and the people living on it. The more formal label of Nueva Filipinas was also used, but Spain did not regard the region as particularly valuable by any name. Colonization was not attempted until the late seventeenth century, and even then it did not take. Not until the early eighteenth century did Spaniards manage to plant durable settlements in what became Texas, making it one of the last places of New Spain's northern frontier to be inhabited by colonists.

The Distant Frontier

The first half-century of Spanish exploration—the early sixteenth century—saw treasure seekers poking about the southern parts of North America looking for what native lore claimed were fantastic troves of gold and gemstones in elaborate cities, the fabled Seven Cities of Cíbola. The cities did not exist, and when it became apparent that great treasure was not in the region, the Spanish quickly lost interest in it, except to lay claim to its huge span on maps that delineated every-

thing from Florida to the Pacific Coast as Spanish. Yet, there were almost no Spaniards in Texas. There were precious few people of any
kind, for that matter.

Nueva Filipinas, never carefully surveyed by the Spaniards, remained a nebulous geographical entity that stretched from the neighboring province of Coahuila at the Nueces River in the south to the
Sabine River in the east and to the Red River in the north. Much of
what is now west Texas belonged to the province of New Mexico and
the southwest portions on the lower Rio Grande to Nuevo Santander.
The first Spaniards who settled the region were Catholic missionaries
working among the Indians. When French explorers, Sieur de La Salle
prominent among them, bumptiously claimed the Mississippi River
Valley for Louis XIV, dubbing it Louisiana, Spain had a more compelling
reason to assert its presence in the eastern regions of Texas. By the
1690s, several Spanish missions had sprung up in Texas, but they were
fragile enterprises and were abandoned as quickly as they were established. Continuing French pressure in the region, however, gave Spain
cause to establish the mission system more energetically. A second period of mission building began in the second decade of the eighteenth
century and placed dozens of these establishments throughout the region, including the most populated at Bexar, first settled in 1718 and
eventually to become San Antonio de Bexar. La Bahía del Espíritu
Santo, which became Goliad, was another sizable settlement, and in
east Texas, Nacogdoches was founded in 1779.

For years these small and scattered missions were the only evidence that Spain rather than France claimed lands that had no firm
border between the contending powers. If anything, the sparse population and apparent worthlessness of the land made it uninviting to
French encroachment and made it valuable to Spain only as a frontier
buffer for the richer, more settled parts of New Spain to the south. Raids
by hostile Indians dampened enthusiasm for increased settlement, and
when Spain obtained Louisiana from France in 1763—a result of the
reshuffling of imperial possessions worldwide after the Seven Years'
War—New Spain restructured its provincial administration and all but
deserted east Texas. In the next thirty years, the population declined,
and the government began secularizing those missions that remained.
Although population numbers began to increase in the early nineteenth
century, the number of Spaniards in Texas was still less than four thou-

sand and had increased only by several hundred at the time of Mexican independence.

The small population of Texas was troubling for New Spain, especially when the United States purchased Louisiana from France in 1803, a portent of profound changes in the region. Madrid had agreed to transfer Louisiana to Napoleonic France in 1803 with the caveat that Napoleon would never sell it to the United States. When Napoleon did just that, New Spain was well aware of the fresh problem it faced on its northern frontier. It was one thing for Louisiana to be owned by a distant European neighbor, no matter how aggressive, but quite another to have it owned by a contiguous country, no matter how young and presumably weak. In fact, vigilant Spanish administrators had immediate cause for worry because the permeable border represented by the old and largely dismantled mission system was simply insufficient to protect Spanish interests in the region. American adventurers at the head of armed bands led expeditions into Texas. Even before the Louisiana Purchase, an American named Philip Nolan was traipsing into Texas to steal horses. Spanish authorities finally caught up with Nolan and executed him to deter other interlopers, but there were indigenous problems to cope with as well. The Hidalgo rebellion of 1810 had support in Texas, and in 1811 Texas governor Manuel María de Salcedo had to put down an incipient revolt in San Antonio de Bexar. Two years later, Bernardo Gutiérrez de Lara, an emissary of Mexican insurgents, joined Augustus W. Magee, formerly a lieutenant in the U.S. Army, to lead a group into Texas from Louisiana. Calling their throng the Republican Army of the North, Magee and Lara occupied key positions along the Nueces River, including Nacogdoches, Goliad, and San Antonio de Bexar, where they killed Governor Salcedo and drafted a constitution for a Texas republic. Because Magee died and Gutiérrez de Lara knew next to nothing about military operations, Spanish forces quickly crushed the revolutionary movement by shattering the Army of the North near the Medina River on August 18, 1813. Six years later, though, Mississippian James Long led a filibuster into Texas, captured Nacogdoches, and proclaimed a republic with himself as president. The Spanish Army again rumbled up from the south, putting Long and his followers to flight, but these exercises were becoming expensive, distracting, and disturbingly frequent.[1]

Realizing that the region's sparse population tempted adventurers from the United States, New Spain wanted to boost settlement in Texas, but the project bucked a dispiriting trend: in three centuries Spain had only been able to establish three permanent settlements between the Rio Grande and the Sabine River. Hispanic settlement was not likely to increase the population in the near future, particularly with the continuing menace of hostile Indians and foreign incursions. The province had never been anything but a distant frontier for New Spain, settled with the aim of protecting the interior from French interlopers, and it remained isolated and thinly populated on the eve of Mexican independence. No one could have imagined that a transplanted New Englander would hatch a scheme to settle Texas and that his son would apply it so successfully that it would people the land with Americans.

Settling Texas

Moses Austin was born in Connecticut, cut his entrepreneurial teeth in Virginia, and created a lead-mining empire in Missouri that earned him a fortune before he had turned forty. At the opening of the nineteenth century, he was worth nearly $200,000 (approximately $3 million in today's purchasing power) and watchful for new opportunities, one of which was to help establish the Bank of St. Louis. The bank's failure during the Panic of 1819, however, left Austin not only penniless but also indebted. During the ensuing economic depression, he assessed both his and fellow citizens' predicament as a challenging opportunity rather than a calamitous setback. Although he was fifty-eight years old, he exuded an uncompromising optimism that would have been remarkable for a man half his age. He saw farm foreclosures that left families displaced and eager for a second chance, he read of the Adams-Onís Treaty that established the western border of the Louisiana Purchase, and he gazed beyond that border to the vast, unpopulated expanse of Spanish Texas. Envisioning both a colony of Americans on those lands and another fortune waiting to be made, he set out to persuade Spanish authorities that his plan to populate their empty northern province was in their best interests.

Austin arrived in San Antonio de Bexar on December 23, 1820, and presented to Governor Antonio María Martínez the plan for settling a grant of land with American transplants. Initially, the governor was unimpressed, but Austin persisted, and three days later Martínez sent the proposal to Spanish authorities with his endorsement. Spanish administrators were willing to entertain Austin's idea of a system that made him the *empressario* responsible for enrolling and settling the colonists. The land would have a stable population of families putting down roots, and though settlers would come from the United States, New Spain, in no position to be particular about the matter, regarded increasing the population as the first priority and assimilation the second. To accomplish the latter, settlers would be required to convert to Catholicism and adopt Spanish as their language. The land grant was approved on January 17, 1821, Austin receiving the good news shortly after he returned home. He lived only a few months more, though, for his health was delicate—he had developed pneumonia during his journey—and his exertions to advance Texas colonization worsened his condition. On June 10, 1821, he died with almost his last words imploring that the colonization plan not die with him. His son Stephen was not eager to promote the Texas idea, but he agreed to abide by his father's dying wish and reaffirmed the arrangement with Spanish authorities. The arrangement was deemed such a worthy solution to the Texas population problem that Mexican independence did not derail it. Iturbide confirmed the arrangement as did the Victoria administration when it assumed power under the Constitution of 1824.

Austin was not the only *empressario*—others such as Green DeWitt and Haden Edwards also negotiated to settle families in Texas—but he was the most successful and influential. Their combined efforts were nothing short of breathtaking. Hispanics, whose numbers on the frontier had always been quite small, virtually disappeared in the ensuing Anglo migrations. By 1830, about seven thousand Americans had settled in Texas, more than double the number of Mexicans, making the *empressario* system one of the most successful relocation experiments ever devised. As the elder Austin had predicted, economic hard times in the United States heightened the lure of Texas—the Panic of 1819 and ensuing depression dislodged many southern farmers—and "Texas fever" raged among Americans eager for a new start. The initials "GTT" (for "Gone to Texas") were carved into the walls of countless deserted cabins across the rural South.

Mexico only marginally benefited from this influx. On the one hand, American immigrants were not always the honest, hardworking families that the *empressarios* recruited. Unsavory types trafficked with Indians in guns and liquor, smuggled slaves, and at most saw Texas as a safe haven from bill collectors and American lawmen. Meanwhile, respectable settlers staked out farms in east Texas that were distant from assimilating influences, such as the Mexican settlements in the western part of the province. Although the rules of the *empressario* system required that settlers speak Spanish and convert to Catholicism, they rarely if ever did either. Instead, they remained stubbornly American in words, deeds, and faith. Mexico City had sugared immigration enticements by exempting American settlers from tariff laws, but those settlers ignored Mexican statutes that were in force as well, especially ones attempting to curb or abolish slavery. In fact, American settlers became cynical about the Mexican government, particularly when their encounters with it through unreliable Mexican courts increased popular discontent. While hostile Apaches and Comanches ranged the western stretches of the province, the Mexican Army had too many officers and too little stomach for policing a distant and perilous frontier, and the Mexican government's turbulent fortunes so preoccupied authorities in the nation's capital that they took little notice of Texan affairs until it was too late to do much about them. Unprepared for the size and speed of the American migration, Mexico City was surprised by the growing Anglo population's demands for increasing autonomy. Texas wanted to break away from Coahuila, joined to Texas because there had seemed little need for a separate provincial government over such paltry numbers. When Tejanos (Texans of Mexican descent) began adding their voices to such demands, Mexico City could not ignore the volatile situation in Texas forever.

Startling evidence of that volatility surfaced in 1826 when an uprising in Nacogdoches persuaded Mexico to stop additional American immigration into Texas. This disturbance, eventually known as the Fredonia Rebellion, was initially over land grants. In 1825, brothers Haden and Benjamin Edwards obtained Mexican permission to place a settlement in eastern Texas around Nacogdoches, but the area was already partly settled. The Edwards brothers tried to force these people off their land, but Texas settlers were difficult people to push around. As they stood their ground, their appeals to Mexican authorities resulted in the cancellation of the Edwards' contract, a setback that Benjamin Edwards sought to correct by taking Nacogdoches by force in December 1826.

Although he grandiosely proclaimed the Republic of Fredonia, other *empresarios* led by Stephen Austin condemned his reckless adventurism because it menaced the land grant system by inviting the ire of the Mexican government. Fredonia was able to defend itself at first, but the impending arrival of Mexican soldiers, accompanied by a glowering Austin, persuaded Edwards to depart in some haste for Louisiana.

The Republic of Fredonia was no more, but its brief existence sounded an alarm. Despite Austin's efforts, Mexico City was convinced that Anglo settlers had gone beyond ignoring the rules of assimilation to displaying open disloyalty. Furthermore, Mexico finally noticed that the Anglo population had grown disproportionately large in comparison to the Mexican one. In late 1827, Gen. Manuel Mier y Terán led an expedition to catalog the natural resources of Texas and survey the U.S. border between the Sabine and Red rivers. Most importantly, though, he was to count the Americans living in Texas. Weather and disease impeded the expedition's work, and it was not until early 1829 that it completed its labors, but the findings were sobering. Mier y Terán was convinced that American immigration was merely a prelude to U.S. efforts to acquire Texas, and he recommended an increased Mexican military presence near settlements. His report also called for efforts to integrate Texas into the Mexican economy, promote Mexican immigration to the region, and prohibit additional American colonization.

Mindful of Texans' prickly mood, the government had exempted them from President Vicente Guerrero's September 15, 1829, decree abolishing slavery, but a law of April 6, 1830, included the main points of Mier y Terán's report and prohibited the importation of additional slaves. The predictable Texan protest would have been more vehement except for the inherent conservatism of the Anglo settlements, which were under the influence of moderates like Stephen Austin. In addition, both the Mexican national and Coahuila state governments erratically applied antislavery provisions in Texas. Accordingly, the 1830 law proved virtually unenforceable as American settlers, many with slaves, continued to enter the province. By the time Mier y Terán returned as Commandant General of the Eastern Interior Provinces in 1830, a post that gave him authority over Texas, the situation had further deteriorated. His attempt to enforce new tariff policies led to civil unrest, and the growing disarray of Mexico's government in the early 1830s worsened matters. Deeply depressed by his inability to control the extant

American population, let alone halt its increase, Mier y Terán committed suicide on July 3, 1832, the first Mexican casualty of an incipient independence movement that neither he nor Mexico City could stop.

The Texas Revolution

Anglos and Tejanos convened in October 1832 and drew up a petition requesting the repeal of the 1830 immigration and slavery law. Austin continued to counsel restraint and called for loyalty to Mexico, but he consented to deliver the petition, obviously thinking that he could make its case without endangering Mexico-Texas relations. Yet, Austin's mission occurred during the instability caused by Gómez Farías's sweeping reforms, and the government was in no mood for distractions from distant provinces. During his sporadic visits to the capital, Santa Anna was courtly, polite, and apparently willing to reach some form of accommodation, but as days stretched into weeks, Austin began to doubt the sincerity of the sometimes-president. Frustrated by the delay, Austin unwisely wrote a letter to associates in Texas expressing his doubts and injudiciously suggesting that at the least Texas should break away from Coahuila. When the letter fell into the government's hands, Gómez-Farías had Austin arrested. The *empressario* spent almost two years in jail before his release sent him back to Texas. By then, he was so embittered by the experience that he was convinced that independence was the only correct course for Texas to pursue, even if it required force.

By the time of Austin's release, Santa Anna had abolished the Constitution of 1824 and had resolved to crush rebellions in all the fractious states. As part of this new policy, Mexican soldiers attempted to confiscate a cannon in Gonzales, Texas, in October 1835, and sparked a sharp little fight in which the feisty men of Gonzales drove off the soldiers and kept their cannon. It was not much of a clash, but open revolt against Mexico did not need a larger one, and events began to move more rapidly than either Santa Anna or Texans realized. In fact, when Austin returned from his imprisonment, many Texans had made up their minds about independence. They united behind Austin and other leaders to drive Mexican military forces from the territory. A week after the fight at Gonzales, Texans seized Goliad, and in November, Anglo and Tejano volunteers commanded by Austin mounted a siege against the Mexican garrison at San Antonio de Bexar. Also in that month, Texas separated from Coahuila when a convention established a provisional government, appointed a council, and elected a governor. Although the stated goal for these actions was to secure rights guaranteed by the Constitution of 1824, no one could have doubted that independence from Mexico was a whispered resolve.

At San Antonio, an ineffectual Austin, still sick from his imprisonment, turned over command to Edward Burleson and set out for the United States to seek financial aid for the rebellion. Finally, under the command of Col. Benjamin Milam the rebels began an assault on December 5. Five days of hard fighting through San Antonio's streets pushed Gen. Marín Perfecto de Cós and his men into the former mission called the Alamo and compelled their surrender on December 10. Cós' capitulation was as humiliating for him as it was pleasant for the Texans, because he was Santa Anna's brother-in-law. After paroling their prisoners, the Texans relished what seemed the relatively easy defense of their rights. Complacency prompted many Anglos either to return to their homes or strike out on ill-advised adventures such as an attack on distant Matamoros. Texans also took comfort in the conventional wisdom that Santa Anna would not commence a campaign until weather improved in late spring.

Santa Anna did not intend to wait before punishing Texan rebels and avenging the embarrassment of his brother-in-law. Fresh from suppressing Zacatecas, he marched an army across a thousand miles of tough terrain in dreadful winter weather to arrive at San Antonio de Bexar in late February 1836. The toll of the march was high—more than half his force had fallen out or deserted—but the Texan situation was even grimmer. When Santa Anna arrived, Col. William B. Travis in command at the Alamo sent urgent appeals for reinforcements, yet all but one of them remained unanswered. Only the thirty-two spirited men of the Gonzales Ranging Company answered Travis' call. Santa Anna commenced an intermittent but destructive bombardment for thirteen days before hurling some two thousand soldiers against the Alamo in the predawn darkness of March 6. The makeshift fort's 187 defenders, the famous Davy Crockett and an ailing Jim Bowie among them, only lasted a few hours, and seeking to overawe remaining rebels, Santa Anna had decreed there would be no survivors among those who resisted.[2] Another part of the Mexican Army meanwhile defeated small

Map 2.1

Texas forces at San Patricio, Agua Dulce, and Refugio. (See Map 2.1.)
A fate similar to the Alamo's awaited Col. James W. Fannin's command
of 280 men when they surrendered at Coleto Creek on March 20. After
briefly being held captive at Goliad while other rebels were rounded
up, these men were also executed. Their number by then was almost
four hundred. Santa Anna meant to frighten the rest of Texas into submission with ruthlessness.

Many did flee, but those who stayed were made more resolute by
the slaughter of the Alamo garrison and Fannin's command. On March

2, 1836, delegates meeting in an unprepossessing shack at Washington-on-the-Brazos had declared Texas' independence from Mexico. They placed the physically impressive Sam Houston, formerly governor of Tennessee and friend of Andrew Jackson, in command of the Texas army. Houston at first alarmed the Texas provisional government as he led his forces on an extended retreat toward the east, but the Texans picked up additional recruits, mainly from the United States, and were rested and ready for revenge when they shocked part of Santa Anna's army near the San Jacinto River on April 21, 1836. To shouts of "Remember the Alamo!" and "Remember Goliad!" Houston's approximately nine hundred men shredded Mexican lines and killed nearly half of Santa Anna's thirteen hundred soldiers in less than a half hour. Santa Anna himself was accidentally captured the next day—he had skulked away from the battle disguised as a common soldier—and was forced to sign the Treaty of Velasco on May 14. In the treaty he agreed to order all Mexican armies out of Texas and to convince the Mexican government to recognize Texas' independence.

The botched campaign against Texas revolutionaries destroyed Santa Anna's reputation in Mexico and ended any influence he had with the government. Although the Mexican military reluctantly withdrew south of the Rio Grande, Mexico City refused to ratify the Treaty of Velasco and continued to insist, as Texans adopted a constitution and set up a republican government, that Texas was still a part of Mexico. In addition, Mexico was convinced that the entire affair had been sponsored by the United States with the aim of obtaining Texas. During the summer of 1836, U.S. Brig. Gen. Edmund Pendleton Gaines briefly led troops into northeastern Texas, confirming for Mexico City that the United States was up to no good in the region.

U.S.-Mexican Diplomacy

The boundaries that the Adams-Onís Treaty established between the United States and New Spain were inherited by Mexico, but American desires to own Texas were never in doubt. John Quincy Adams had not wanted to give up Texas to Spain in his negotiations with Onís, and when he became president in 1825, he tried to purchase it from Mexico. Mexico's rejection of the offer did not discourage the U.S. government from repeating it in 1827 and again in 1829 when Andrew Jackson became president. The persistent American offers filled both President Guadalupe Victoria and his successor Vicente Guerrero with considerable apprehension. U.S. minister Joel Poinsett certainly hoped and more than suggested that his influence with the Mexican government would make negotiations for purchasing Texas relatively easy.

Actually, the two countries needed a formal treaty to sanction even the boundary established by Adams-Onís, but Poinsett was reluctant to suggest, as his government wanted, that Mexico discard the 1819 treaty boundary and recognize a line south of the Sabine River. The money Adams was willing to pay at this point—a million dollars—was insufficient in Poinsett's view, and rather than risk insulting the Victoria administration into intransigence, he let the matter lay. Moreover, Poinsett became convinced that the Texas question was preventing the resolution of other important agreements. He was probably correct, because after he finally agreed in January 1828 to the Adams-Onís line, he was able to arrange a commercial treaty only weeks later. Although the U.S. Senate ratified both treaties that spring, the Mexican Senate displayed its growing distrust of Poinsett by delaying its deliberations. Guerrero took office in the meantime and resolved to have the treaties concluded by calling the Mexican Congress into special session in August 1829, but the timing was unfortunate. The Spanish invasion of Tampico prompted the president to declare a national emergency, and Mexico's attention was consequently on other matters. Besides, the continuing delay underscored the fact that Poinsett had been deeply involved in the Masonic controversies—he had helped establish the York-rite lodges—and increased the perception that he habitually meddled in Mexican affairs. In short, his behavior had irreparably alienated a significant portion of the Mexican political establishment.

Andrew Jackson thus became the U.S. president with the boundary still officially undetermined. Jackson hoped to exploit Mexico's poverty and its national emergency over the Spanish invasion to America's advantage. He planned to offer $5 million for Texas, or as much of it as Mexico would part with, a bargain he claimed would provide Mexico with the means to fight Spain while cementing Mexican-American amity. It was an extraordinary offer completely unacceptable to the Mexican government. Poinsett was utterly discredited, and Jackson replaced him with Anthony Butler, a second-rate political operative and land speculator infamous for an ambiguous morality that Mexicans found immediately objectionable. Butler suggested bribery as a way to advance negotiations, a recommendation that Jackson read with a sly smile, scrawling on the back of Butler's communication, "A Butler. What a scamp."[3] Mexican officials were considerably less amused. They demanded Butler's recall.

Butler did more than offend Mexicans. He revealed an increasingly impatient American interest in Texas that deeply troubled them. Like any young country, Mexico was touchy about its territory. One of the charges at deposed president Vicente Guerrero's trial was that he had secretly conspired with Poinsett to sell Texas to the United States. No evidence has ever surfaced to support that charge, but Guerrero's execution sent a clear message to any subsequent official regarding the matter: Texas was not for sale upon pain of death. Under those circumstances, the fate of Texas, already filling up with Americans, remained uncertain. Painfully obvious, though, was that Mexico, beset by internal turmoil and incapable of governing far-flung provinces, owned a remote piece of real estate that was wanted by the United States, a country rapidly and aggressively expanding its borders.

Consequences of Texas Independence

The Texas Revolution naturally appealed to American traditions of self-government and resistance to tyranny, but more important was the fact that an overwhelming majority of Texans were Americans whose relatives in the United States were outraged by the atrocities at the Alamo and Goliad. Popular assemblies throughout the United States adopted pro-Texan resolutions, citizens groups raised money, and eager men and boys mustered themselves into volunteer companies that, had the fighting lasted longer, might actually have seen action across the Sabine River. In the face of such popular sentiment, the U.S. government was lackadaisical in enforcing its 1818 neutrality law.

Texas independence nonetheless presented the United States with a serious diplomatic dilemma, for merely acknowledging the Texas Republic was sure to enrage Mexico. On the other hand, any American plan to incorporate Texas into the United States held the potential for grave domestic repercussions. Many Americans wanted Texas, and almost all Texans wanted to join the United States, but just as many

Americans were adamantly opposed to annexing Texas. At the center of the dispute was slavery. The United States had already experienced a serious political crisis over slavery during the debates on Missouri statehood in 1819. The resulting Missouri Compromise established the dividing line between free and slave states at 36° 30', the southern border of Missouri, with the stipulation that slavery would not be permitted north of that line in the remainder of the Louisiana Purchase. Texas already had slavery, of course, and was entirely below 36° 30'. Abolitionists, taking their cue from suspicious Mexicans, claimed that the Texas Revolution had been nothing more than a plan by southern slaveholders to expand their economic system and increase their political influence. The North-South divide on the issue became so impassioned that Andrew Jackson resolutely steered the Democratic Party clear of it. He even waited to extend diplomatic recognition to the Texas Republic until he was about to leave office in March 1837. Jackson's successor, Martin Van Buren, was equally aware of the political predicament Texas promised, and so the issue receded from the center of public discussion and political contention for the next several years.

Seeming American indifference compelled prideful Texans to take annexation off the table in late 1838. Yet many problems beleaguered Texas independence, including an empty treasury, mounting debts, hostile Indians, and Mexico's continued assertion that Texas was not independent. In fact, Mexico seemed bent on eventually avenging its humiliation and reclaiming its territory. In the face of such threats, Texans felt compelled to keep a larger army than they could afford because nobody knew when Mexico might attack. Keeping the Lone Star Republic jittery were two desultory Mexican invasions that were unimpressive other than to demonstrate how ill equipped Texas was to defend itself. Some form of outside assistance was essential. Rebuffed by the United States, Texas looked to Europe, first to secure recognition and then to craft treaties and negotiate loans. Europe was interested, particularly the British, who weighed Texas on the scale of imperial affairs. Texas in Britain's orbit could block U.S. expansion, which, if unchecked, would threaten Britain's influence in both the Caribbean and the Pacific. Texas could provide British textile mills with cotton to lessen an uncomfortable reliance on cotton from the plantations of the American South. Texas could also serve as an open, tariff-free market for goods from British factories. American abolitionists violently opposed embracing Texas because of slavery, but British abolitionists saw an opportunity to advance their cause there. Perhaps Texas would be amenable to giving up slavery for British friendship, abolishing the hated institution in exchange for money and protection. Other European capitals, jealous of Yankee commerce and wary of Yankee expansionism, weighed their opportunity in Texas as well. France followed Britain's lead to extend recognition to the Republic and sign treaties to bolster its commerce.

Annexation

The implications of these events for the United States eventually outweighed the diplomatic and domestic perils of annexation. Even so, several twists of fate were required before annexation was viable.

In 1840, the Whig Party won the presidency, primarily over issues surrounding the economy, but the victor, William Henry Harrison, caught cold at his inauguration and died of pneumonia thirty days later. Harrison's vice president was Virginian John Tyler, vaulted unexpectedly into office and was almost immediately a disappointment to the Whig Party, for Tyler quickly adopted stances more in tune with states' rights Democrats. As Whigs fumed over their inability to enact a coherent legislative program, they derided Tyler with mocking titles such as "His Accidency" and finally cast him out of their party. These antics delighted Democrats, but they did not welcome Tyler as one of their own. Consequently, Tyler found himself a president without a party, and though that handicap was a considerable disadvantage in many respects, on the matter of Texas, it became a unique advantage. With nothing to lose by further alienating the Whigs, he was freed from soothing the party's anti-Texas attitudes and could pursue annexation unencumbered. Whigs accused him of pushing for Texas annexation either to court Democratic support or to form a coalition of expansionists into a third-party movement that would nominate him for a second term. And though Tyler likely contemplated the possibility of his actions redeeming his political fortunes, the man who named his Virginia home "Sherwood Forest" because he saw himself as a political renegade like Robin Hood, was increasingly indifferent to the chatter of parties and the reproach of critics. Tyler became fixated on annexing Texas.

Texas was understandably guarded about new offers of American annexation, but circumstance and necessity combined to persuade Texas that the time for resolving relations with the United States was at hand. Independence had been a difficult ride for Texas. Sam Houston, the Republic's first president, was succeeded by a transplanted Georgian named Mirabeau Buonaparte Lamar, who lived up to his bombastic name by implementing big (and costly) plans. Lamar reacted petulantly to American reluctance over annexation by claiming that Texas did not need the United States. He established a new capital named Austin in untamed western Indian country and envisioned extending Texas' borders to the Pacific, but his schemes merely scraped the bottom of an empty treasury, excited Indians to additional hostilities, and resulted in a ruinous attack on Mexican Santa Fe. By the end of Lamar's presidency, Texas was in such a muddle that its citizens were clamoring for a solution. Although Sam Houston, embittered by American actions, was reportedly unfriendly to renewed annexationist overtures from the United States, his return to office coincided with a growing pro-annexationist sentiment throughout the republic.

For their part, President Tyler and Secretary of State Abel Upshur worked unstintingly to line up the necessary two-thirds Senate majority to ensure ratification of an annexation treaty, but the administration's plans were seriously threatened by a freak accident. In February 1844, a presidential party cruised the Potomac River on the USS *Princeton* when a cannon exploded during a firing demonstration and killed Upshur. Tyler scrambled to rescue Texas annexation in the wake of this tragic event, but he seemed to make a major mistake by appointing John C. Calhoun as Upshur's replacement. Calhoun, a South Carolinian whose political philosophy had increasingly inclined toward southern sectionalism and states' rights, had watched Britain's abolitionist goals in Texas with alarm. After taking over at the State Department, he unwisely lashed out at Sir Richard Pakenham, the British minister to the United States, in a letter that exalted the beneficence of slavery. The language was bad enough, and the gesture was both undiplomatic and impolitic, but the letter's attitude did the most damage. Abolitionists were reanimated in their opposition to annexation—the abolitionist poet John Greenleaf Whittier railed at "slave-accursed

Texas"—convinced that they now had proof that the initiative was a southern conspiracy.[4] Worse for the administration, this perception spread from the abolitionist fringe and took hold among the northern public.

In such an unpromising atmosphere, the Texas annexation treaty made its way to the Senate. The treaty's timing was bad for reasons other than Calhoun's outburst, for debates over it coincided with the presidential campaign of 1844. Inevitably, expansionism became the centerpiece of a bitter election. Antislavery forces latched on to a demand for "All Oregon," a reference to the enormous (and slave-free) region in the Pacific Northwest disputed by the United States and Great Britain. Texas annexation was equally contentious, and an attempt to retire it from political discussion wrecked Martin Van Buren's chance for the Democratic nomination. A letter he published in the *New York Globe* opposing annexation gave the appearance that Van Buren had made a cynical bargain with Whig nominee Henry Clay to avoid the Texas issue in the coming campaign. Simultaneously a letter by Clay appeared, stating, "I consider the annexation of Texas . . . as a measure compromising the national character."[5]

Andrew Jackson was representative of Southerners enraged by Van Buren's apostasy and abruptly withdrew support for his candidacy. Emerging from the remaining pack of contenders was America's first dark-horse candidate, Tennessean James K. Polk, a man of limited abilities but boundless ambition whose nomination seemed a triumph for the annexationists. It was the season's only triumph for them, however, as the Texas annexation treaty proved a predictable casualty of the disagreeable debate. On June 8, 1844, the Senate rejected it by a crushing two-thirds majority.

Undeterred, Democrats redoubled their efforts for annexation. To placate the northern wing of the party, the Democratic platform stridently called for attaining "All Oregon" with the famous cry of "Fifty-Four Forty or Fight!" hoping that Oregon would serve as a counterweight for Texas. As for the mood of the country, it obviously inclined toward those promising to advance what newspaper writer John L. O'Sullivan would call America's "manifest destiny" to extend its borders across the continent.[6] That autumn, voter impatience with Clay's indecision about Texas in particular and Manifest Destiny in general cost him the election and placed Polk in the White House.

Polk's margin of victory was slight and put in doubt the success of another annexation treaty. Lame-duck John Tyler, in office until Polk's inauguration in March 1845, nevertheless chose to interpret Polk's election as a mandate for expansion. Tyler was also concerned that Britain would accelerate its plans to solidify and bolster Texas' independence before Polk took office. Tyler's fears were not unfounded, for Britain had openly advanced several plans to keep Texas out of the American Union. In the spring of 1844, Foreign Secretary Lord Aberdeen thought he could capitalize on American anti-annexationist sentiment by proposing that the United States join Britain, France, Texas, and Mexico in a pact to guarantee Texas independence. Aberdeen's plan, however, had only lukewarm backing from France, and all stripes of American opinion suspected Britain's ulterior motives. Richard Pakenham, the British minister in Washington, measured American Anglophobia and counseled Aberdeen to postpone any movement on the plan until after the 1844 election. If Britain were perceived as meddling in Texas, Democrats, already bellicose about Oregon, might rally even their opponents to their cause. The greatest hope for Britain was Clay's election, something that London counted on in an obvious miscalculation. Polk's victory, in fact, set the British government back on its heels because it now had to cope with growing Anglo-American tension over the Pacific Northwest. Aberdeen placed Texas on a back burner.

But only briefly. In late January, he dispatched a special emissary to Mexico City to persuade the Mexican government to recognize Texas' independence in exchange for Texas' pledge to rebuff American annexation offers. Finally persuaded to agree to this British plan, Mexico at long last admitted the nine-year-old reality of Texas' separation. By then, it was too late.

Texans made the most of Polk's apprehensions about Britain. In fact, they correctly judged themselves in a seller's market where their agents could tout the benefits of a Lone Star Republic to the British while describing the benefits of a Lone Star State to the Americans. Confronted with the specter of a British satellite inclined to abolitionism on his southwestern border, Tyler felt that a solution to Senate obstructionism was especially urgent. With good reason he doubted that anyone could cobble together a two-thirds annexationist majority there, so the administration resorted to a joint resolution, which required only simple majorities in both houses. The annexation resolution sailed through the expansionist House on January 25, 1845, by a comfortable vote of 120 to 98, but it barely squeaked through the bitterly divided Senate on February 27, 1845, by a margin of two votes (27 to 25). Regardless of the mixed nature of the vote, the matter was done. Just days later on March 1, 1845, as almost the last official act of his presidency, Tyler signed the joint resolution. The apparent disregard of constitutional protocol to satisfy expansionist expediency infuriated abolitionists, but their voices could not carry in the heady atmosphere of Manifest Destiny. As far as the U.S. government was concerned, Texas was slated to become part of the Union.

The British plan of exchanging Mexican recognition for Texas allegiance instantly became a dead letter. After the United States made its firm offer of annexation, Mexico's tardy concession never stood a chance of attracting significant support among Texans who harbored an abiding anger toward their former owner. There might have been a lingering resentment about the United States' belated proffer and some Texans would retain an enduring nostalgia for the might-have-beens of independence, but they were in the minority. America held the attraction of a shared culture, language, and heritage as well as the promise of financial and material aid against a host of enemies, Mexico chief among them. That summer a Texas convention voted almost unanimously to reject the Mexican offer and accept the American invitation.

The Developing Crisis

With annexation, Texas immediately became the center of a serious controversy between the United States and Mexico. The Mexican government had plainly stated that annexation would be regarded as an act of war, and Mexican minister to Washington Juan Almonte wasted no time in breaking diplomatic relations. Just days after John Tyler signed the annexation resolution, Almonte closed his embassy and departed for home. Reaction in Mexico City was equally decisive. Acting Mexican president José Joaquín de Herrera proclaimed "the clear right to use all her [Mexico's] resources and power to resist, to the last moment, said annexation."[7] In due course, the American minister to Mexico left his post as well. Mexico and the United States were not speaking.

They needed to, and for reasons other than the fact that Mexico had something that Polk wanted. In addition to any territorial plans the Polk administration had for the Southwest, the troubling boundary dispute between Texas and Mexico now had the potential to get out of hand. Spain's colonial system and Mexico's provincial arrangements had always marked the Nueces River as Texas' southernmost boundary. Santa Anna's capture after San Jacinto, however, had caused him to legitimize the Rio Grande as the boundary, a claim stubbornly sustained by Texas. The amount of territory in question was significant, for the Rio Grande extended much farther west than the Nueces, pushing northward from El Paso to Santa Fe and beyond. In the years following the Texas Revolution, the point was somewhat academic because Mexico insisted that Texas was not independent. Texas felt the matter was anything but academic, of course, and once Texas became part of the United States, James K. Polk supported the Texas claim.

Financial issues loomed too, and Mexico had a history of allowing its debts to cook up trouble. The country's frequent internal disorders occasionally injured foreigners residing in Mexico, destroying their property and physically injuring them. Andrew Jackson in 1837 surveyed the situation and suggested that such depredations merited "immediate war."[8] The French actually acted on such an impulse to send a sizable naval squadron to Veracruz in 1838, ostensibly to collect debts owed to a French baker whose shop had been destroyed in Puebla. Before the so-called Pastry War was over, the blockade of Veracruz had become a full-scale invasion. The French squadron destroyed the town and damaged its famous fortress, and French soldiers occupied the area. In this sorry episode, Santa Anna rehabilitated his reputation by appearing on the scene with no government authority but claiming that he would liberate Mexico from these trespassing bill collectors. He led a futile attack that left him seriously wounded, requiring his leg to be amputated, but his behavior was hailed by all of Mexico, and later the disembodied leg was given a state funeral. Having taken the only seemingly resolute action in what was an otherwise embarrassing display of Mexican impotence, Santa Anna emerged from the Pastry War physically hobbled but with his status as national hero fully restored. As for the French, they left Veracruz of their own volition, but not before the Mexican government had promised to pay 600,000 pesos in damages and submit to arbitration conducted by the British.

Andrew Jackson's threats of war remained only threats, though, as American claims were referred to commissioners from both countries in 1839. The commission calculated the bill at some $2 million. As the French could have attested, Mexican finances could not afford a fraction of that figure, and even with the best intentions, no Mexican government was able to pay off the debt. Although Mexico made efforts to stay current with payments, they were frequently insubstantial, and a considerable balance remained outstanding in 1845, with Mexico in arrears.

California

Of overarching importance for Polk was the matter of the West Coast. As the administration worked to settle differences with Britain over Oregon, Polk weighed with undisguised enthusiasm the commercial and strategic potential of American ports along the coast south of Oregon. The lucrative China trade, already partly tapped by intrepid New England merchant shippers, was a powerful incentive to round out the contour of America's continental destiny, a contour that Polk believed must include California to have any logic. Acquisitive Americans in the East had long been gazing on California. Andrew Jackson offered Mexico a half million dollars for San Francisco alone in 1835, but selling anything to the Americans was out of the question. John Tyler had tried another tack in 1842 when he proposed a favorable Oregon boundary settlement with Britain in exchange for British help in acquiring part of California from Mexico, but the complicated plan came to nothing. Meanwhile glowing reports of California's salubrious climate, abundant natural resources, and impressive ports boosted American interest. San Francisco, according to American minister to Mexico Waddy Thompson, was "capacious enough to receive the navies of all the world."[9] Feverish American enthusiasm was starkly revealed in 1842 when rumors that war had broken out with Mexico prompted U.S. Navy commodore Thomas ap Catesby Jones to seize Monterey and proclaim California as American territory. A day later Jones learned that there was no war, took down the U.S. flag, and braced for the reprimands his embarrassed government leveled at him while it was extending abject apologies to Mexico. American regrets were grudgingly accepted, but Mexico considered the incident as foreshadowing America's secret plans.

Mexico had reason to be wary, for California had the earmarks of becoming another Texas. Actually, there were two Californias for Mexico—the Baja peninsula was one and Alta California, or upper California, the other. The latter was a distant land made exotic by the foreign interlopers who became permanent residents, people from Russia, Britain, and the United States. The population of Alta California numbered about twenty-five thousand in the 1820s, the Hispanic portion of which was quite small and included soldiers garrisoning presidios at San Francisco, Monterey, Santa Barbara, and San Diego. Californios clustered around pueblos and Franciscan missions, and they were owners of prosperous ranchos whose heyday came after the Mexican government secularized church holdings in 1833.

A number of Americans had wandered into the region, which was even more distant from Mexico City than Texas and, as noted, boasted even fewer Mexicans besides. In addition, the omnipresent British were making Americans edgy. The U.S. Navy's precipitous seizure of Monterey was sparked by alarm over British naval activity in the Pacific, judged by Commodore Jones as a sign of British designs on California. If we recall that American diplomats were equally unsettled by British influence in Mexico and Texas during these years, we can sympathize with that judgment. We now know that the British government was more interested in establishing a foothold in Texas than California, but Americans at the time were not taking any chances. In the wake of the Monterey incident, the Tyler administration made Thomas O. Larkin, an American resident of Mexican California, U.S. consul in Monterey, and shortly after taking office in 1845, Polk designated Larkin as a confidential agent with the job of secretly promoting American interests in California. Polk's fear that Britain was eyeing his prize spurred him to arrange a rapid and thorough settlement of the matter with Mexico. Polk was consequently compelled to reopen diplomatic relations with Mexico. The failure to reopen those relations would be a direct cause of war.

Conclusion

U.S. expansionists wanted Texas from the time of the Louisiana Purchase, and many thought John Quincy Adams's arrangement in

1819 that relinquished claim to the region a bad bargain. Blind to the gathering forces in the North, the Mexican government in the 1820s could not forecast the dangers of agreeing to large American settlements in Texas. At the end of the decade, when Mexico tried to restrict American immigration and monitor those settlements, it provoked a growing discontent and courted disaster. Insistently American in their culture and political beliefs, Texans were increasingly vexed by Mexican efforts to enforce unpopular laws and control previously unregulated behavior. Their revolt became a successful revolution for independence, conducted in emulation of the American patriot example, a sentiment that eventually overcame domestic and diplomatic obstacles to American annexation.

Yet annexing Texas meant alienating Mexico just when newly installed President James K. Polk was eager to realize America's continental aspirations by acquiring the Pacific Coast. Negotiating with Mexico was made impossible by the Texas problem, but Polk was undaunted by the challenge. He instructed Zachary Taylor to assemble a so-called Army of Observation at Corpus Christi. He ordered Commodore David Connor's squadron to stand off Veracruz and dispatched Commodore John Sloat's squadron to the California coast, just in case. Then, in the best tradition of a man bargaining from a position of considerable power, James K. Polk made Mexico an offer it could not refuse.

Notes

1. Long was eventually captured and would die in a Spanish prison in Mexico, but his wife Jane was living near Galveston when she gave birth to his daughter in 1821, reportedly the first American born in Texas.

2. Santa Anna permitted some twenty women and children to leave during the siege. After the battle, he spared the wife of one of the defenders, Suzanna Dickenson, and Travis' slave Joe, less from compassion than to have them relate to Texas revolutionaries elsewhere what they had seen.

3. Anthony Butler to Andrew Jackson, March 7, 1834, in vol. 5, *The Correspondence of Andrew Jackson*, ed. John Spencer Bassett (Washington: The Carnegie Institution of Washington, 1927–1928), 251.

4. Whittier is quoted in Margaret L. Coit, *John C. Calhoun: American Portrait* (Boston: Houghton Mifflin Company, 1950), 372.

5. Clay's letter appeared in the *National Intelligencer*, April 17, 1844, while Van Buren's was published the same day in the *New York Globe*.

6. John L. O'Sullivan, "Annexation," *United States Magazine and Democratic Review*, July 1845.

7. Steven R. Butler, ed., *A Documentary History of the Mexican War* (Richardson, TX: Descendants of Mexican War Veterans, 1995), 5.

8. Andrew Jackson, Special Message of February 6, 1837, in vol. 3 *A Compilation of the Messages and Papers of the Presidents, 1789–1908*, ed. James D. Richardson (Washington: Bureau of National Literature and Art, 1908), 278.

9. Thompson is quoted in R. G. Cleland, "Asiatic Trade and the American Occupation of the Pacific Coast," *Annual Report* (American Historical Association, 1914), 287.

CHAPTER 3

WAR

Negotiations Fail

In September 1845, President James K. Polk proposed to his cabinet that he send John Slidell to Mexico to establish the Rio Grande border and negotiate the purchase of Alta California and New Mexico. Polk was prepared to authorize Slidell to go as high as $40 million for the territory, but he believed the Mexican government would accept less. An even larger concern than money, though, was the necessity of overcoming obvious Mexican hostility. Polk wanted to make sure the Mexican government was willing to talk before dispatching Slidell. A message to the American consul in Mexico City, John Black, instructed him to feel out the Mexican government on the matter. Black's queries resulted in a series of misunderstandings that would have been comical if their consequences had not been so serious. As it was, Slidell's upcoming trip was more than a complete waste of time; it gave Polk an initial, if flimsy, pretext for war.

After Black met with Mexican foreign minister Manuel de la Peña y Peña, the Mexican government said that it would meet with a U.S. commissioner "to settle the present dispute."[1] Peña y Peña also requested that the United States demonstrate good faith by removing the implicit menace posed by U.S. Navy commodore David Conner's squadron that had been standing off Veracruz since the break in diplomatic relations. This seemingly positive change in U.S.-Mexican affairs prompted Conner to move away from the Mexican coast, and the good news that Mexico was willing to talk was sent to Washington. Missing from these glad tidings, however, was any tangible understanding concerning what Mexico was willing to talk about, let alone to whom. Nevertheless, when Black's news reached Washington, the Polk administration misunder-

stood what the Mexican government was willing to do. Peña y Peña had
no intention of reopening formal diplomatic relations with the United
States. The trouble over Texas, especially the Texas claim about the Rio
Grande boundary—the "present dispute" in the language of the Mexican communiqué—was the only matter to be discussed. As far as Mexico was concerned, Texas would have to accept the Nueces River
boundary as a condition of Mexico resuming formal relations with the
United States. In any case, not an acre of Mexican territory was for sale.

The Polk administration, however, oddly perceived that Peña y
Peña's message reestablished formal diplomatic relations, a state of affairs that made everything negotiable. Slidell's formal instructions accordingly designated him as a minister, the highest rank accorded to
any American diplomat.[2] The matter of Slidell's title alone meant that
the Mexican government could not talk to him. To do so would reopen
formal diplomatic relations without resolving the principal reasons for
breaking them, which were the substantial injury caused by Texas annexation and U.S. support for the Rio Grande boundary. Mexico's
stormy political climate would not allow a government to survive that
abandoned the country's interests.

Despite indications that Polk was being either obtuse or disin-
genuous, he was not completely ignorant of Mexico's delicate domestic situation. For example, he told Slidell not to bring up the purchase
of New Mexico and Alta California if doing so would impede discussions about the Rio Grande boundary. On the other hand, Polk knew
what he wanted and was clearly willing to do whatever was necessary
to get it. He had already set in motion a secret initiative that he hoped
would turn California into another Texas by inciting an indigenous rebellion there, overthrowing Mexican authority and requesting U.S. annexation. Thomas O. Larkin, the American consul at Monterey,
California, was told to alert residents, many of them immigrants from
the United States, of American willingness to accept California into the
Union. Yet, the fact that Polk also instructed Larkin not to do anything
to offend the Mexican government indicates that the president expected
Slidell to make real progress. In short, Polk apparently did not appre-
hend the technical diplomatic problem the dispatch of an American
minister posed.

For President José Joaquín de Herrera's government, Slidell's arrival posed more than a technical diplomatic problem. The prospect of

receiving an American minister caused a first-rate domestic crisis. Herrera's opponents vehemently objected to any negotiations with the United States and certainly to any accommodation regarding the Rio Grande boundary. Feverish intrigue in Mexico City made secrets impossible, and despite great exertions to keep Slidell's visit confidential, both his impending arrival and his instructions were common knowledge. Even before Slidell set foot in the capital, the Mexican press and people were in full cry protesting Herrera's apparent willingness to talk to him.

The president was in trouble for other reasons too. Like so many of his predecessors in that unhappy republic, Herrera had come to power because of a revolt (his was on December 6, 1844) and was referred to with the customary euphemism of "acting president" (meaning, latest usurper) until his formal election in August 1845. The trappings of legitimacy were fragile adornments, though, when even a sizable number of those who had supported the 1844 revolt now saw Herrera's *moderados* (or moderates) as unable to tackle the hard business of toughening up Mexico. After the annexation confrontation with the United States had turned out so badly, Herrera's presidency survived only because his opponents were at each other's throats.

Political Factions at War's Eve

Part of Herrera's opposition consisted of the *puros*, who believed that as long as an incompetent army and its vainglorious officers defended places like Texas, the nation was in physical danger from voracious neighbors. Reflecting the soreness of the recent Texas wound, the *puros* asserted that Mexico simply had to reconquer Texas, a resolve that resonated with the urban and rural poor, giving the *puros* a large constituency that made them a political faction too powerful to ignore. And in the Mexican tradition, they were not above resolving differences with force. Led by Valentín Gómez Farías in league with supporters of former dictator Antonio López de Santa Anna, *puros* had unsuccessfully attempted to overthrow Herrera on June 7, 1845. Herrera's government had discovered the plot beforehand and had exiled Santa Anna before the attempted coup.

Thus Herrera hung on, his principal support coming from the *moderados* who also believed that both church and army had too much influence, but who harbored deep prejudices against Mexico's lower classes and equated reform with incipient anarchy. A third faction, the conservatives, agreed with the *moderados* about the unrestrained poor endangering stable government, but conservatives wanted to reestablish a monarchy and strengthen the army and church, believing that was the only way to maintain stability and improve Mexico's future.

Despite their failed coup just months before, the *puros* posed the biggest threat to Herrera's government in the fall of 1845. Angry over the government's failure to act decisively the previous spring when the United States announced the annexation of Texas, they railed that Herrera was a weakling. Mexico, they claimed, had senselessly destroyed "an army of twelve to fifteen thousand well-equipped and well-disciplined troops" and thus ruined the best chance of successfully challenging Mexico's grasping northern neighbor.[3] They were at least correct that Herrera and Peña y Peña wanted to placate the United States in some way, for Herrera knew that the Mexican Army was no match for its United States counterpart. Despite the *puros'* militant demands for a showdown, Herrera did not have the money to make the army stronger. He consequently had to walk a fine line between accommodating the United States to avoid war and soothing combative *puros* to stay in power. The only certainty that emerged as he undertook this difficult chore was a universal hatred for the United States.

In the end, Herrera had no choice but to satisfy his critics, but first he tried to buy some time. When Slidell arrived in Mexico City, Herrera's government objected to his credentials to postpone the opening of any negotiations, averring that Slidell's title of minister obviously exceeded the terms Peña y Peña had set forth in October, a violation that required the government to take the matter under advisement. On December 16, 1845, the Mexican government cited Slidell's designation as a minister rather than commissioner as just cause not to receive him. Unfortunately for Herrera, his faltering tightrope act made everyone equally angry and produced precisely the opposite effect he had desired. He had wanted to appear strong to his domestic enemies, but they thought him weak. He had wanted to appear conciliatory to the Americans, but they thought him belligerent. For his part, Slidell grumbled that Mexico's rebuff was nothing more than a contrived technicality and irritably insisted that everybody had known he was making the trip to talk about issues other than Texas. The United States had not misunderstood the agreement for negotiations, he claimed; the Mexican government had been duplicitous in withdrawing it for political reasons.

Herrera's government teetered on the brink of collapse. Herrera had not dealt decisively with the *puro* rebels in June, and now he was hedging and stalling about the Slidell mission. Such signs of weakness and indecision encouraged the opposition to make another attempt to bring down the government. His political assets hemorrhaging away, Herrera increasingly but unwisely relied on the army to sustain his presidency. Most officers and the bulk of the army had stayed loyal during the June coup attempt, but events were rapidly souring their relationship with both the executive and the legislature. Conservatives under Maj. Gen. Mariano Paredes y Arrillaga, commander of the Army of the Reserve, suspected that *puros* might be planning another coup and began planning one of their own. Paredes y Arrillaga used the Slidell fiasco to incite popular anger at Herrera and exploited the ensuing unrest as an excuse to bring his army toward Mexico City, a subterfuge for military force so transparent that it fooled nobody, including Herrera. In a desperate effort to save his government, Herrera tried to counter this military threat by activating the civic militia or *cívicos* in Mexico City. Yet the middle class, fearing both armed mobs and armies, opposed this gesture and made it futile. When Mexico City's army garrison joined Paredes y Arrillaga, Herrera fled the city on December 29, 1945, and Paredes y Arrillaga became acting president of Mexico on January 2, 1846. He bluntly proclaimed that he would defend Mexican claims to Texas. He accordingly made sure that both Mexico and James Polk clearly understood that the new government did not intend to sanction the Texas affair, let alone part with any additional territory.

When Polk received the news that Slidell had been rebuffed, he sent word to Zachary Taylor, commander of the oddly named Army of Observation, to move south and occupy a position on the Rio Grande. It was a provocative move and many have judged it as an attempt to start a war with the aim of obtaining territory Polk had earlier hoped to acquire by negotiation. Presumably even more telling was the fact that Polk did not yet know about the Paredes y Arrillaga coup and the new government's confrontational stance when he ordered Taylor south. Yet it is difficult to say with certainty that Polk was deliberately trying to goad Mexico to war. After all, he knew that the two principal opposition factions in Mexico, the *puros* and the conservatives, had called for war with the United States. Furthermore, Slidell's treatment by Herrera's *moderados* suggested they were more interested in soothing *puros* than ironing out problems with the United States. Given that information, Polk could merely have been exercising prudence by having Taylor's army protect territory that Mexico had sworn to reclaim.

Unfortunately, after news of the December coup reached Washington, neither Polk nor Paredes y Arrillaga could concede much without appearing weak, something neither could afford in what was turning out to be a very high-stakes game of diplomacy. In fact, Polk sent Slidell a new commission that he hoped would satisfy the new Mexican government, but this time it included a veiled threat that if the envoy was not received, America would fight to preserve its honor. The change in tone and posture was telling. Polk was apparently optimistic about the Slidell mission at its beginning, but events had gradually sapped the optimism and made the president mindful of the calendar. The new Mexican government, he concluded, would probably not negotiate.

The Polk administration consequently negotiated with someone else. From his exile, the ever wily Santa Anna had indicated through an intermediary that he would be willing to give the United States the territory it wanted in exchange for Polk helping him return to power. Of course, Santa Anna was also promising disappointed *puros* that he could provide the military leadership to unseat the conservatives and retake Texas. Nobody could tell which pledge, if either, was truthful, but as Santa Anna offered deals and made promises to anyone willing to listen, the Paredes y Arrillaga government refused to talk to the one person who could avert a plunge into war. Despite his new commission, John Slidell sat idly in Mexico City, an object of popular scorn and a target for Mexican anger. As Santa Anna played his two-faced game and Mexico and the United States glowered at each other but did not talk, news reached the Mexican government that Taylor had moved toward the Rio Grande. Paredes y Arrillaga and his advisors deemed the maneuver an act of war.

Confrontation

While politicians and diplomats struggled to make sense out of how Texas annexation and the Rio Grande boundary claim would affect U.S.-Mexican relations, the U.S. Army and Navy moved into position to fight a war. For six months Taylor's army had been camped outside Corpus Christi, Texas, where almost four thousand bored and uncomfortable men awaited decisions being made in Washington and Mexico City. Before this duty, these men had mainly garrisoned frontier posts to guard against Indian attacks. Only a few older officers, veterans of the War of 1812, had ever experienced a battle against regular military forces.

The army had a considerable job preparing to fight Mexican regulars. When it assembled at the sleepy village of Corpus Christi, even its best officers could only form their men "after a fashion."[4] Constant drilling and marching did little to improve morale as summer's almost unbearable heat and humidity gave way to a cold, wet fall. The tiny town of Corpus Christi afforded few amusements, and even homegrown pastimes such as horseracing and amateur theatricals became tedious, tempting both officers and men to drink too much whiskey, visit prostitutes, bicker among themselves, and occasionally settle quarrels with brawls.

One dispute among the officers grew out of Brevet Brig. Gen. William Jenkins Worth's arrival in October 1845 and threatened to disrupt the entire army. Worth, a career regular officer of many years' service, viewed the prospect of war with Mexico as a chance "to play a leading part in the great orchestra of the great National Drama."[5] Nonetheless, his entrance on the stage at Corpus Christi sounded a sour note by confusing the army's command structure. Zachary Taylor's second-in-command, Col. David E. Twiggs, insisted that he should remain in that post even after Worth's arrival, and when Taylor agreed, the issue became a tangle of army technicalities and bruised egos. The technicalities concerned brevet ranks. Congress had statutorily limited the number of officers in the army, and the small size of the pre–Civil War force often deprived meritorious officers of promotion, even when they had performed exceptional service. Brevet (or temporary) ranks provided a way around the restrictions by bestowing the rank's title and occasionally its authority without conferring its pay grade or allowances. Because frugality had prompted Congress to the limit the size of the officer corps, the government had no objection to this financially meaningless tweaking of the law.

Many of the officers who received brevet ranks, however, regarded them as much more than honorifics. Worth, who had received his brevet promotion for his service in the Second Seminole War, was one of them. The problem was that Twiggs was two years senior to Worth as a colonel, Worth's actual rank. From Washington, General of the Army Winfield Scott tried to resolve the chain-of-command problem at Corpus Christi by arbitrarily ruling that brevet ranks carried seniority, but the man in command at Corpus Christi, Zachary Taylor, thought differently. Taylor also had been brevetted brigadier general for his service in Florida (he was senior to both Twiggs and Worth as a colonel), but he argued that linear (or the actual legal) rank determined seniority. When the controversy reached Secretary of War William L. Marcy's desk, he adroitly kicked the matter upstairs to the president. Meanwhile, Worth was threatening to resign his commission, and officers from colonels down to second lieutenants were taking sides, signing petitions, and writing congressmen. Their interest was more than academic, for everyone had a stake in the dispute's resolution. Whether they favored brevet or linear rank, they wanted the matter settled permanently and petitioned Congress to pass a law clarifying the process. Congress demurred, but Polk finally ruled that linear rank took precedence, a decision that reached the army as it was preparing to carry out the president's order to move to the Rio Grande. Worth at least waited until the army reached the Rio Grande, but he then wasted no time before storming off to Washington to plead his case, a petulant act that many officers found disreputable. Typical was junior officer George Gordon Meade, who believed Worth's behavior made "him unfit to command."[6] It was not a good start for a campaign, presuming there was going to be one.

On the Rio Grande

Camp life at Corpus Christi was tedious, but at least it featured pleasant sea breezes off the Gulf of Mexico. In contrast, the march south to the Rio Grande was anything but agreeable as the army headed inland to a barren landscape short of water. Mexican patrols watched the American advance and at least once made contact with a detachment from Taylor's main column. Lieutenant Ramón Falcon was coldly cordial, but he warned American officers that they had best leave Mexican soil. Taylor's army continued its way south.

Lieutenant Falçon's relatively friendly advice was illustrative of both his government's policy and its problems. Paredes y Arrillaga had taken power on the promise to retake Texas, and he could not countenance American occupation of the territory between the Nueces and the Rio Grande without seriously eroding his political support. But in actuality, he could do little more than Falçon's little patrol had done. Paredes y Arrillaga discovered that Herrera's assessment of the army's shortcomings was regrettably accurate. Not only was retaking Texas out of the question but also merely challenging Taylor's advance presented a serious problem. Compelled to take some sort of action that at least appeared to contest the area between the Nueces and the Rio Grande, Paredes y Arrillaga reinforced the Mexican garrison at Matamoros with two thousand troops under Gen. Pedro de Ampudia.

It was the best he could do because years of neglect, in part caused by Mexico's struggling economy, had reduced the Mexican Army to a pathetic state. Soldiers went without pay, wore ill-fitting and ragged uniforms, and choked down wretched food that sometimes made them sick. The Mexican soldier's life was hardly the stuff of recruiting posters, and even those citizens of humblest means would not serve unless conscripted. Confronted by the United States, Paredes y Arrillaga resorted to drafting men convicted of vagrancy, a tactic that boosted the army's roster but did nothing to increase its formidability. Instead, the twenty thousand men of the Mexican Army—on paper a daunting opponent for Taylor's much smaller numbers—were actually a scattered, badly disciplined, disaffected rabble with little motivation for fighting anyone, especially Americans.

Taylor did not know any of this, however, and his comportment on the march to the Rio Grande was that of a man walking among snakes in the dark. Before establishing a position on the Rio Grande, he carefully secured a line of supply and communication with the coast. First he took possession of Point Isabel to provide a disembarkation point on the Gulf of Mexico, and only then did he move most of his army to the Rio Grande just across from Matamoros. Repeated warnings from the Mexican military that these actions constituted an act of war were a bit unnerving, but Taylor at least appeared unfazed. He hoped and perhaps expected that talks with Mexican military officials at Matamoros could prevent hostilities.

When Taylor arrived, Matamoros had not yet received the reinforcements under Ampudia, so the garrison's commander, Gen. Francisco de Mejía, nervously watched Taylor put up a camp and raise the U.S. flag just across the river. Soon an American messenger splashed across the Rio Grande and met with Mejía's second-in-command, Brig. Gen. Rómulo Díaz de la Vega. Luckily, French speakers on both sides made communication possible by the cumbersome exercise of translating American statements into French and then into Spanish and repeating the process in reverse for Mexican responses. The language barrier did not conceal, however, that the Mexicans were extremely unhappy. They refused to accept American assurances of peaceful intentions. They made plain that they wanted the U.S. forces to withdraw. Until he was reinforced, however, Mejía could do little else but watch the Americans begin the construction of an earthwork stronghold they had already dubbed Fort Texas.

After Ampudia arrived with the long-awaited reinforcements in the second week of May, the poorly trained and ill-equipped Matamoros garrison at least outnumbered Taylor's Army of Occupation. For his part, Taylor could count the increasing disparity and urged the War Department to send him additional troops. Americans in Fort Texas might have been edgy, but Mexicans in Matamoros were discontented. Ampudia's reputation for cruelty made him unpopular in the army, and Gen. Mariano Arista soon replaced him as commander of the Army of the North.[7] Paredes y Arrillaga's minister of war, José María Tornel, instructed Ampudia to take no action against the Americans until Arista arrived. Arista, on the other hand, had instructions to attack Taylor's army. Although Ampudia and Arista disliked one another, they would have to cooperate to defend against Taylor's invasion.

Before Arista arrived, Ampudia followed the government's orders for restraint, but he also threatened Taylor with war if he stayed on the Rio Grande. The threats and the increased size of the Matamoros garrison prompted the Americans to remain vigilant by conducting patrols along the Rio Grande, and a tense uneasiness settled in at Fort Texas. Some American soldiers reacted to the prospect of combat by deserting. Mexican promises of land bounties to American deserters were mighty enticements for those immigrants who were in the army to make a living rather than selflessly serve their country. In addition, many immigrants in the 1840s were Catholics from countries such as Ireland. Those who were capable soldiers found nothing troubling about joining a Catholic army with the prospect of later settling in a Catholic country. These deserters became a part of the Mexican Army popularly referred to as the *Battalón de San Patricio* or Saint Patrick's Battalion, in which they fought bravely for Mexico up through the final campaigns of the war.

Mariano Arista took command at Matamoros on April 24, 1846. He was a man of varied parts, a career officer who had spent three years in exile in the United States after participating in a failed coup in 1833. He knew Americans about as well as he knew the region he was now ordered to defend, and none of that knowledge encouraged him much. Matters on the Rio Grande presented something of a military problem, for Fort Texas had taken sufficient form to discourage a direct assault on it. Nuance seemed the better strategy, so the following day Arista sent Gen. Anastasio Torrejón with about sixteen hundred Mexican cavalry to menace Taylor's supply line to Point Isabel. He hoped to draw the Americans out of their fortifications. As he moved into position, though, Torrejón did more than draw Taylor out of Fort Texas. He started the war.

The Mexican cavalry stumbled on an American patrol consisting of companies C and F of the U.S. 2nd Dragoons led by Capt. Seth B. Thornton. (See Map 3.1.) When Torrejón attacked, killing most of the patrol and capturing the rest, including Thornton, everything on the Rio Grande instantly changed. True enough, Mexico had considered Taylor's appearance on the river an act of war, but not until the attack on Thornton's patrol was Taylor convinced that the two countries were likely to start shooting at each other.

Taylor immediately sent word to President Polk about the attack and asked for volunteers from Louisiana, the nearest state, to augment his forces. With Torrejón's men threatening his supply base at Point Isabel, Taylor took most of his force toward that place, leaving about five hundred men with artillery support under Maj. Jacob Brown at Fort Texas. In the meantime, Arista prepared to go on the offensive. He left a holding force at Matamoros under Mejía and moved the bulk of his men across the Rio Grande to take Fort Texas, but when he realized that his original plan had worked—Taylor had moved out to protect his supply line—he left Ampudia with about twelve hundred men to menace the Fort Texas garrison and advanced a little over three thousand men to prevent Taylor's return.

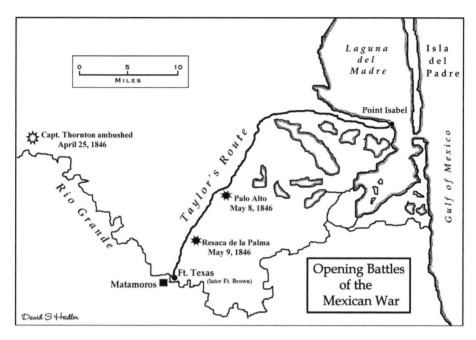

Map 3.1

Arista thought better of this plan almost immediately. Instead of merely threatening Fort Texas, he sent back part of his army to force its capitulation. After bolstering Point Isabel and acquiring supplies, Taylor planned on May 7 to return to Fort Texas with some urgency because he knew it was besieged. Yet he also learned the following morning that Arista's large force had moved between him and the fort. In fact, the Mexican Army was positioned across the main road at Palo Alto, just one mile in Taylor's front. The Americans advanced, approaching the Mexicans about 2:00 P.M., and deployed their artillery to match salvos from Mexican batteries. Arista's left flank was directly on the road, so at first Taylor's artillery and then his infantry concentrated on hitting that section of the Mexican line. Meanwhile Arista dispatched his cavalry to encircle the U.S. position, a move the Americans thwarted with their artillery. In addition, marshy terrain along the American front considerably hindered Mexican assaults, and thick smoke as well as grass fires started by the artillery barrages briefly halted the battle, a delay that gave the Mexicans time to regroup. Resuming the battle, Arista concentrated his artillery fire on the weaker American left and launched his infantry against the American batteries, but Taylor withstood the barrages and repulsed the threat to his guns. The Mexicans remained stubborn despite these setbacks, and the best Taylor could do was push Arista back a bit in some hard and deadly work. The first battle of the war ended with Arista still between him and Fort Texas.

That night some of Taylor's officers recommended that the army dig in where it stood, but he worried that Fort Texas would become the first large casualty of the American campaign. Taylor decided that even if Arista received reinforcements during the night (he did, as it happened), the Americans had to fight through to the fort. The next morning scouts discovered that Arista's fresh manpower was only part of the problem. His new position, an old riverbed called Resaca de la Palma or Resaca del Guerrero by the Mexicans, was a depression about ten feet deep in places and several miles long, a natural fortification that offered daunting protection, much of it sheltered by trees that provided additional cover. Yet Taylor had no choice but to attack. Getting through Arista's skirmishers in the thick chaparral before the *resaca* proved very nearly impossible, and a party of American dragoons failed to capture some of the Mexican artillery. Yet their effort revealed the weak positioning of those batteries, and a determined infantry assault finally did seize them, a feat that unnerved much of Arista's army. Mexican panic and flight followed. One of Taylor's officers grimly tallied the battle's cost: "the road and adjacent thickets are filled with their [Mexican] dead," he noted, without exaggeration.[8] American burial details labored for two days clearing the landscape of corpses. In the two days of battle at Palo Alto and Resaca de la Palma, the United States had lost 175 killed and wounded to the Mexican Army's at least 600 killed and wounded and close to 200 missing. Arista had outnumbered the Americans, but he had made costly tactical mistakes. In addition, the Mexican Army's poor morale and inferior weapons, especially its substandard artillery, were crucial elements contributing to its defeat.

Arista's withdrawal across the Rio Grande to Matamoros also took the pressure off of Fort Texas, soon reached by Taylor's main force and renamed Fort Brown in honor of its fallen commander. Mexican bombardment had taken a toll on the small but plucky garrison, and Major Brown on May 6 had "received a severe wound, which caused his death at two o'clock on the 9th."[9] From across the river, Arista weighed his chances of defending Matamoros given his poor showing and large number of casualties at Palo Alto and Resaca de la Palma. Taylor clearly planned to cross the Rio Grande. He sent word to Arista advising him to surrender his army and all public property, including weapons, but the Mexican commander chose retreat over capitulation. He began moving his army out of Matamoros on May 17, including its artillery and the few supplies he had remaining, but the artillery slowed his march and was the first thing this forlorn force jettisoned, submerging it upriver. As for food, his men marched out of Matamoros hungry and expected to remain so because the Mexican government had made no reliable arrangements to supply them.

Taylor crossed the river and occupied Matamoros on May 18, 1846, transforming it overnight into a teeming conglomerate of "regular and volunteer officers, regular and volunteer soldiers, speculators, sutlers, camp followers, Texas rangers, loafers, gamblers, and what not."[10] Maintaining order and protecting Mexican property and citizens tested American officers and made Taylor eager to move out of the town. At least he began regularly receiving a measurable quantity of reinforcements and supplies. That he received anything was something of a marvel. Taylor's initial report about the attack on Thornton's patrol had spurred Gen. Edmund Pendleton Gaines in Louisiana to muster forces there and request troops from neighboring states. In fairly short order, reinforcements were arriving at Point Isabel even as guns were sounding at Palo Alto and Resaca de la Palma. Yet, this initial speed of mobilization was illusory, for the War Department was unprepared to equip additional soldiers or supply them with food. Many state militias called up by Gaines were ordered to stand down until the department could organize itself for war. Some doubtless found it shocking that the long-anticipated contest with Mexico had finally come, and the nerve center of the American military was not ready.

War

While some people in the Polk administration acted surprised that the war had started, Polk was not among them. If anything, Polk was delighted—at least as much as this careful and colorless man could feel delight. His was generally a flat disposition that measured words and actions with finely tuned prudence, occasionally giving way to fits of temper, such as when he had heard in April that Slidell had been rebuffed by Paredes y Arrillaga's government. Shortly after his return to Washington, Slidell related to Polk the sorry tale of his misadventures in Mexico, and the president seized on the idea of using the diplomatic slight as a cause for war. He conferred with advisors on the matter and decided to prepare a war message for Congress, describing the insult of John Slidell as an affront to the United States. To be sure, Slidell's discomfiture lacked the usual requirements for such events. Mexican violations of diplomatic etiquette were not likely to invoke the same level of outrage among the political establishment as a Mexican military attack on American soil, but at the time it was all Polk had. Luckily for him in only a few hours he had something much better when Taylor's report about the attack on Thornton arrived in Washington that very day. Polk immediately revised the grounds for his request to Congress to make war on Mexico because it had "shed American blood upon the American soil."[11]

Members of Congress who had disagreed with moving Taylor to the Rio Grande questioned Polk's assessment of the situation. Others were not necessarily opposed to war with Mexico but believed that it posed serious risks and should be postponed. They pointed nervously to an ongoing dispute with Great Britain over the Oregon boundary, one that could lead to war. Great Britain could then ally with Mexico, bringing Britain's navy and industrial capacity to Mexico's assistance.

Polk nevertheless submitted his message to Congress on May 11, 1846, pointing out that a state of war already existed because of the Mexican attack. He insisted that he had tried to resolve the U.S.'s differences with Mexico, but Mexico had refused to receive his emissary, let alone open a productive discussion. He insisted that Taylor's move to the Rio Grande was not an act of aggression but instead was a proper defense of Texas from Mexican invasion, an invasion whose likelihood had now been unfortunately proved. Under the circumstances, Polk said, Congress had the duty to make the war formal with a declaration as well as support with adequate appropriations for what Polk described as Taylor's beleaguered army. Polk raised the specter that Taylor and his men were in great peril before overwhelming Mexican forces that could have already destroyed them, and he requested $10 million and authorization to raise fifty thousand volunteers. Linking supply for Taylor's army to the declaration of war became the key strategy of Polk's congressional operatives when the message was submitted. Nobody knew of course that as of May 11 Arista was preparing to evacuate Matamoros and Taylor's army was hardly beleaguered, but the sense that there was an emergency on the Rio Grande allowed Polk's supporters to stipulate that the House of Representatives could debate the issue for only two hours, time they mostly spent reading the president's war message and its supporting documents. By a 123 to 76 vote, an attempt to detach the question of supplying Taylor's army from a vote declaring war failed, forcing all but 14 of the 76 to vote for the war message or appear indifferent to American soldiers under fire in the field. Former president John Quincy Adams was among the nays. When the Senate also voted on supplying Taylor and declaring war as one measure, Polk confidently predicted that "the fear of the people" would bring even his most unyielding Whig critics into line.[12] He was right: the Senate voted 40 to 2 in favor of the war.

Whigs were not alone in their anger over Polk's stratagem. Some northern Democrats also found the affair distasteful. Manifest Destiny certainly gripped the nation in 1846, but so did a growing uneasiness as more than abolitionists began to suspect that Polk intended to expand slavery into the Southwest and relinquish American interests in Oregon. Even some Southerners, who certainly wanted to increase their influence, feared that Polk was moving too quickly. Burned by the commotion he had caused with his indiscreet letter to Pakenham, John C. Calhoun was reluctant to bring slavery to the center of national discussion again, a situation he knew would animate determined abolitionists. And aside from any sectional concerns, many weighed the potential international repercussions as the nation went to war with Mexico, for in the spring of 1846, war seemed just as likely with Great Britain.

Oregon

There seemed to be cause for worry over the Oregon dispute, for within days of the attack on Captain Thornton's party, the United States was also taking an aggressive stand against the British. In April 1846, Polk received congressional authorization to give the British the required one-year notice ending joint Anglo-American tenancy of the Oregon country, an agreement in place since 1827.

The Polk administration's posture in the Oregon dispute was in part dictated by domestic politics. Northern Democrats had been placated in the 1844 campaign with a platform that called for acquiring "All Oregon," which was really a pledge to antislavery elements that the Pacific Northwest would be used to balance the annexation of Texas with its slaves. The domestic advantages of the "All Oregon" policy ran considerable international risks, especially since it was framed in the cantankerous slogan of "Fifty-four Forty or Fight!"—a reference to the 54th parallel, the northernmost possible boundary of Oregon, which would have included a sizable portion of British Canada. Polk certainly realized these hazards and was at least willing to retreat from demands for the 54th parallel. Yet, Polk would be criticized by antislavery proponents for even this reasonable concession, for they claimed he relinquished a chance for gaining substantial free territory from Britain while inflexibly insisting on adding to slave territory taken from Mexico. There were key differences between the quarrels with Mexico and with Britain, however. In the case of Oregon, there was no annexation controversy, and diplomatic relations with London were occasionally strained but never broken. For their part, the British, possessors of a global empire and massive navy, did not have to prove their power in a fight over a remote territory that was, after all, not deemed essential to their national or imperial interests. Rather than chance an expensive and pointless war, Britain chose negotiation.

Consequently, one month into America's war with Mexico, promising talks with Britain began in early June with the aim of resolving the Oregon dispute. The British proposed a boundary at the 49th parallel that would give the United States control of the Columbia River and Puget Sound in exchange for Britain retaining Vancouver Island and the right for its fur-trading business to use the Columbia. Although the British offer almost precisely matched previous American demands, Polk at first worried that accepting it would violate his party's new pledge for "All Oregon." Yet his advisors convinced him that war with Mexico had made these latest guarantees unrealistic, particularly when rejecting Britain's offer risked a fight the United States could not likely win. The question was not whether to accept Britain's offer, but how to accept it without seeming to abandon the rallying cry of "Fifty-four Forty or Fight!"

Polk solved the quandary with a procedure not used since George Washington's administration. The Constitution instructed the president to obtain not only the "consent" of the Senate for treaties but also its "advice." Washington on only one occasion had sought the Senate's advice and had been infuriated by the result, which included questions from touchy senators about his allegedly interfering with legislative debate. Washington never again sought the Senate's advice on treaties but merely submitted them for ratification, and succeeding presidents had followed his example. Yet before signing the Oregon Treaty, Polk revived the practice of asking for the Senate's advice just this once, for if the Senate told him to accept the treaty, the Senate would be responsible for its terms. Although Midwesterners believed the arrangement with Britain ignored their interests and antislavery men wailed that it directly disregarded them, the Senate advised the president to accept the treaty and then ratified it on June 18, 1846. Without wasting more than an ounce of his political capital, Polk had adroitly steered the country from a fight with Britain and could now concentrate its full power on defeating Mexico.

The news was simply devastating for Mexico where considerable hope had been placed in an Anglo-American argument necessitating an Anglo-Mexican alliance. Now with the news of the Oregon Treaty, the reality sunk in that there would be no Royal Navy to break the American blockade, and there would be no redcoats to distract the American military. Mexico was alone, and in that isolation, it was all but certain to lose the war.

The Army of the West

As soon as Polk signed the declaration of war, he sent orders to Col. Stephen Watts Kearny at Fort Leavenworth to use his regulars and Missouri volunteers to protect trade caravans traveling from Missouri to Santa Fe. Missourians and their powerful senator, Thomas Hart Benton, had been apprehensive that a war with Mexico would disrupt their lucrative trade along the Santa Fe Trail, and ostensibly the Kearny mission was to calm their fears. In reality, though, Polk intended to seize New Mexico and use it as a base for conquering California. Soon Kearny would receive orders detailing Polk's true intentions.

Kearny commanded the 1st Dragoons, a unit whose sterling reputation was a reflection of its talented and experienced commander.

Unlike most army officers of the day, Kearny steered clear of politics and instead concentrated on fashioning one of the best frontier army units in American military history. He was more than ready then when he received orders to move out his troops, but he had to wait for a thousand volunteers coming from Missouri. In preparation for his mission, he began to organize supply lines to cover the broad reach of the Santa Fe Trail to Bent's Fort, the last stop on American soil in what is now southeastern Colorado, and a familiar trading post for Indians, trappers, and mountain men.[13] The campaign promised to be a thorny task. Despite his uncompromising professionalism, Kearny could do little to improve the army's poor supply system, and his march to New Mexico was sure to be plagued by acute shortages as he traveled through an area largely devoid of settlements, let alone towns. He also was supposed to collect his army from remote posts dispersed across the western frontier, even though some of these troops had already received a summons to join Taylor on the Rio Grande. Kearny had the difficult job of not only assembling these scattered units at Fort Leavenworth but also preventing other officers from hauling them off to Texas.

And then there were the volunteers. Kearny had to cope with a large number of new men unaccustomed to the hardships of an extended march. He sympathized with those unfamiliar with military discipline and ruled his volunteers with a soft hand, but he also wanted to prepare them for coming ordeals. His regulars spent the few weeks before their departure for the West training these men in the rudiments of frontier campaigning. Most volunteers were Westerners themselves, denizens of the American wilderness, and they proved quick studies, but nobody could predict how they would fare when rations became short and water dear.

They did all right. Organized as the First Missouri Mounted Volunteers, they elected their own colonel as approved by law. He was Alexander W. Doniphan, a thirty-eight-year-old Missouri lawyer and politician whose military experience was exclusively his service as brigadier general of the Missouri State militia. Doniphan's honesty and integrity were widely acknowledged, and he was famous for defying the governor's direct order to persecute Mormons when they came into Missouri in 1838. With that kind of grit, he had earned both the admiration and affection of his men, and they pledged to follow him anywhere. To everyone's surprise, possibly including their own, they did just that and more. Serving under Doniphan were two graduates of West Point, Charles Ruff as lieutenant colonel and William Gilpin as major, both of whom had resigned from the U.S. Army to move west. These two exemplified their regiment as much as Doniphan did. They and the men they commanded all had reasons for living in the West, the same reasons for joining this regiment, marching off to parts unknown, enduring incredible hardships, and standing up to terrifying dangers. They characterized another aspect of Manifest Destiny, a better one than the dubious exercise of supposed racial superiority that fueled other, ugly expressions of this new national credo. While some people back East contended that America's push for more territory was a veiled effort to extend the influence of slavery, few of these Missourians owned slaves or wanted to. Instead they believed that they were doing something grandly magnificent by extending America to the Pacific Ocean, acting as small pieces of human endeavor in a great, fated design. Nothing else can account for what they accomplished against impossible odds, what they bore against unbearable adversity. In the tradition of laconic, understated observations typical in the West, the First Missouri Mounted Volunteers would do.

The First Missouri and Kearny's 1st Dragoons appropriately became the Army of the West. After sending supplies ahead, the force slowly began moving out of Fort Leavenworth on June 5, the last units of it hitting the trail at the end of June. (See Map 3.2.) The lead elements of Kearny's army were sent to guard trading caravans, some carrying munitions, to prevent New Mexican governor Manuel Armijo from confiscating such cargos to use against Kearny's army. In addition, Kearny instructed Capt. Benjamin Moore in command of this vanguard to confiscate caravan goods belonging to the governor to use as a bargaining chip for his cooperation. Armijo had something of a reputation.

Meanwhile, five hundred members of Brigham Young's Church of Jesus Christ of Latter-day Saints joined the Army of the West. Popularly known as Mormons, they were persuaded to join the American forces to prepare the way for Mormon immigration to California. Although Mormon leaders expected these men to be mustered out in California to put matters in order for the larger migration to come, most followers of Young eventually established their main settlement on the Great Salt Lake in modern Utah. In addition to the Mormons, other

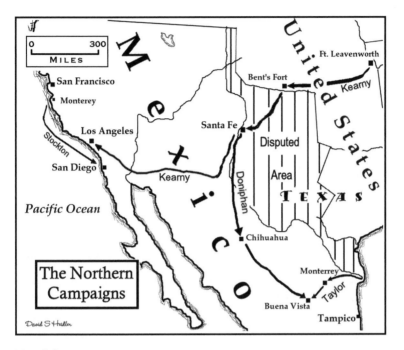

Map 3.2

volunteers continued to drift into Fort Leavenworth after the main army's departure and were quickly sent along to join Kearny. Eventually his total strength was about twenty-five hundred. The more than five hundred miles to Bent's Fort was more than a month's journey, an especially grueling introduction to overland marching for the volunteers. Kearny rested his men around Bent's while gathering information, but many volunteers were not allowed to enjoy the trading post's hospitality. As rumors filtered back that the officers were enjoying the company of ladies and drinking "mint juleps, made with brown sugar and Taos whisky," morale plummeted.[14]

The Army of the West started for Santa Fe on August 2 none too soon. A few days' march brought them into Raton Pass, a journey every bit as miserable as the one to Bent's Fort but now marked by short rations and dangerous terrain. Kearny had sent scouts and civilian agents ahead to determine Mexican military strength at Santa Fe and to gauge the mood of its people. A number of Americans lived in and around Santa Fe, and Kearny wanted both to warn them of his approach and to inform them that he intended to establish an American government in New Mexico. His scouts returned with the welcome information that American residents would be most pleased with his plans and with the news that Governor Armijo intended to oppose them with force—or at least claimed he would. Manuel Armijo's role in the American invasion has invited considerable speculation, including suspicions that he was bribed by Americans to leave Kearny's advance unchecked. The son of a wealthy New Mexican *hacendado*, Armijo did have a weakness for making money in suspect ways, whether by cheating at horse racing, skimming acreage from official land grants, or raiding the treasury of the local Catholic Church.

Whatever the case, Armijo's scouts counted Kearny's numbers, and the information apparently persuaded the governor to defend Santa Fe at Apache Canyon, a narrow pass twelve miles outside of town. There he planned to assemble about three thousand men, but whether he actually intended to use them does not seem to have mattered. Most of them had no stomach for the task. Risking their lives for an inattentive government far away in Mexico City seemed the height of folly, especially when their economic interests tied them more closely to American merchants. The *puros* philosophy of government was quite attractive to them in the abstract, and now that they contemplated facing American guns, it became physically compelling as well. Armijo knew about this disaffection and placed little confidence in his makeshift force, but he tried to bluff Kearny until reinforcements arrived from Chihuahua to the south.

Armijo accordingly put on a brave face when Kearny's emissaries arrived in Santa Fe demanding its surrender. The governor told them that he was prepared to lead the people of New Mexico into battle against American aggressors but to prevent needless bloodshed he would meet with Kearny at Las Vegas, a town east of Santa Fe. When the governor did not keep the appointment, Kearny continued his march on Santa Fe, pausing in every town along the way to extract pledges of loyalty to the United States from local Mexican officials. By August 17, Armijo's improvised army was rapidly dissolving, and rather than leading what was left of it to some meaningless heroics, he decided to take himself to Mexico. Fleeing south in advance of the American arrival, he met Col. Mauricio Ugarte, commander of Mexican troops in Chihuahua, who was coming to Santa Fe's aid. Armijo justified his unseemly flight by exaggerating Kearny's numbers, doing so with such conviction that Colonel Ugarte also decided to head back south.

Kearny consequently took New Mexico without firing a shot. Mexican officials remaining in Santa Fe sent word that there would be no resistance and, on August 18, 1846, Kearny, who had just received news of his promotion to brigadier general, rode into Santa Fe. Curious children followed the army as in a parade, causing one of Kearny's officer's to observe that "children are everywhere the same, when soldiers or any other show" comes to town.[15] The U.S. flag soon fluttered over the governor's residence, a symbol given meaning during the days that followed as Kearny established an American government in New Mexico and conveyed President Polk's assurances that everyone's rights would be preserved. On the surface all seemed calm and most New Mexicans seemed either happy or at least placid.

Not everyone was pleased and some would not remain docile, but poor communication and a lack of organization frustrated an active resistance to the American presence until after Kearny was gone. For the time being, Kearny could report that everything had proceeded much more smoothly than expected. Matters went so smoothly, in fact, that Kearny moved with speed, and questionable legality, to establish a law code and appoint Charles Bent territorial governor, actions that would be legitimate only after Congress had established a territory. Kearny was in too much of a hurry to heed such technicalities. He also believed he had more men than either the New Mexico garrison or the California expedition would need, so he sent Doniphan's Missouri volunteers to rendezvous with an expedition out of San Antonio under Gen. John Wool. Kearny then made hasty arrangements to take the balance of his force to California, the real object of his campaign all along. Many volunteers, including the Mormons who were so eager to make the trip because of its destination, had not yet arrived, but Kearny needed to start for the mountains before autumn snows clogged the passes. He expected latecomers to catch up on the trail.

Santa Anna

During that summer, Santa Anna was also on the move, shifting his place of exile to Havana, Cuba. The Polk administration had considered the benefits of helping him return to power in the spring of

1846, and once hostilities broke out, the president was eager to pursue the plan. In July, an American agent met with Santa Anna in Havana and promised that U.S. ships blockading the Mexican coastline would allow Santa Anna back into the country in exchange for his ending the war on terms favorable to the United States. Santa Anna exuded an ebullient if unctuous friendliness, offering ideas about how seizing Tampico would put military pressure on Paredes y Arrillaga and even pointing out suitable landing spots for an attack on Veracruz. Of course, the chance of Santa Anna regaining power was as remote as it was likely, but the certainty of his keeping his word was less than slight. One could fault Polk for being curiously blind to this charlatan's capacity to lie, but at the same time, the United States really had nothing to lose by playing all possible angles. Any arrangement with Santa Anna or for that matter with Paredes y Arrillaga would require a substantial sum of money. Vague signals suggested that the existing government of Mexico might be willing to negotiate an end to the war, but having an alternative government waiting in the wings seemed sensible foresight.

The Wilmot Proviso

Kearny's march was a clear signal that the administration intended to acquire far more than the Rio Grande boundary. The administration's settlement of the Oregon question in June convinced many Northerners and Midwesterners that Polk was more interested in acquiring the Southwest than the Northwest. Now even northern and midwestern expansionist Democrats grumbled that the president was ignoring their interests to advance his Southwest and California agenda.

Many northern Democrats, caught up in the spirit of Manifest Destiny, had supported the war as good for both country and continent, but during the summer of 1846 they began having second thoughts. The southern wing of the party seemed to be dictating administration policy at the expense of northern interests. These northern Democrats were not disaffected, at least not yet, but they were gloomy about a number of issues, the war among them. The rift in Democratic unity spelled trouble for the administration. When Whigs complained about plans for a new national bank being repeatedly quashed, nobody on the other side of the aisle much cared, but Democrats from manufacturing states began listening to Whigs who pointed out that reducing protective tariff schedules had only benefited the South. Everyone noticed that the admission of Florida and Texas had given slaveholding states a majority in the Senate, and a sizable number of northern Democrats began to wonder if the war's real aim was to increase an already palpable southern dominance of the government.

Of course, not all northern Democrats felt this way. Some saw any territorial expansion, no matter where it occurred, as good for the country. Whigs also were divided along sectional lines over the most contentious issues. The radical northern faction of the party, often called Conscience Whigs and led by John Quincy Adams, was stoutly antislavery and prepared to oppose any measure or deed that increased the power of slaveholding interests, but most northern Whigs opposed the war anyway. Even if a purported slave power conspiracy was only a figment of abolitionists' imaginations, moderate Whigs objected to the breach of Mexican territory as indefensibly arrogant. Southern Whigs were beset by a host of contradictory impulses, but in general, the war simply alarmed them because it tended to dredge up dangerous debates over slavery. Democrat John C. Calhoun felt a kinship with the southern wing of the Whig Party, for he too believed that adding western territory to the United States would hopelessly divide the country over the slavery issue.

For weeks after the declaration of war, differences among its opponents hindered the creation of a coherent opposition to the Polk administration, though some representatives tried. Abraham Lincoln, a first-term Whig congressman from Illinois, repeatedly introduced resolutions demanding that the administration specify the exact spot where Mexicans had attacked Taylor's forces, information that Lincoln believed would reveal that Taylor had provoked the incident by being in Mexico. Yet Lincoln's initiative never caught on with other Whigs and his dogged persistence about it soon made him a laughingstock in Democrat newspapers as they mocked his "spot resolutions."[16]

In August 1846, though, serious trouble for the Polk administration came from the Democrat's side of the aisle. Polk and his cabinet had decided to ask Congress for money to ease negotiations that would end the war, secure Mexican recognition of the Rio Grande boundary, and arrange terms for the purchase of New Mexico and Alta California. When Polk sent the appropriation request to Congress on August 8, the wide array of administration critics found common ground in their belief that the money was actually meant to purchase territory from Mexico. Yet how could anyone vote down money that was described as necessary to make peace without appearing as reflexive partisans? That night, Democratic congressman David Wilmot of Pennsylvania and other northern Democrats hit upon the answer. Wilmot proposed an amendment to the appropriation bill calling for the prohibition of slavery in any territory acquired from Mexico. Polk condemned what he called "a mischievous and foolish amendment," and southern Democrats clenched their fists as their worst fears about the ensuing debate were realized.[17] The northern majority in the House passed the Wilmot Proviso by a vote of 83 to 64, but Southerners in the Senate were able to hold the measure at bay. Whatever Wilmot's motives in this affair— and some have described them as completely altruistic—the result was extremely disruptive, for the proviso killed the appropriation bill while taking on a life of its own. Though never enacted, the Wilmot Proviso became a point of reference for the debate over slavery, a long-lived quarrel that took on new meaning as the American military snatched up new territories.

Mexico's Distressed Government

The U.S. government was troubled by the war, but the Mexican government was undone by it. From the start of his ascension to power, Paredes y Arrillaga had been part of a Centralist scheme aimed at restoring monarchical rule in Mexico. Early military embarrassments at Palo Alto and Resaca de la Palma derailed the monarchists' plans and weakened Paredes y Arrillaga's government. In a pathetic effort to reclaim popular support, Paredes y Arrillaga became a newly converted champion of republicanism, but he was a wretched war leader apparently incapable of expelling the Americans from Mexico let alone Texas. On April 23, he responded to Taylor's move to the Rio Grande by issuing a confused and tortured proclamation declaring the country in a state of defensive war. Because the Mexican Congress would not meet until June, he explained, conducting an offensive war would be unconstitutional. Yet even after Palo Alto and Resaca de la Palma, even after Taylor occupied Matamoros, Congress did not declare war. The most aggressive action Congress could manage was to give Paredes y Arrillaga command of the army with instructions to defend the nation.

The poor military performance, lingering suspicions concerning plans for a monarchy that Paredes y Arrillaga could not explain away, and equivocation about Texas predictably doomed the government. *Puros* and *moderados* alike wanted to overthrow it, and supporters of the exiled Santa Anna had been courting both factions for months while mounting a publicity campaign to reform his image with the public. A coup in the spring of 1846 proved premature and failed, but military setbacks reinvigorated the government's opponents. Through his agents Santa Anna again formed an alliance with *puro* leader Gómez Farías and was depicted as Mexico's savior-in-waiting, for "only a man with his heroic halo could inspire a shred of hope."[18] Small rebellions sprouted throughout Mexico, and Paredes y Arrillaga's feverish effort to stamp out subversive plots in Mexico City only delayed the inevitable. His departure to take command of the army under the congressional directive was either an act of sheer impudence or hopeless naïveté. He left the government in the hands of Nicolás Bravo. On August 4, 1846, a successful uprising overthrew what was left of that government, and Santa Anna was soon on his way home, courtesy of the U.S. Navy.

Notes

1. K. Jack Bauer, *The Mexican War, 1846–1848* (New York: Macmillan, 1974), 22.

2. The U.S. diplomatic service did not bestow the rank of "ambassador" until the end of the nineteenth century because it was regarded as a vestige of aristocratic privilege. American diplomats were at a disadvantage throughout the 1800s because they were socially inferior in foreign capitals to those occupying ambassadorial rank. Correspondingly, foreign governments would send to Washington only diplomats of reciprocal rank, meaning that their embassies in the United States were frequently staffed with young or marginally qualified "ministers." Serious diplomatic disputes usually required the appointment of special envoys.

3. Pedro Santoni, *Mexicans at Arms: Puro Federalists and the Politics of War, 1845–1848* (Fort Worth: Texas Christian University Press, 1996), 54.

4. Ethan Allen Hitchcock, *Fifty Years in Camp and Field: Diary of Major-General Ethan Allen Hitchcock, U.S.A.* ed. W. A. Croffut (New York: G. P. Putnam's Sons, 1909), 198.

5. George Winston Smith and Charles Judah, eds., *Chronicles of the Gringos: The U.S. Army in the Mexican War, 1846–1848, Accounts of Eyewitnesses & Combatants* (Albuquerque: University of New Mexico Press, 1968), 57.

6. George Gordon Meade, *Life and Letters of George Gordon Meade, Major-General, United States Army* (New York: Charles Scribner's Sons, 1913), 1: 88.

7. In 1844, Ampudia executed Francisco Sentmanat, the former governor of Tabasco, and had his decapitated head boiled in oil and put on public display, a barbarous exhibition that repelled many Mexicans, including parts of the army.

8. Rhoda van Bibber Tanner Doubleday, ed., *Journals of the Late Brevet Major Philip Norbourne Barbour, Captain in the 3rd Regiment, United States Infantry, and His Wife, Martha Isabella Hopkins Barbour, Written during the War with Mexico, 1846* (New York: G. P. Putnam's Sons, 1936), 60–61.

9. Smith and Judah, *Chronicles of the Gringos*, 62.

10. George Wilkins Kendall, *Dispatches from the Mexican War*, ed. Lawrence Delbert Cress (Norman: University of Oklahoma Press, 1999), 50.

11. Richardson, vol. 4, *Messages and Papers of the Presidents*, 442.

12. James K. Polk, *Polk: The Diary of a President, 1845–1849, Covering the Mexican War, the Acquisition of Oregon, and the Conquest of California and the Southwest*, edited by Allan Nevins (New York: Longmans, Green, 1952), 88.

13. A reconstructed version of Bent's Fort is located on the original spot and operated by the National Park Service.

14. Richard Smith Elliott, *The Mexican War Correspondence of Richard Smith Elliott*, eds. Mark L. Gardner and Marc Simmons (Norman: University of Oklahoma Press, 1997), 56.

15. Smith and Judah, *Chronicles of the Gringos*, 122.

16. The reaction to Lincoln's speech is described in David Herbert Donald, *Lincoln* (New York: Simon & Schuster, 1995), 124–26.

17. Polk, *Diary*, 138.

18. Santoni, *Mexicans at Arms*, 106.

TEXAS: CHURCH OF ALAMO, SAN ANTONIO DE BEXAR.

The Alamo—Once a Spanish mission, the Alamo in San Antonio de Béxar became an improvised citadel at the beginning of the Texas revolt against Mexico. In March 1836, all 187 of its defenders fell to Mexican forces commanded by Antonio López de Santa Anna, a defeat that inspired Texas revolutionaries to succeed in their bid for independence. (Library of Congress)

GENERAL D. ANTONIO LOPEZ DE SANTA-ANNA.
PRESIDENT OF THE REPUBLIC OF MEXICO.
By A. Hoffy, from an original likeness taken from life at Vera-Cruz.

The above is a correct likeness from our personal observation

E. W. Moore
Com. late Texas Navy

Alex. C. Blount

Published July 1847, by A. HOFFY, N.º 29, South Third S.t near Chesnut, Philad.ª
& by JOHNSON & BROCKETT, N.º 28, South Seventh S.t bet. Chesnut & Walnut.

Antonio López de Santa Anna—Dashing and unprincipled, Santa Anna exemplified the worst aspects of the criollo ruling class in the early years of the Mexican Republic. He would rule Mexico no less than eleven times, each of his tenures marked by his duplicity and Mexico's waning fortunes. (Library of Congress)

SALE OF DOGS.

Martin Van Buren's Misstep—The cartoon lampoons Van Buren's maladroit position on Texas before the 1844 presidential contest in which he tried to steer a middle course between abolitionism and annexation. Here he is a dog with a fox's tail leading Andrew Jackson astray while James K. Polk and George M. Dallas are held out as "pups well broken." Jackson's forsaking of Van Buren did indeed lead to Polk's nomination with Dallas as his vice presidential candidate. (Library of Congress)

Texas Coming In—The annexation of Texas caused a serious domestic divide, here depicted as Polk welcomes the ship of Texas, manned by Stephen Austin and Sam Houston, while prominent Whigs led by Henry Clay hold on to a rope that pulls them into the torrential "Salt River," forcing them to keep their grip or be swept away. Meanwhile, abolitionist William Lloyd Garrison in the lower left-hand corner swears that he will not keep company with a "blackleg," a term that meant professional gambler, a reference to Clay's penchant for cards as well as his risking principle on the annexation question in his bid for the presidency. (Library of Congress)

James Knox Polk—The first "dark horse" presidential candidate in American history, Polk won the presidency in 1844 and interpreted his victory as an endorsement of expansion. He commenced an aggressive round of diplomacy that secured the Oregon country from Britain by treaty, but he was less successful in restoring relations with Mexico, and the result was war. (Library of Congress)

GENL ZACHARY TAYLOR.
THE HERO OF BUENA VISTA.

Published by James Baillie, 87th St near 2d Avenue, N.Y.

Zachary Taylor—Affectionately nicknamed "Old Rough and Ready" by his soldiers, Taylor was sent to Corpus Christi and then to the Rio Grande as part of Polk's policy of applying pressure on Mexico. His presence on the Rio Grande sparked the war, and he fought its first major engagements with enough skill to win accolades at home. Polk soon was suspicious of Taylor's political ambitions. (Library of Congress)

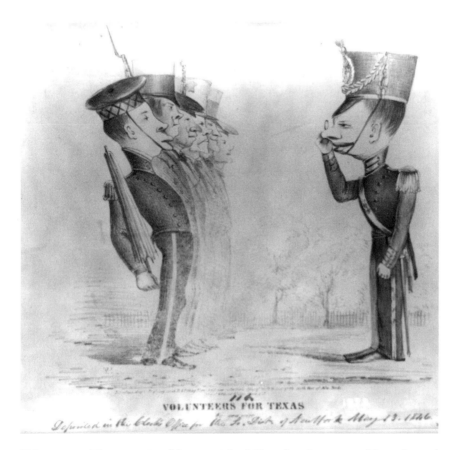

VOLUNTEERS FOR TEXAS

Volunteers—The questionable martial skills of volunteer soldiers bound for Taylor's army were satirized in this cartoon in which most are lacking uniforms and the first man in the ranks carries a parasol rather than a musket. The officer fares no better as he inspects his new charges through a monocle, his most prominent feature a weak chin. Actually, the volunteers exhibited such undisciplined and occasionally criminal behavior that they caused considerable trouble for the army and were never popular with regular troops or officers. (Library of Congress)

DISTINGUISHED MILITARY OPERATIONS WITH A HASTY BOWL OF SOUP.

Hasty Bowl of Soup—Playing on Winfield Scott's claim that he had been so busy preparing for the war that he had only left his desk for "a hasty bowl of soup," the cartoonist parodies President Polk's decision to supersede the politically popular Taylor with Scott by having Scott smother Taylor with a bowl of soup. (Library of Congress)

FLIGHT OF THE MEXICAN ARMY.
AT THE BATTLE OF BUENA VISTA FEB 23 1847

Flight from Buena Vista—Santa Anna's first military campaign of the Mexican War was aimed at destroying Zachary Taylor's depleted and overextended army, but the battle fought at Buena Vista ended with Taylor's army intact and Santa Anna forced to retire from the field. The depiction here characterizes that withdrawal as a "flight," which is an exaggeration, although the bad effect on already battered Mexican morale was no less telling. (Library of Congress)

SANTA ANNA DECLINING A HASTY PLATE OF SOUP AT CERRO GORDO.

American Victory at Cerro Gordo—Winfield Scott's significant victory over Santa Anna at Cerro Gordo is here satirized by again invoking the "hasty bowl of soup" catchphrase that hounded Scott throughout the war. Scott is lampooned for his enjoyment of extravagant pleasures, and Polk's imprudent decision to allow Santa Anna back into Mexico expecting that he would end the war is disparaged with the passport that appears in the lower right-hand corner. (Library of Congress)

GEN? SCOTT'S GRAND ENTRY INTO THE CITY OF MEXICO, SEP? 14th 1847.

Published by James Baillie; 87 & 90, 1207 & 72. Avenue, New York.

Scott Enters Mexico City—The march to and the taking of Mexico City were lauded as among the most notable military achievements of the age by no less than the Duke of Wellington. Scott's triumphal entry into the Mexican capital signaled the end of fighting but not necessarily the end of the war, which required hardheaded diplomacy that stretched into weeks. (Library of Congress)

CHAPTER 4

The Northern War

Santa Anna Returns

Mexico's change of government coincided with the country's deteriorating military situation. While awaiting his return, Santa Anna's followers worked with Gómez Farías to organize a provisional government under the leadership of José Mariano Salas. A primary reason for the rebellion was to place Santa Anna in command of the nation's armies to deal with the invasions of New Mexico and northern Mexico. Meanwhile, Salas and Gómez Farías worked to restore the people's trust in the government by reinstating civil liberties and allowing a free press, things Paredes y Arrillaga had suppressed. The new government assured the people that "the democratic principle is completely saved in our plan."[1]

Politically astute Mexicans trusted Gómez Farías, but they had strong doubts about Antonio López de Santa Anna. The ex-dictator received a subdued welcome when he landed at Veracruz on August 16, a sign of chilly sentiments toward him throughout Mexico. Santa Anna proclaimed his desire to make Mexico a true republic, but in the same breath he announced the need for a temporary dictatorship to prosecute the war. Instead of proceeding to Mexico City, though, he left Gómez Farías and Salas waiting there, occasionally sending emissaries to convey his desires. More importantly, he did not protest when the interim government restored the Constitution of 1824, and he reassured everyone that he was a firm supporter of the *puros'* policies. These were clever moves, for Santa Anna's apparent acceptance of arch-federalism calmed rural states eager for more autonomy and made them less likely to seek independence during the distraction of the war. People who had expected the worst from him had reason to be confused—and hopeful.

It was a confusing time in Mexico. Despite their rhetoric and enacting reforms that some criticized as too indulgent in wartime, the *puro*–Santa Anna alliance also installed some repressive measures to keep order and prevent the opposition from staging another coup. *Puro* leaders expected unquestioning loyalty from government employees and spoke of forging a united war effort, but they allowed public meetings to degenerate into tantrums against the Catholic Church and conservatives. The *puros* were obviously trying to generate popular support for the war, but their main accomplishment was to terrify the church and the upper classes whose money they needed to fight it. The *puros* also alienated other important groups. To stir patriotic support for Mexico's defense and enlist the men to mount it, the Salas regime reinstituted the civic militia or *cívicos*, a move that alarmed middle-class citizens who understandably feared impoverished mobs with guns.

The advent of the *cívicos* also upset regular army officers who carped about the potential diminution of their status. The restoration of the *cívicos* was not the only reason army officers were disgruntled. The *puros'* true federalism promised a sharp decrease in army funding. The disaffection in the army was dangerous because unlike the amorphous discontent brewing in other parts of Mexican society, the army was an organized institution accustomed to using its muscle to protect its privileges. Santa Anna was thoroughly attuned to the army's rumblings, and he rebuffed advice to assume the interim presidency. Instead, he announced that he would don his general's uniform and lead Mexico's brave soldiers into battle. Santa Anna needed the support of the military not only to fight the Americans but also to realize his personal plans in Mexico.

Finally on September 14, 1846, Santa Anna rode with great pomp and ceremony into Mexico City. On the surface all seemed harmonious between Santa Anna and his *puro* allies, and the celebrations for this hero's return suggested that Mexico was at last inspired for the great exertion of expelling the Yankee invaders and reclaiming its territory. With the country under attack on several fronts and blockaded by the U.S. Navy, however, the celebrations could not last forever, and the inspiration would need to be translated rapidly into successful action. Even his critics might have thought that Santa Anna was the man for this hour; all of Mexico hoped he was.

Volunteer Trouble

After occupying Matamoros, Taylor began incorporating into his small army the numerous volunteers being sent to him, mostly Southerners mustered in for only six months. They were different from the long-term volunteers authorized by Congress upon the declaration of war. Instead, these first arrivals were adventurers eager to fight Mexicans and return home with a fund of stories for friends and family. Discipline, especially the kind imposed by military regulations, was more than an alien concept for them; it was a repugnant one, and Taylor soon had reason to regret ever having seen them. Most of their infractions were of the drunken and disorderly variety, such as frequenting local prostitutes and brawling with whomever was handy. If the volunteers were not running rampant, they were doing nothing at all. "They expect the regulars," said one disgusted officer, ". . . to play waiters for them."[2]

Some behavior was impossible to dismiss as merely annoying or rambunctious. Violence toward local inhabitants was especially troubling, and increasing numbers of volunteers multiplied problems, causing officers to complain that they would prefer a small army to a large one composed of criminals. In fact, the volunteers' treatment of Mexican civilians appalled regular officers. One of the least odious crimes was simple theft, but some volunteers committed far more serious offenses, and the army seemed helpless to stop them. Rape was quite common, and occasionally Americans were caught killing Mexican civilians for sport.

This behavior by a few bad characters was horrifying enough, but the tacit complicity through inaction of otherwise decent people was a troubling illustration of the observation that true evil occurs when good men do nothing to stop it.[3] Taylor's lament that after entering Mexico he had virtually no authority over miscreant volunteers was unconvincing. The vast majority of Americans certainly condemned mistreatment of civilians, but traditions of racialism and supposed ethnic superiority prompted many to view Mexicans as inferior beings, particularly those from the lower classes.[4] Both the incidents and the blind eye that American authorities turned on them created a simmering resentment toward occupation forces that occasionally boiled over in acts of retaliation against the most convenient targets, even if they had committed no outrages. And, of course, Americans sometimes reacted to such attacks with brutal retaliation, the most notorious case being the Agua Nueva massacre.

In December 1846 Arkansas volunteers under the command of Gen. John Wool raped several women in the village of Agua Nueva. A month later one of Wool's soldiers was killed, and shortly afterward several of the Arkansans opened fire indiscriminately on a crowd of Mexicans. According to some accounts, they saw a Mexican with something belonging to the dead soldier, but even if that were true, it hardly justified the ensuing slaughter as the Mexicans tried to take shelter in a cave. There the Arkansans murdered at least two dozen Mexicans. The killers were dismissed from the service and sent home, which was hardly a sufficient punishment.

Even the relatively dutiful volunteers who later entered the army under longer terms of enlistment were never popular with regulars. Except for their generals, volunteers elected their officers, and the frequent result was a shameless pandering by aspirants who refused to enforce even rudimentary discipline. Such problems surfaced in every theater of the war and virtually ruined many volunteer units, making them unfit for service under regular officers. Some edged toward mutiny. All too typical was one volunteer among the relatively exemplary Army of the West who complained about the general's insistence that the men wear proper uniforms: "When volunteers . . . leave their homes and friends, sacrifice pecuniary considerations, . . . they have the right to equip and clothe themselves as to them shall seem fit and proper."[5]

An additional complication arose from the fact that many volunteer officers were local or national politicians who wielded enough influence to obtain a commission but had no experience for the military authority it provided. They also had a strong incentive to exaggerate their importance in campaigns and invent tales of their heroics in battles. When they wrote letters home and dispatched anonymous reports containing these exaggerated stories to American newspapers, they often omitted any mention of regulars and their officers, causing considerable resentment toward themselves and their men. Many feuds between high-ranking officers later in the war were rooted in these types of incidents.

Zachary Taylor himself was not immune to laudatory press coverage. After Palo Alto and Resaca de la Palma, newspaper congratulations began stirring his political ambitions, and he frequently dealt with the volunteer problem mindful of how his actions played back home. Yet, there were limits to his patience, especially because he had orders to fight the Mexican Army and consequently required some measure of peace within his own to do so. Because volunteers with six-month enlistments would not be around long enough to campaign in the interior, Taylor decided to send them home and await the long-term volunteers. Getting rid of these troublesome men was a blessing on several levels for as they defied discipline, preyed on civilians, and damaged morale, they also ate up Taylor's supplies. He was happy to see them go.

The Monterrey Campaign

The War Department informed Taylor of plans for another U.S. column under Gen. John Wool to move out of San Antonio against Chihuahua and eventually join forces with him in northern Mexico. Meanwhile, Taylor intended to press the Mexican military in the region by taking the city of Monterrey. Beginning in early July 1846, he began establishing a staging area at Camargo up the Rio Grande, using regulars exclusively, perhaps to defuse tensions with volunteers but certainly to ease his supply troubles. (See Map 4.1.) Eventually, some long-term volunteers joined the regulars at Camargo and were part of the army on its march to Monterrey. Everybody suffered from the climate. In July and August, daily temperatures rose well above 100 degrees, and when undisciplined volunteers kept untidy camps, the heat and filth spread disease. A recently arrived soldier was shocked when he accompanied a doctor to a hospital tent. Cynically responding to the suggestion that something should be done for a delirious man near the tent's entrance, the physician muttered, "He will die in two days."[6] Illness promised to take a larger toll on Taylor's army than the enemy, and he was forced to leave many sick soldiers in Camargo when he started for Monterrey in the third week of August.

Taylor reorganized his army into three divisions, two consisting of regulars and one of volunteers. David Twiggs and the querulous William Worth, who had hurried back to the army after learning it was fighting, commanded the regulars, and Gen. William O. Butler the vol-

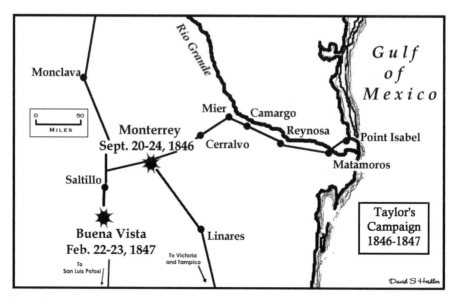

Map 4.1

unteers. Taylor had six thousand men with which to dislodge the seven thousand soldiers protecting Monterrey, again under Pedro de Ampudia, who had been reinstated to command the Army of the North after Arista's disappointing performance. Francisco Mejía had labored to improve Monterrey's defenses and when Ampudia arrived at the end of August, he also sought to extend them. More importantly, however, he disobeyed orders from Santa Anna in Mexico City to take the army to Saltillo. Ampudia and Mejía had reasonable grounds for ignoring the instructions, for both believed that a retreat would completely destroy the army's already ragged morale. Yet they also were mindful of how defeating an American army deep in Mexican territory would boost their political fortunes.

Taylor learned from spies and scouts about Monterrey's impressive fortifications and that they were being improved daily, so he wasted no time in starting his final push from Cerralvo on September 11. The Mexican Army was equally impressed with Monterrey's defenses, as it happened, and became prisoners to them. When Ampudia planned to hit Taylor at Marín on the road between Cerralvo and Monterrey, his officers refused to take their men out of the city's fortifications. Ampudia sent out Torrejón with part of his cavalry to slow Taylor's march, but the cavalry felt naked and edgy. After briefly riding out to Marín, Torrejón brought his men back without firing a shot.

Despite these troubling signs, the Mexican Army in Monterrey actually had a considerable advantage over the invading Americans, including superior numbers in strong defensive positions. Strong points guarded the city's entrances and its closely situated, low adobe buildings on straight streets gave Mexican infantry an abundance of sites to mount fearsome defenses. Ampudia hoped to have even additional infantry if reinforcements could be brought from Saltillo, a prospect that suggested he could trap large parts of the American army in the streets of Monterrey and cut it to pieces. In fact, outnumbered by Ampudia and fighting on the offensive, Taylor's sole advantage was his superior artillery. Americans knew that attacking the well-fortified Mexican position would mean heavy casualties. One of Taylor's officers made a fatalistic entry in his journal on the eve of the battle, musing that his "life is the rightful property of my country, and cannot be taken from me, or preserved, except by the fiat of the great God who gave it." He would be killed the next day.[7]

Fortunately for the Americans, the Mexicans labored with almost superhuman resolve to annul their advantages. Ampudia argued incessantly with his subordinates over every tactical detail, and his soldiers were subjected to confusing, contradictory orders that left them badly deployed. His cavalry units, which formed a significant part of his army, were an exasperating bunch whose timidity had already given Taylor a disconcerting mobility. They also refused to fight on foot, which made them worthless should the Americans push their way into the city.

On the morning of September 21, Taylor used his mobility to dash Ampudia's hopes for reinforcements from Saltillo. He sent Worth's division to block the Saltillo Road while Twiggs' division staged what was supposed to be a diversion against fortifications guarding Monterrey's northeastern entrances. Worth began his westward movement on the night of the 20th, and although the Mexicans deduced what he was up to, they did nothing other than send a few hundred cavalrymen on a pointless ride. After he cut the road, Worth sent three regiments of infantry against Federación, a fortified summit west of town. By early morning of the 22nd and after heavy fighting, Worth's men had taken the position, giving American forces control of the heights looking at Monterrey from the west. They immediately turned captured Mexican batteries on the town's outer works.

While Worth's men made their attacks, Taylor sent Twiggs' and Butler's divisions against Monterrey's east and north, mainly as a diversion but with instructions to exploit any weaknesses in Mexican defenses. Despite withering fire from a strongpoint called Tenería, Twiggs' men fought their way into the town but immediately found themselves in narrow streets under a deadly crossfire from low rooftops. They withdrew. Later that morning Tenería was secured, partly through the daring of Col. Jefferson Davis' Mississippi Volunteers, which allowed the Americans to make another more concentrated attack on the next stronghold, El Diablo.

Twiggs admitted later that he was "quite unwell" and consequently absent during all these early proceedings, but he finally arrived on the field and directed the attack on El Diablo.[8] He explained that before a battle he customarily took copious amounts of laxatives to loosen his bowels because he subscribed to the old soldiers' belief that a bullet would pass through the lower abdomen without severing relaxed intestines. Twiggs had overdone the treatment, however, and was indisposed that morning until the battle was well under way. Finally feeling a bit more like himself, he organized his artillery to draw fire from El Diablo and thus opened the way for part of his division to gain the stronghold's rear, overrunning it. After some hard and resourceful fighting, Twiggs' men secured these important outer works but were short of ammunition and unable to mount a decisive push into the town.

The following day, September 22, Taylor made plans for what he hoped would be the decisive assault on Monterrey. Keeping Twiggs' regulars in reserve, Taylor wanted Worth to attack from his positions to the west while the volunteers stormed the town from the east. Expecting such a move, Ampudia relocated his troops to the upper, interior part of the town, and the Americans consequently met with little resistance at first. Soon, however, they found themselves in a nasty house-to-house struggle that slowed their progress almost to a standstill. It took all day to reach within one or two streets of Monterrey's plaza square, and by then darkness stopped the fighting.

That night emissaries from Monterrey's civil government visited Taylor's headquarters. They wanted to send away Monterrey's residents, but they also brought a message from Ampudia, which removed the need for civilian evacuation. Ampudia offered to turn Monterrey over to the United States if he and his men could leave with their weapons. Taylor hesitated before giving up a total victory, but Ampudia's message did at least propose a way to end the immediate fighting and possibly could open preliminary negotiations to end the war. Each side appointed three commissioners who met the next day to hammer out an agreement. The joint commission agreed to allow the Mexican Army to leave the city and march some forty miles south of Monterrey with their small arms and one artillery battery. Neither force was to advance on the other during an eight-week truce unless either chose to terminate it with proper notice.

Taylor's men, exhausted by the vicious fight, saw nothing controversial about this agreement, and Taylor was satisfied as well. He had never been under the impression he was supposed to conquer Mexico. Instead, defeating the Mexican Army on three separate occasions certainly seemed sufficient to force the Mexican government to the bargaining table, which had been the aim of American efforts from the start of the diplomatic crisis over Texas. Taylor, however, had failed to weigh several factors, including the political realities in Mexico City and the evolving mood of his own government, particularly as James K. Polk personified it. The new Mexican government had to sustain itself against dangerous critics, and even though Santa Anna had made indirect promises to the Polk administration that he would work for a negotiated peace, such pledges were worthless because they were politically untenable, even if Santa Anna had made them sincerely, which he had not. As for attitudes in Washington, Polk wanted California, and Taylor's armistice did nothing to acquire it for him. In fact, Polk flew into a towering rage when he heard that Taylor had allowed Ampudia's army to walk away unscathed. He curtly instructed Secretary of War William Marcy to hasten orders to Taylor canceling the armistice. With opponents biting his ankles at home and uninformed generals making policy on the battlefield, Polk angrily turned away from talking to fighting and the hard but crucial business of defeating Mexico. He was determined to leave office with his promises about the acquisition of California and New Mexico fulfilled. He believed that the United States had been diplomatically insulted by Mexico. Even the return of Santa Anna, abetted by the United States, had resulted in continued snubs. Putting Mexico on its knees, he insisted, not polite truces and continued postponements, would win the war and the California prize.

A Change of Plans

Polk knew enough about Mexican geography to realize that Taylor in the northern part of the country could not apply direct pressure on Mexico City, but he had hoped that Taylor would capture or at least distract the Army of the North to prevent it from interfering with another campaign under contemplation. Santa Anna himself had suggested to Polk's emissary in the summer of 1846 that an American landing at Veracruz would permit a direct march on Mexico City and compel Mexico to conduct meaningful negotiations. By fall, Polk had come to regard a Veracruz landing as just the strategy to turn the war around. Even before he learned of what had happened at Monterrey, Polk wrote in his diary, "If this be practicable, it is of the greatest importance that it be done."[9]

Taylor also knew he could not threaten Mexico City. The mountainous terrain he would have to travel consisted of narrow, defensible passes, and an arid desert promised only to amplify the problems of his inadequate supply system. Plunging deep into central Mexico was impossible, but northern Mexico offered ample means for fulfilling Polk's desire for continued pressure on Mexican armies. Talk of Taylor as the Whig candidate for president in 1848 was a siren song for the gruff, old general, and he knew that he needed to keep his name before the public to ensure his nomination. Sitting idly in Monterrey while other commanders won glory on the field and prominence in newspaper accounts would not do.

Polk, however, wanted it that way. The Democrat president also heard talk of Taylor as the next Whig nominee, and though Polk had pledged to limit himself to one term, he was not going to have his administration smooth Taylor's way to a Whig presidency. To isolate him in northern Mexico far from battles and newspaper coverage, the War Department intended to leave Taylor with just enough men to hold his position. Most of his regulars would be taken from him to attack Veracruz and march on Mexico City. The troublesome volunteers would remain as the bulk of Taylor's army.

Isolating Taylor served a political purpose, but military necessity dictated the attack on Veracruz, for Polk concluded there was no other solution than to launch an assault on Mexico City. Deciding who was to lead the campaign, however, was not so easy. In October 1846, when Polk's cabinet first began discussing the Veracruz landings in earnest, General of the Army Winfield Scott presented a plan that included the number of men necessary for the entire campaign, an inventory of equipment and supplies, and the best way to accomplish the landing. Scott had even factored in the lethality of Mexico's low coastal areas during summer, urging that the invasion take place immediately so that the army could be well inland before yellow fever season began in late spring.

Scott had been thorough because he wanted to command the expedition. He doubtless regretted not assuming command over Taylor, his junior, at the start of the war, but he indulged a bad habit for over planning every aspect of any undertaking, and his delay in starting for Mexico gave the ever-vigilant Polk time to nurture suspicions about Scott's political ambitions. The president did not let him go. Scott then all but destroyed his standing with the administration and his reputation with the public by resorting to another lifelong bad habit, that of writing angry letters. His exchanges with Secretary Marcy infuriated Polk. Finally aware that he had overstepped, Scott tried to repair the damage by depicting himself as a painstaking public servant, claiming that his incessant planning for the war had only allowed him to leave his office "to take a hasty plate of soup."[10] Scott, already known as "Old Fuss and Feathers" because he reveled in ceremony and sported gaudy uniforms, thus gave his critics a catcall with which to ridicule him, and the newspapers fervently embraced it. It was an unlikely way to regain the favor of the president or secretary of war.

By fall 1846, Scott was trying to restore his image with a supreme show of competence emphasized by carefully drawn plans and detailed specifics. Polk still found Scott extremely annoying, and the general was openly a Whig, but none of the volunteer generals—mere politicians who had received their appointments because they were loyal Democrats—had the experience to organize, let alone command, a complicated military operation. Appointing a lieutenant general to outrank Major General Scott was briefly considered, and Democrat senator Thomas Hart Benton, a War of 1812 veteran of sorts, even suggested himself as the man for the job, but Polk thought the idea would take too long to implement and involved unacceptable risks in any case. The new rank of lieutenant general would require congressional approval, and Congress would not be back in session until the end of the year. The blatantly political nature of the move might also stimulate the kind of opposition Polk had faced in August over his appropriation request.

The president really had no choice but to give the command to Scott, doing so on November 19, 1846. Just as Scott's supporters had to admit that he was personally irritating, Scott's detractors had to acknowledge that he was militarily capable. The general proved everyone right by supervising all particulars of the expedition with prickly vigilance. Specially designed landing crafts would be used for the first entirely amphibious invasion of foreign soil in American military history, and Scott attentively charted the progress of these boats from planning through construction. They were to be launched from the U.S. naval squadron then being assembled and enlarged in the Gulf of Mexico, the same squadron that would carry Scott's army of approximately ten thousand men and all the supplies and equipment required to besiege Veracruz. With paraphernalia and transport ready, the question was where to get seasoned and experienced men to carry out Scott's demanding mission.

Zachary Taylor had also recommended a Veracruz landing to put direct pressure on Mexico City, but he had no inkling of how far plans had progressed in Washington to do just that. Once aware of the campaign, he probably should have guessed that his army was the logical answer to Scott's manpower problem. Part of Taylor's volunteer force had already been detached to cooperate with the navy in occupying the Mexican coastal city of Tampico, an obvious staging area for a Veracruz landing. When he received orders to cancel the Ampudia armistice, he planned to reopen his campaign to conquer northern Mexico, although the War Department told him to hold his position at Monterrey. Just before Christmas, however, he moved part of his army to secure the town of Victoria and not until afterward did he receive a letter from Scott explaining that the Veracruz–Mexico City campaign would require most of Taylor's regulars. Scott had been as tactful as was possible for a man of his lumbering discretion, but the effort did not placate Taylor, who derisively dismissed "Scott's sugared letter."[11] Scott tried to throw "Old Rough and Ready" another bone, writing again to say that he wanted to meet with Taylor to discuss strategy and assuring him that spring would bring him reinforcements that would allow him to renew his campaign, but Taylor would have none of it.

He was expecting reinforcements sooner than Scott was promising anyway. Gen. John Wool had earlier moved down from San Antonio with the original objective of Chihuahua. He learned, though, that Mexican forces there had moved out of that town. With no place else to go, Wool suggested that he and Taylor combine forces, and as Taylor watched his army trickle to the south, he readily agreed.

Changes in Mexico City

Santa Anna made a triumphant entrance into Mexico City shortly before the Mexican Army's defeat at Monterrey, but interim President Salas remained in office as a figurehead while the Santa Anna–Gómez Farías coalition made the government's important decisions. In the meantime, Santa Anna spent a couple of weeks arranging a clever plan that he hoped would secretly quicken his stride to eventual dictatorship. Most telling was his restoration of an advisory committee known as the Council of State, first established by the Constitution of 1824. Santa Anna hoped that the gesture would allay fears that he intended to wield autocratic authority as he had in 1844, and he reached out both to the *moderados* by including the faction's prominent members on the council and to the *puros* by suggesting that Gómez Farías become its president. Of course, the council had virtually no power, and to serve as its meaningless president, Gómez Farías had to leave the truly influential position of minister of finance. But Santa Anna was persuasive in appealing to the nostalgia for 1824, and he suggested that if Gómez Farías refused the council presidency, it would go to his political enemy, *moderado* leader Manuel Gómez Pedraza. Under the Constitution of 1824, the president of the Council of State had been the sitting vice president, and Gómez Farías took comfort that his designation as the council's presiding officer meant that Santa Anna intended for him to be in line for the presidency. With Santa Anna planning to take command of the army in the field, Gómez Farías would not let Gómez Pedraza assume the position, although by taking it himself, he was effectively removed from influencing governmental affairs.

After Santa Anna left with reinforcements to take command of the

Mexican Army at San Luis Potosí, the *puros* and *moderados* commenced an unremitting argument that boded ill for the government's stability. *Moderados* attempted to discredit Gómez Farías by resigning their posts in droves, but the stubborn *puro* leader remained determined to make the coalition work even though the "opposition had no other objective than to get rid of him."[12] The two factions chiefly quarreled over the issue of suffrage for the September congressional election. The *puros*, backing the August 6 decree that had proclaimed the new government, promised all adult males the vote regardless of their ethnicity, class, or landlessness, but the *moderados* were convinced that such widespread participation would yield an overwhelming *puro* victory. Inevitably, *moderados* cried fraud when the elections were held, and unfortunately a few unavoidable irregularities gave credence to the accusation for the disgruntled and disaffected. The legislature chosen in this election would not convene until December, but it was already under a cloud of suspicion regarding its legitimacy.

In addition to the ongoing feud between the *puros* and the *moderados*, the governing coalition itself began to unravel as Gómez Farías bickered with interim President Salas. Gómez Farías was convinced that Salas intended to reverse democratic reforms enacted by the revolution. He and his fellow *puros* also suspected that the *moderados* intended to disband the civic militia because of their fear of armed mobs. When disputes almost led to armed clashes between lower- and upper-class militia units, the *puros* asked Santa Anna to assume all executive power and end the threat of civil war in Mexico City.

At first he refused, but after gauging the political winds, he had a change of heart, especially when it became apparent that the *puros* would form a significant portion of the legislature, just as the *moderados* had predicted. As the Congress prepared to meet and select the president and vice president, Santa Anna reassured his *puro* friends that he was devoted to their cause, and in December 1846, after considerable maneuvering by *puros* and *moderados*, the Congress accordingly elected him president of Mexico and Gómez Farías vice president. Yet, disillusionment had set in by this point because the two principal executive officers of the Mexican government knew that each of their goals for the country was considerably different. Only the bleak military situation forestalled a decisive confrontation. The *puros* put aside their absolute insistence for semi-independent state governments in the interests of national defense, and Santa Anna took command of the army, delaying his grab for total power. In Santa Anna's absence, Gómez Farías acted as the head of the government, as he had done more than a decade before, giving him and his *puro* followers an opportunity they had not had in years. Whether *puro*, *moderado*, or conservative, however, all were ultimately hostages to the distant war that would soon be on their doorsteps.

New Mexico and California

Puro federalism was popular in the rural outlying parts of Mexico because those regions felt neglected by the central government in Mexico City. Few national tax dollars found their way to these remote places, and Mexico's mountains and deserts made communication between the distant states difficult and slow. Few soldiers were sent to protect inhabitants from Indians, bandits, or, for that matter, the United States. New Mexico and California had at best remained in intermittent contact with Mexico City, California more so because of its ports, but after hostilities began these states were virtually cut off from communication with their central government.

In the summer of 1846, Brig. Gen. Stephen Watts Kearny easily occupied and annexed the major towns in New Mexico and by September was establishing posts to hold the territory as he prepared part of his force for the march to California. Indians rather than Mexicans posed the main difficulty in New Mexico, and Kearny was convinced that he was leaving more than enough men to maintain the peace. Yet when Kearny left for California in September 1846, New Mexico was hardly pacified. Agreements with roaming tribes were deceptive measurements of peace, for New Mexico had a sizable Indian population that lived in ancient permanent towns and villages around larger Mexican settlements. These towns feared for their status under American control and were increasingly suspicious of Charles Bent's civilian government. As more Missourians under Col. Sterling Price arrived, the Indians seemed calm, but they actually were biding their time in the face of American power. That time ran out on January 19, 1847, when they launched an uprising that killed several Americans, including Governor Bent. The general insurrection by Indians and New Mexicans

that followed lasted for weeks until American forces were able to restore an uneasy peace.

Doniphan's Expedition

Col. Alexander Doniphan and his men had planned to leave New
Mexico and link up with Wool shortly after Kearny's departure for California, but the unexpected difficulties with New Mexico's Indian population delayed them. Doniphan consequently spent most of that fall
leading columns into Indian country to negotiate peace agreements
with Indian leaders. He did not leave to rendezvous with Wool until
December, and by that time, Wool had changed his plans and was moving to join Taylor near Monterrey. The intended combination of
Doniphan's forces with Wool's was never to happen, but the Missourians would make their mark nonetheless.

In mid-December Doniphan began moving his almost nine hundred Missouri Volunteers from Valverde, New Mexico, south toward
Chihuahua. On Christmas Day, they defeated a reluctant Mexican force
of garrison troops and militia at the battle of El Brazito, a farcical affair that gave Americans control of El Paso and "completely disorganized and dispersed" Mexican resistance in the area. Doniphan lingered
in El Paso for more than a month as he was reinforced and resupplied.[13]
He started out again on February 8, 1847, and was nearing Chihuahua
three weeks later.

At Chihuahua, Doniphan faced a more imposing opponent than
unorganized militia. The town's defender, Gen. José Antonio Heredia,
had almost three thousand men and a seemingly impregnable position
on the Rio Sacramento. To avoid a frontal assault, Doniphan moved
around Heredia's left on February 28, 1847. Heredia sought to counter
the maneuver with his cavalry, but the riders were late and only briefly
skirmished with the Americans. Doniphan then fortified a strong position from which he launched attacks against the Mexican defensive
works throughout the day until his artillery's superiority ultimately
forced the Mexicans to retreat. The battle, later dubbed Rio Sacramento,
was costly for Heredia, who lost more than five hundred men killed,
wounded, or taken prisoner. Doniphan lost only one killed and less
than a dozen wounded. On March 2, the Americans marched into Chihuahua unopposed where they stayed for several weeks while being re-

supplied. By this point in the expedition "shoes were a luxury, and hats a very doubtful article."[14]

Still hoping to fulfill the original purpose of his campaign by combining with Wool, Doniphan sent word asking Wool what to do. Meanwhile, his men took in Chihuahua, after a fashion. They were at first welcome because they had money and stimulated the economy, but these rough frontiersmen were also tough customers, particularly when they drank, and they occasionally smashed up each other and Chihuahua as well. The town's beautiful public areas particularly suffered. When Doniphan finally heard from Wool in April to bring his men to Saltillo, five hundred miles away, the people of Chihuahua were not unhappy then to see them go. The Missourians were done with fighting in this war, and from Saltillo they were sent home over a more secure route. Finally discharged at New Orleans in June, their march had seen two battles and covered more than two thousand miles.

California

The difficult mountain passes leading into California, the impracticality of supplying a large number of troops on the march, and the expectation that many Californians would welcome annexation and hence not fight led Kearny to take only a small contingent of dragoons, about three hundred riding mules, and some engineers on his march to California. They set out on September 25 hoping to reach the mountains before the first snowfall. About a week and half out of Santa Fe, Kearny encountered legendary mountain man Kit Carson, who conveyed the information that California was already in American hands. Kearny later learned that Carson's announcement was premature.

Nonetheless, much had occurred in California since Kearny had received his orders to take it, much more than even the Polk administration knew. Communication was slow in days when the telegraph was a new invention and running wires even between the large cities of the Northeast was still under way. Even so, Polk had tried to anticipate a war's consequences in California. Before the conflict began, he had sent a warning to Commodore John D. Sloat's naval forces in the Pacific that Mexico's strong reaction to Texas annexation might mean war. In that event, Sloat was to take San Francisco. For his part, Sloat tried to monitor relations between the two governments by having his squadron visit Mazatlán on Mexico's west coast. Learning that Slidell had been sent to negotiate any unresolved differences, he assumed that war had been averted.

Actually, while Sloat's men indolently enjoyed the sun on the coast of Mexico, momentous events were unfolding in California. Capt. John C. Frémont of the U.S. Army Topographical Engineers, dispatched to explore some of the rivers of the Oregon country, inexplicably deviated from his orders and entered California near Sutter's Fort in December 1845. Frémont, already a famed explorer and son-in-law of powerful senator Thomas Hart Benton, might have received instructions from his father-in-law to find a good overland route to California. Benton and his friends would have an advantage in acquiring land once the United States took possession of the region. Although legend had established him as the "pathfinder of the West," Frémont proved more gifted at stirring up trouble than finding travel routes.

In any case, Frémont was simply a ham-fisted faker. He improbably claimed to have taken a wrong turn that landed his expedition in Alta California rather than Oregon, and he used this absurd story to justify a journey to Monterey for rest and resupply before striking out northward to his professed destination. Mexican officials in Monterey had no reason to suspect him or refuse his request, for many Americans had innocently wandered into California over the years. These Mexican officials certainly did not think Frémont and his soldiers would stay, but as days wore into weeks, they had reason to worry. Frémont began poking around, first taking his exploring party to the Pacific and then unaccountably moving south, away from Oregon rather than toward it. Watching these strange movements, Mexicans at last were openly alarmed. American consul Thomas O. Larkin was dismayed as well. Larkin was a transplanted New Englander, and despite an adventurous life, there was still a good bit of Yankee prudence to the set of his jaw. As the president's confidential agent, he was certainly aware of Polk's designs on California and worked tirelessly to avoid an armed conflict that might derail the peaceful acquisition of the province. In any case, he knew that Frémont did not have enough men to supplant Mexican authority by force. Frémont knew this as well and consequently moved north out of Mexican territory, at least for the time being.

Mexican authorities remained edgy, however, and Larkin was soon in contact with Commodore Sloat to request that the navy send at least one ship to northern California to protect American citizens in case matters turned ugly. Sloat obliged even as he remained uncertain about moving his entire squadron toward California. Before hearing from Larkin, Sloat had been visited by Lt. Archibald Gillespie of the U.S. Marine Corps. The Polk administration had sent Gillespie into Mexico to gather information and then travel to California with instructions for Larkin. Adding to his air of mystery, Gillespie also had purportedly personal letters for Frémont, even though the captain was not supposed to be in California. Gillespie presented himself to Sloat on February 9, 1846, and asked for transportation to California. Sloat provided it, but it was all a bit much for the aging, cautious commodore. The example of the impetuous Thomas ap Catesby Jones was a fresh reminder of the pitfalls of rash action, and Sloat puzzled over what he should do without a declaration of war. There was also the question of the British. The United States and the British had not yet settled the Oregon boundary dispute, and it appeared that if the United States cast a proprietary eye on California, the British would preemptively seize it. It was all such a tangle; Sloat decided to sit tight until he heard something definite.

Lieutenant Gillespie, on the other hand, did not intend to pause for an instant. Ferried to California, he met with Larkin during the third week in April to tell him that Polk wanted them to encourage an independence movement in California. Gillespie then struck out for Oregon to find Frémont. There he delivered the letters to the army captain and possibly conveyed instructions, but if so, there is no record of their substance. Shortly after meeting with Gillespie, though, Frémont was back in California.

By May 17, Sloat learned that fighting had broken out on the Rio Grande and began preparations to move his squadron to California and carry out his orders to seize San Francisco. Sloat was so deliberate in his preparations—some would have described it as dawdling—that the Polk administration had time to compose new orders for him. Secretary of the Navy George Bancroft reaffirmed the instruction to take San Francisco but added Monterey as a target too. Bancroft told Sloat that after securing these California ports, he was to put them under a government sponsored by the United States, a fine distinction that Sloat did not at all understand, as events would reveal.

For his part, Captain Frémont had been busy since reading his mail, purportedly from his wife and father-in-law. The letters and his conversation with Lieutenant Gillespie had a strangely galvanizing effect on him. His return to California was marked by apparent plan and purpose. He met with American settlers who expressed worry that deteriorating U.S.-Mexican relations would mean their expulsion from California. Mexican officials already suspected that Frémont was up to no good, and soon they were convinced of it when Frémont clearly became the unofficial leader of American settlers willing to revolt. Soon American raids on Mexican positions compelled authorities to assert themselves, but their efforts were ineffectual. The Americans celebrated their heady victories over the Mexicans by abruptly declaring California independent, choosing July 4, 1846, as appropriately symbolic. They called their new nation the Bear Flag Republic because they had fomented their makeshift revolt under a banner whose most prominent feature was a large grizzly bear. Neither they nor the flag were much to look at—a few hundred scraggly frontiersmen with a crudely sewn pennant—but for the moment they were successful because local Mexican authorities were both surprised and frightened, certain that the United States was behind everything and was intent upon unfolding even more elaborate plans. That certainty was later confirmed by Sloat's squadron pounding up the Pacific Coast and Kearny's Army of the West marching in from the east. Far from their government in Mexico City, Mexican officials in California did not know what to do.

In early July, Commodore Sloat finally appeared off Monterey where he heard about the Bear Flag revolt. He promptly seized the port and issued the stunning announcement that he was annexing California in the name of the United States, even though neither his original orders nor the ones yet to arrive authorized wholesale annexation. Sloat also announced a policy of religious toleration and guaranteed private property as he selected the town's new civil government from his crew. He especially hoped that news of Monterey's fall would convince Bear Flag revolutionaries to change their goal from independence to that of securing the remainder of California for the United States. After detaching part of his command to take San Francisco, he sent emissaries to Bear Flag strongholds at Sonoma and Sutter's Fort to ask for cooperation. Most Bear Flaggers gladly abandoned the independence movement to help conquer California as American citizens. Captain Frémont was among them. Sloat's good cheer over this development, however, rapidly evaporated when he met Frémont. He was dismayed to learn that the army captain had possessed no authority to lead an American rebellion, Bear Flag or otherwise. In fact, Commodore Sloat was most alarmed that he had even indirectly abetted Frémont's activities, especially with his precipitous (and equally unauthorized) annexation announcement. Much to Sloat's relief, Commodore Robert F. Stockton, who was scheduled to replace him, arrived on July 15, and Sloat, eager to head home, quickly turned the entire operation over to him, an operation that Sloat might have described by then as a career-wrecking mess. Stockton, however, was more sanguine about everything that had happened and proved much more sympathetic to Frémont. He was correspondingly much more willing to take risks to obtain all of California for the United States. He gave the rash explorer command of the former Bear Flaggers, now designated as California U.S. volunteers. He also rewarded Frémont with a field promotion to major and made the intrepid Lieutenant Gillespie a captain of the new unit. His aim was to use everyone at hand in the job of acquiring California, a move he was confident would earn him glorious acclaim throughout the country.

Stockton was a man of action accustomed to troubling situations. He had been in command of the USS *Princeton* when the ill-fated firing demonstration killed Secretary of State Abel Upshur and others during the Potomac River cruise in 1844. Nobody had blamed him for that particular disaster, and he was positive that courting another one in California would leave him similarly unscathed. In this attitude, he was a marked contrast to his cautious predecessor. With the exception of the impulsive annexation proclamation, Sloat had stepped lightly in the California matter, always with the goal of winning over its Mexican population to replicate the way Tejanos had been part of the Texas Revolution. Stockton chose to intimidate California's Mexicans, a tactic that courted disaster indeed.

Mexican officials in the southern regions of California knew that Americans would soon assail them as well. Gen. José María Castro and Gov. Pio Pico planned to defend Los Angeles with their meager forces because they really had no other choice. Governor Pico and wealthy California landowners had little affection for and scant loyalty to the Mexican government, but they did fear for their property and the lucrative maritime trade they had cultivated with other nations if the United States took control of the province. For Pico and his supporters, the developing American offensive was a long-anticipated and universally dreaded inevitability. The influx of American settlers had troubled them for years because of the specter of California's becoming another Texas. Nonetheless, Pico had been powerless to stop Americans from squatting in the remote regions of northern California, though he plainly made them feel unwelcome and made no secret of his desire to evict them. Mutual suspicion had bred mutual resentment, and now those Americans were armed and supported by the U.S. government. If successful in seizing California, they were likely the ones to be serving eviction notices. Governor Pico and General Castro had no choice but to defend Los Angeles.

Pico appealed to resident Mexicans (*californios*) to rally them to California's defense. Americans would suppress Catholicism, he warned, and even force conversions to Protestantism. Worse, they would bring slavery to California. These alarms had little effect, though, and few answered Pico's call to arms. Only when American forces directly threatened them did *californios* resist, but that was not the way to repel invaders.

As it happened, Pico's greatest aid in raising a defense was Stockton's arrogance. In part, the commodore's overconfidence resulted from the ease with which California's major northern ports had been taken. It seemed to follow that conquering all of California would be equally effortless. Yet, Stockton's rough dealings with *californios* raised their fears that he would break Sloat's promises about their property and their religion. Some reconsidered their diffident response to Pico's earlier pleas.

Stockton did not seem to mind that he was going to have to do with guns what might have been accomplished with persuasion. If anything, he relished the opportunity to contrive unnecessary and complicated tactical maneuvers. Instead of simply chasing Castro's tiny hundred-man Los Angeles garrison out of California, Stockton planned to capture it with an elaborate pincer movement composed of Frémont's volunteers on one side and sailors and marines on the other. The USS *Cyane* took Frémont to San Diego so he could move on Los Angeles from the south while Stockton moved in from the coast about twenty miles from Los Angeles. By the first week of August, as American plans became evident, Castro sent word to Consul Larkin that he wanted to discuss terms. Stockton refused to hold negotiations, however, unless California's Mexican government declared itself independent from Mexico City. With no peaceful way to end this impasse and lacking sufficient numbers to defend Los Angeles, Castro and Pico abandoned the town.

On August 13, Stockton and Frémont led their little armies into Los Angeles without firing a shot. Stockton immediately began organizing a civilian government and set September 15 as the day for territorial elections. He had not been authorized to take such steps, and California was not officially a territory of the United States, even if he said it was, for Stockton was apparently unaware that only Congress had the power to annex territories and organize their governments. Stockton was too busy to worry about such proprieties. He appointed Frémont his military commandant, a temporary title he invented for just this occasion, for he intended to make Frémont territorial governor after the elections. As the Americans soon discovered, the *californios* had other ideas.

Trouble in Los Angeles

Stockton was so confident that California was secure that he believed fifty men were a sufficient garrison to control Los Angeles and the surrounding region, an indication of how deluded he was about the volatile situation he was leaving behind. He planned to take the rest of Frémont's people to launch an attack on Mexico's west coast at Acapulco. He consequently left former lieutenant, now captain, Gillespie in command of only a token military presence. Gillespie also inexplicably believed he could control a potentially hostile population that outnumbered his garrison thirtyfold, for he adopted an imperious manner that quickly alienated already resentful *californios*. They were soon involved in a violent uprising led by Cérbulo Varela and José María Flores, a former officer in the Mexican Army. Gillespie sent a plea to Stockton for help and tried to find a more defensible position until reinforcements arrived, but he ultimately had to surrender his command. Captain Flores was generous, allowing Gillespie to take his men to the coast, but southern California, just that quickly, was no longer in American hands.

Gillespie and his men waited aboard an American merchant ship off San Pedro until a relief expedition arrived on October 6, 1846. The following day, Capt. William Mervine of the USS *Savannah* led about three hundred men to retake Los Angeles. Opposed by *californio* cavalry and one artillery piece—one more than Mervine had—the Americans were forced to return to San Pedro and wait for Frémont and Stockton who were coming south with more volunteers, sailors, and marines. A rumor that the Monterey garrison would be attacked delayed Frémont, and after assessing the bleak situation at San Pedro, Stockton decided to shift his base to San Diego.

For a time, both sides warily watched one another. In Los Angeles, Flores knew that his situation became untenable the moment Stockton in the south and Frémont in the north chose to converge on his position. To discourage that maneuver, he sent guerrilla bands to threaten the small American garrisons Stockton had established across the countryside, hopeful that the menace would force Stockton and Frémont to stay put. The raids stunned the Americans as their smaller units were forced to surrender or to pull back to larger American garrisons. For several weeks then, in the late fall of 1846, Flores could take comfort in having held his own while keeping the Americans off balance. In early December, however, an unexpected turn of events made even his most resourceful efforts hopeless.

Kearny Arrives

After more than two months on the trail, Stephen Kearny arrived in California with his three hundred dragoons and immediately sent scouts ahead to test the accuracy of Kit Carson's news. Instead of finding the fight for California finished, the scouts found Stockton stuck in San Diego with glum news about a lost Los Angeles and a perilous countryside. After the two officers exchanged messages, Stockton sent Gillespie with about forty men to persuade Kearny to move against the *californios* who ranged between Los Angeles and San Diego. When scouts reported the presence of *californios* at San Pascual under the command of Capt. Andrés Pico, the brother of California's erstwhile governor, Kearny needed no additional encouragement.

On the morning of December 6, 1846, Kearny's dragoons and Gillespie's men attacked Pico's camp, but the *californios* had enough time to gather their lances and mount their horses. Kearny's men had never fought lancers, but that disadvantage was only part of their problem. They also were riding newly broken horses they had just acquired upon entering California, and the mounts proved skittish and unreliable. The nasty little fight that ensued—known as the battle of San Pascual—cost Kearny eighteen men killed and thirteen wounded, himself among them. It might have been worse, but Kearny's artillery arrived and forced Pico to withdraw. Still the Americans were in a bad way after the fight, and a lack of wagons for the wounded slowed their progress back to San Diego to a snail's pace. Pico's men constantly assailed them, and "soon both animals and men began to suffer."[15] Urgent calls for rescue eventually brought a relief party from Stockton, which brought Kearny and his men into San Diego on December 12, considerably banged up and noticeably chastened.

The significance of this Mexican victory was uncertain, though. The Pico brothers had shown that the average *californio* did not want American rule, but the men who defeated Kearny's troops were small landowners, agricultural workers, and shopkeepers. Large landowners, with a few important exceptions, saw the war as trouble best avoided. Some actually believed that an American government would better serve their interests. Thus while *californios* were irresolute, Americans were determined to persevere, if not always congenially.

As soon as Kearny recovered from his wound, he and Stockton began making plans to retake Los Angeles, but it soon became apparent that the two men could barely stand one another. Their uneasy relationship always promised to turn turbulent, especially over issues of command. Kearny's orders clearly placed him in charge of military forces in California and made him military governor of any annexed territory. Stockton, however, argued that since he had been first on the scene, had done all the work, and still commanded the largest force, he should be in charge and serve as governor. Kearny might have pointed out that Stockton's tactics and attitude had managed to lose much of the territory won by others, but he refrained from making the observation, just as he did not take issue with Stockton's insistence that he be allowed to name his successor as military governor. With remarkable self-control, Kearny held his tongue and temper, judging the recapture of Los Angeles as the more important issue, for the time being. He deferred to Stockton's direction of that campaign under the rationale that the commodore was contributing the most men to it.

The expedition of approximately six hundred men began its march at the end of December and was nearing Los Angeles in early January to the dismay of Captain Flores. He knew that his small numbers would not be able to withstand an attack, and risking his own capture was highly dangerous. He had been among those paroled after the Americans had first taken Los Angeles, and his subsequent activities clearly violated his pledge to lay down arms, a capital offense if a captor wanted to make an issue of it. Flores proposed negotiations, but Stockton refused and continued his advance. Forced to fight, Flores tried to exploit Stockton's chief vulnerability, which was the necessity to cross rivers on the way to Los Angeles. Flores staged an ambush at Bartolo Ford, starting the battle of San Gabriel, in which he deployed his small artillery pieces and lancers to block the American crossing. Superior American artillery and Kearny's dragoons pushed back the *californio* defense, and when his counterattack failed, Flores pulled back to the environs of Los Angeles. There he made a final attempt on January 9 to stop the Americans but it too failed. As the *californios* fled northward, Stockton's martial medley of dragoons, sailors, marines, and volunteers entered Los Angeles. It was the morning of January 10, 1847.

Frémont was heading south to cooperate with Stockton's force, but his remarkably slow pace unexpectedly put him directly in the way of Flores' little fleeing army. With the possibility of capture, his violated parole loomed again, and Flores did not wait to discover Frémont's views on the matter. When his men surrendered, he was not among them. Frémont, already late for his appearance at Los Angeles, was eager to be shed of these new impediments, so he paroled the *californios* and hurried on his way.

He might have wished he had not. Small uprisings continued throughout California, but the province was all but pacified, meaning that the American commanders now had plenty of time to quarrel over issues of command and insubordination. Caught in the middle of the argument was Capt. John C. Frémont, and it was little comfort that his predicament was largely his own doing. Continuing his efforts to establish a civil government and his own primacy, Stockton named Frémont governor on January 16. Kearny now drew the line. Only he had the authority per his official orders, he insisted, to form a government. Furthermore, he now insisted he was the superior officer in the province. It was one thing for Commodore Robert F. Stockton of the U.S. Navy to disagree with Kearny; quite another for Capt. John C.

Frémont of the U.S. Army to inform a brigadier general that Frémont considered himself subject only to Stockton's orders. The resulting situation thus became more than an instance of interservice rivalry going from bad to worse. It was exasperating to lock horns with a naval commodore, but it was beyond comprehension to have such impudent defiance from an army captain.

In practical terms, though, Stockton had Kearny in an awkward position. The navy had more men to support the commodore's disobedience, leaving Kearny with only papers to support his case. It was out of the question, of course, to level guns at another American force, even if it was the navy, particularly when they were all trying to control a hostile population. The best Kearny could do was walk away, taking his dragoons to San Diego while awaiting further instructions.

At San Diego, the Mormon Battalion finally showed up, in fairly bad shape from their adventures on the trail. After departing Santa Fe the previous October, the Mormon Battalion undertook an arduous march in trying conditions. Kearny had wanted them to find a wagon route for settlers heading to California, but they found almost everything else on the way, almost all of it bad. Stampedes, foul weather, and starvation made for a torturous trip, and they were finally obliged to barter for food with Indians. According to a member of the battalion, on one occasion they had "purchased some meal and beans and sold our clothes off from our backs to do that."[16] When these starving men finally arrived in San Diego in January 1847, they were not likely to awe anyone, whether restive *californios* or insolent naval commodores.

The situation resolved itself at the end of January in any case. Stockton was himself superseded by a senior naval officer, Commodore W. Brandord Shubrick, whose arrival barely preceded new orders from Washington reiterating and firmly establishing the army's control of California's government. Now firmly in command, Kearny immediately set about restoring the army's universe. He curtly ordered Frémont to report to headquarters at Monterey. It took more than a few threats to make the errant captain comply, which did not help his case. After turning command over to Col. Richard Mason, Kearny, with a detachment of 1st Dragoons as escort, took Frémont back to Fort Leavenworth where he was charged with mutiny, disobedience of orders, and insubordination. The trial at the end of 1847 found Frémont guilty and cashiered him from the army, but Frémont's father-in-law, powerful

Missouri senator Thomas Hart Benton, had the sentence overturned. Frémont resigned his commission anyway, his own pride, in this case as in all others, his worst enemy. He continued to explore the Rockies, and his exploits were romanticized in the writings of his wife, Jessie Benton Frémont, who possessed a talent for the florid style of nineteenth-century adventure tales.

As for Stephen Kearny, he was widely regarded as one of the most talented officers of his time, and his level temperament earned him posts as the civil governor of Veracruz and Mexico City during the brief American occupation. Yet his exploits were costly and consuming. Soon after the war, malaria accomplished what a thousand-mile march, raucous volunteers, hostile Mexican forces, and impertinent fellow officers had not been able to. Kearny died in 1848 at fifty-four years of age.

Notes

1. Pedro Santoni, *Mexicans at Arms*, 130.

2. Quoted in James M. McCaffrey, *Army of Manifest Destiny: The American Soldier in the Mexican War, 1846–1848* (New York: New York University Press, 1992), 120.

3. The sentiment is often attributed to the eighteenth-century British statesman Edmund Burke, but numerous researchers have not been able to locate the quotation in any of Burke's letters, writings, or published speeches.

4. The term *racialism* rather than *racism* best describes this mind-set, for it was not based solely on prejudice and bigotry. Instead, a considerable body of eighteenth- and early-nineteenth-century scientific "evidence" had led educated people to conclude that superior cultures were the by-product of superior races, an erroneous notion nevertheless embraced as informed and proven.

5. John Taylor Hughes, *Doniphan's Expedition* (College Station: Texas A&M University Press, 1997), 56.

6. Franklin Smith, *The Mexican War Journal of Captain Franklin Smith*, ed. Joseph E. Chance (Jackson: University Press of Mississippi, 1991), 9.

7. Doubleday, editor, *Journals of Philip Norbourne Barbour*, 108.

8. Zachary Taylor to Adjutant General, October 9, 1846, in T. B. Thorpe, *Our Army at Monterrey* (Philadelphia: Carey and Hart, 1847), 158.

9. James K. Polk, *Polk: The Diary of a President, 1845–1849, Covering the Mexican War, the Acquisition of Oregon, and the Conquest of California and the Southwest*, ed. Allan Nevins (New York: Longmans, Green, 1952), 155.

10. Bauer, *Mexican War*, 74.

11. Zachary Taylor to James Buchanan, August 29, 1847, in Zachary Taylor, *Letters of Zachary Taylor from the Battle-fields of the Mexican War*, ed. William K. Bixby (Rochester, NY: Genesee Press, 1908), 180.

12. Santoni, *Mexicans at Arms*, 146.

13. Hughes, *Doniphan's Expedition*, 134.

14. J. McCaffrey, *Army of Manifest Destiny*, 161.

15. James Madison Cutts, *The Conquest of California and New Mexico by the Forces of the United States in the Years 1846 & 1847* (Albuquerque: Horn & Wallace, 1965), 174.

16. McCaffrey, *Army of Manifest Destiny*, 156.

CHAPTER 5

SCOTT'S CAMPAIGN

As soon as Santa Anna took control of the Mexican Army, he began a vigorous campaign to rebuild and strengthen it. He relieved General Ampudia of command, established headquarters at San Luis Potosí, and began raising money from every source he could touch, including the church. Yet restoring his hodgepodge of an army to a respectable fighting machine would take more than a new leader and some cash. Its professional soldiers were proud but demoralized by the humiliating defeats on the Rio Grande and at Monterrey. Its conscripts, taken from the ranks of the poor or emptied from Mexican jails, were a dispirited rabble eager to desert. Santa Anna did not only need more men, he needed fresh and better ones, even if that meant relying on mobilization through unpopular conscription. That autumn, directives went out to state governments to provide quotas of soldiers, and while some complied, some did not. Those states that did send men seldom armed them.

Santa Anna took heart from this otherwise disheartening situation, though, by clinging to the belief that one great victory would convince the United States to halt the war. His optimism was not merely wishful thinking. The American response to his pledge that he would set a reasonable price for the land Polk wanted if the United States helped him return to power, was revealing, in his mind. The United States obviously wanted a negotiated settlement, possibly indicating that America's political resolve for the war was more fragile than firm. Growing opposition to the war in the United States, especially evident in the divisive debates over the Wilmot Proviso that August, suggested that bad news from the battlefield might break that political resolve, especially if news announced a major defeat dealt to Zachary Taylor's army. Santa Anna accordingly took heart and laid his plans.

At Saltillo, Taylor heard reports from spies and scouts that Santa

Anna was raising money and troops to amass a revitalized army at San Luis Potosí even as he, Taylor, contemplated losing many of his regulars to Scott's Veracruz expedition. He wanted to secure more of northern Mexico before those men left. For starters, he ordered Gen. John Wool to establish a base for his two thousand men at Parras while he himself began moving a division toward Victoria. He could only hope that Santa Anna was not yet ready to fight.

Santa Anna, however, could not wait, ready or not, for he was under political pressure to act. The Mexican Congress named him president in the expectation that he would fulfill at least some of his promises for martial success, just as Taylor's move to occupy additional portions of northern Mexico spread the Americans rather thin and made them a tempting target. With Wool at Parras and Taylor on the way to Victoria, Santa Anna intended to freeze Taylor with a small diversionary strike while attacking Saltillo, defended by a lone American division under William Jenkins Worth. Surprise was Santa Anna's greatest ally in the proposed undertaking, but keeping his plans secret proved impossible. Worth learned of the plan and immediately sent word to Taylor and Wool that Saltillo was in dire peril. When sufficient parts of the American army unexpectedly gathered again at Saltillo, Santa Anna had to postpone his offensive. Taylor now at least knew that Santa Anna was willing to venture forth from San Luis Potosí. Yet, even as Taylor resolved to keep his guard up, his strength was dwindling. General Scott, hurriedly assembling troops at Tampico in preparation for the Veracruz landing, sent orders to Taylor's regular officers to start moving their men toward the coast. Worth's division was the first to go on January 9 followed by Twiggs' division from Victoria on January 14. It was bad enough losing the men in the face of Santa Anna's pending menace, but it became much worse when an America courier was killed by Mexican troops. On him they found copies of Scott's orders detailing detachments from Taylor's army. The information was soon in Santa Anna's hands. He now had everything he needed to know about Zachary Taylor's shrinking army and how to crush it.

Buena Vista

Santa Anna moved his army of over twenty-one thousand men out of San Luis Potosí at the end of January. He sent almost seven thousand mounted troops under Gen. José Urrea to block Taylor's route to Matamoros and hence sever the American supply line and prevent its use as a likely avenue of retreat. He moved the balance of his army against Taylor at Saltillo, a march of almost two hundred and fifty miles across mostly desert in the dead of winter. Santa Anna knew that his unhappy, physically miserable, ill-supplied, and largely untrained troops were likely to desert at every opportunity, so he made plain that anyone caught away from camp would be shot immediately. Threats notwithstanding, many managed to melt away during a march so grueling that many others simply died along the way. By the time Santa Anna was nearing Taylor, desertions and the elements had whittled his army down to about seventeen thousand men.

Taylor knew that Santa Anna was coming, though he doubted a Mexican army could cross the inhospitable desert between San Luis Potosí and Saltillo before spring. Nevertheless, Mexican patrols had been riding north since mid-January, some large enough to threaten Taylor's outlying positions and even capture small American detachments. Just to make sure he was not surprised, Taylor gave Gen. William O. Butler's volunteers the job of guarding the supply line from Monterrey to Matamoros. Wool's volunteers would defend the area around Saltillo. Meanwhile, Taylor moved his almost five thousand men forward, initially to Agua Nueva, but the ground there troubled him. It exposed his flanks, and as soon as he learned of Santa Anna's approach, he moved back toward Buena Vista, a ranch that guarded the entrance to Angostura Pass. Because Wool was more familiar with the lay of this land, Taylor let him choose the best positions for the upcoming battle. Wool made a soldier's job of it, placing men and artillery to take the greatest advantage of the main road's narrow passage through a plateau and gulches. On the morning of February 22, 1847, the American force, outnumbered and outgunned, discovered just how advantageous the ground was.

That morning, Taylor returned from checking the lines to Saltillo to find a demand from Santa Anna that he surrender. Perhaps it is true, as some stories have it, that aides had to clean up Taylor's colorful response, but the version sent to Santa Anna was curtly succinct in any case: "Sir: In reply to your note of this date, summoning me to surrender my forces at discretion, I beg leave to say that I decline acceding to your request."[1]

Santa Anna likely expected as much. He already had battle plans to divide his army, sending part of it against Taylor's main lines along the plateau while the other attacked through Angostura Pass to turn Taylor's flank. If these maneuvers worked, they would send Taylor's soldiers running back to Saltillo where Mexican cavalry would be waiting. Their slaughter would then be a mere matter of the killing.

Santa Anna launched the plan at midafternoon on February 22 by trying to turn the American left flank, but Taylor successfully repulsed the assault and with that, fighting ended on the first day. The next morning Santa Anna sent in more troops against the American left, causing Taylor to reinforce that portion of his line. Santa Anna then hurled a massive assault against the weakened American middle on the plateau, and by midmorning superior numbers had almost earned the Mexicans an overwhelming victory. As Taylor's center nearly broke and his left crumpled in on itself, he pulled the soldiers on the collapsing left back to the ranch at Buena Vista to mount a last stand amid his supply wagons.

The next desperate hours saw Americans defending their tenuous positions with astonishing tenacity and extraordinary courage. At a crucial moment, Col. Jefferson Davis led his Mississippi volunteers and other volunteer units in a charge that helped save the day. As Santa Anna failed to exploit the advantages he had gained on the plateau and the American left, Taylor's officers regrouped and moved their men into new defensive positions. Subtly but perceptibly, the momentum of the contest shifted from the Mexican attackers to the beleaguered Yankee defenders.

Santa Anna surely sensed this. Up on the plateau, he resolved to hammer through the American lines using the sheer weight of his numbers to force a decision. He came very close to succeeding. American batteries became the most important part of Taylor's defense in this bloody hour, and many of the men manning those guns died at them, including the son of Senator Henry Clay. But they bought precious time with their lives and by late in the day, the American artillery proved decisive in this contest as it had in others. American lines remained intact, and at the end of fighting on the 23rd, Taylor's mangled men held the field.

The battered and begrimed soldiers who heard the dying reports of muskets and the thumping cannons go silent in that twilight had done more than survive Buena Vista. Early bulletins to the United States told of Taylor being badly defeated, but corrections were soon to follow. It was hardly a smashing victory, but Taylor's men had stood firm against extraordinarily long odds, and when word reached the United States of the actual outcome, Taylor was celebrated as a national hero. His men had done more than hold on at Buena Vista, and one of their most stunning achievements was to make their commanding officer the next president of the United States.

At the moment, though, that result was as indistinct as was everything else for the Americans, including the uncertainty about whether the battle at Buena Vista was actually over. Yet, Santa Anna knew it was. His men were spent. They had gone into the battle exhausted from the terrible march to it and had carried out a complicated plan to envelope Taylor's position that left them as scattered as they were fatigued. Santa Anna knew that he would not be able to resume the attack on Taylor right away, and that meant not at all. His first instinct was deceit, however, and he sent word to Mexico City that he had won a spectacular victory over Taylor's army and would soon complete the job of destroying it. Instead of destroying anything, Santa Anna began moving his army back to San Luis Potosí. He took comfort, such as it was, that Taylor in his isolated position and with his paltry numbers posed no threat to the rest of Mexico.

Taylor spent the next few weeks restoring supply lines that had been wrecked by Mexican cavalry, but the war was over for him and his small force. He received reinforcements but mounted no new campaigns. Santa Anna eventually moved most of his army out of San Luis Potosí to oppose Scott's invasion, but Taylor remained primarily on the defensive in northern Mexico. At Buena Vista, he and his brave men had won their part of the war.

Turmoil in the Mexican Government

Santa Anna's lies could no longer disguise the fact that both he and Mexico were in serious trouble. His army had endured two incredibly taxing marches in only a few weeks and was in no condition to fight off a new invasion. Yet when Winfield Scott's army landed in early March, the Mexican Army was going to have to mount a defensive campaign to guard the route to Mexico City from Veracruz. In addition, as Santa Anna confronted the problems of broken morale and inadequate supply, the Mexican government rapidly went to pieces.

As acting president, Valentín Gómez Farías had as his most pressing responsibility financing the war. He worked, however, under the shadow of his reputation for zealous reform, and his political opponents were quick to suspect him of using his power to push a *puro* program. Although Gómez Farías constantly exhorted everyone to work together in this time of national emergency, his frustration got the better of him. It was nothing new for a Mexican government to pressure the church for loans, but Gómez Farías broke the rules by seizing church property to pay for the war. The church had grumbled over forced loans, but outright confiscation turned grumbling into resistance, and the church soon encouraged opposition to Gómez Farías' government. It did not have to look far. *Moderados* also dreamed of toppling the government. They left Gómez Farías' cabinet and sabotaged his efforts to maintain the coalition. The final blow came when Santa Anna announced from the field that he too did not support Gómez Farías.

What happened next was so familiar that it all but followed a well-rehearsed script for overthrowing a government. The conspirators included high-ranking army officers, *moderados*, and church leaders. Their plan to stage a coup against Gómez Farías was an open secret, and when he tried to move *moderado* civic militia units to the coast, it seemed he was trying to prevent their use in an attempted coup rather than, as he claimed, deploying them to repel the expected U.S. landing at Veracruz. The conspirators acted swiftly, staging what became known as the *Polkos* Revolt on February 27, 1847. When Gómez Farías contemplated using the civic militia to maintain order, the middle class, including the *moderados*, were panicked by the possibility that armed mobs would be turned loose in the streets. Their worst fears about the acting president seemed confirmed.

The worst was yet to come, though, for Gómez Farías refused to go quietly. As chaos engulfed the capital, several army officers reneged on promises to provide military support for the rebels, and Santa Anna's followers, fearing that the *polkos* intended to depose their leader too, refused to join the rebellion. By such slender threads, Gómez Farías clung to power.

The situation settled into the stalemate between the *polkos* and *puros* until Santa Anna tipped the balance away from both the government and the rebels. He rode into Mexico City as the proverbial man on horseback, his popularity surging because of his victory at Buena Vista (the capital had not yet heard the truth of that matter), and primed to resume the role of Mexico's savior. Taking control of the government, he allied himself with the *moderados* by repudiating Gómez Farías and regained the church's support by returning its confiscated property. He instead resorted to the extortionate but relatively palatable practice of the forced loan.

The American invasion at Veracruz required Santa Anna to lead the army east and again relinquish the presidency during his absence from the capital. Gómez Farías was completely out of favor and likely to provoke another revolt, but he was not out of office. Santa Anna solved that problem by having Congress abolish the vice presidency, thus legislating Gómez Farías out of the government. Congress then chose Gen. Pedro María Anaya to act as president while Santa Anna saved the country by confronting Winfield Scott on the National Highway that led from the Gulf Coast to Mexico City, the heart of the nation.

To Mexico City: Opening Phases

Scott Lands at Veracruz

The U.S. Navy had played an important role blockading Mexican ports and seizing California, but its participation in the assault on Veracruz was crucial. The navy was responsible for moving Scott's army from several embarkation points, including Tampico, to assemble it at the Island of Lobos off the coast at Veracruz. (See Map 5.1.) The navy also helped to scout possible landing beaches and then transported the army, its animals, equipment, and the specially designed landing craft to them. It played a significant role in the subsequent siege of Veracruz. Yet, the entire operation was an ambitious undertaking, and despite the indispensable contributions the American gulf squadron made to it, the navy did not have enough ships to move thousands of men and their equipment to the Island of Lobos expeditiously. As a result, all the men

Map 5.1

and their supplies were not in place until the yellow fever season loomed.

The delay was quite serious because of its potential consequences. Yellow fever is most virulent in low, tropical regions during the spring and summer months because mosquitoes carry it. People in the nineteenth century did not know about mosquitoes acting as carriers, but they had made the correlation between warm weather and the disease. Although the United States had suffered yellow fever outbreaks in its coastal areas, most Americans had never been exposed to the disease, and Scott was rightly concerned that it could destroy his army before it began the march to Mexico City. He regarded it as urgent to take Veracruz during the winter months and quickly move inland to higher, healthier ground before the yellow fever season began. As his army slowly trickled toward the Island of Lobos, Scott watched the calendar with mounting anxiety. Not until the first week of March did he have a force large enough to make his landing. It remained to be seen if he was too late to avoid the sickness that was so dreaded that coastal Mexicans had given it a vile name, "the black vomit."[2]

Getting ashore to assault Veracruz was a difficult step, and Commodore David Conner, commander of the American gulf squadron, suggested that Collado Beach south of Veracruz would serve the purpose. On March 6, Conner took Scott and his staff on the little steamship *Petrita* to scout the area. Conner was right; the site at Collado was ideal with calm waters that promised an easy transit for landing craft as they pulled toward shore. Even better, the Mexican military had made no effort to establish any defenses on that part of the coast. Possibly the elation over discovering such a promising spot distracted everyone on the return trip, for the *Petrita* cruised too close to the guns of Veracruz and was soon under dangerous fire. The little steamer was a small target and quickly moved out of range as cannonballs sent spray towering around her, but the consequences of a direct hit were sobering. Scott might have perished along with his senior officers Robert Patterson, William Jenkins Worth, and David E. Twiggs, losses that would have made the Veracruz landing and all that followed it unlikely, altering the course of the war. The junior officers aboard the *Petrita* included George Gordon Meade, Pierre G. T. Beauregard, Joseph E. Johnston, and Robert E. Lee, all destined for prominence in another war.

Scott wasted no time, loading his transports for the trip to Collado Beach on March 7 and setting March 9 for the landing. The first division under William Jenkins Worth was given the job of establishing the beachhead. After Worth had secured the beach, he was to be followed by the volunteer division under Robert Patterson and then the rest of the regulars under Twiggs. As the first wave of Americans neared the shore, Mexican cavalry seemed to be patrolling the area, but they fled even before the Americans began splashing toward the beach. As soon as the American soldiers reached land, they planted an American flag in the sand. It was visible to the other transports, a signal that this first difficult part of the operation was not to be dangerous. In fact, by midnight that day, Scott had almost nine thousand men ashore without suffering a single casualty. It was an astonishing example of defensive indifference by the Mexican defenders of Veracruz.

Brig. Gen. Juan Morales commanded the fortifications at Veracruz with about thirty-three hundred men within some of the strongest fortifications in the Western Hemisphere. San Juan de Ulúa, an impressive fort that sat offshore on a reef northeast of Veracruz, was meant to protect the port from a seaborne attack, but its guns could inflict enormous punishment on Scott's troops as they moved around the western edge of the town to establish a siege. Yet, Morales was glum. His ill-equipped men were no match for Scott's army in the open field, which made his fortifications as much a prison as a bastion. In addition, neglectful Mexican administrations had allowed the fortifications in Veracruz to fall into disrepair, and though Morales tried to shore up some of his works, there was nothing he could do about his substandard and unreliable artillery. Even under the threat of San Juan de Ulúa's heavy guns, Scott had been able to move his men into position, to stop the flow of fresh water into the city, and cut Morales off from the outside. The Mexican commander knew that unless he received equipment and considerable reinforcements from Mexico City, his days defending Veracruz were numbered.

Morales was prepared to count every one of them, though. With siege lines in place, Scott on March 22 gave Morales an opportunity to surrender, but he gamely refused. Scott knew that a protracted siege would be successful and require only negligible force, but he also knew he did not have the time, so he resorted to his artillery. American land batteries opened up on the city, and the navy's long-range guns began lobbing in huge shells from ships anchored a mile off the coast. Commodore Matthew C. Perry had replaced Conner as commander of the naval squadron the day before and quickly got into the spirit of things by loaning Scott some heavy naval guns and their crews to augment the army's batteries. As vicious northerly winds churned the sea and made the gunnery work on land difficult, the artillery barrages nevertheless lay the town in ruins and shook its fortifications. The massive naval guns were especially terrifying and when Scott added rockets to the artillery bombardment on the 24th, the town's inhabitants neared the breaking point. Morales stood firm, however, more afraid of Santa

Anna's wrath than Scott's guns. The civilian population prayed for deliverance.

Scott had worries of his own. The Mexican forces in Veracruz regularly returned fire, causing one American soldier to comment wryly that "the air was rent with the whistling of balls, the roaring of our own mortars, and the bustle and confusion incident to such an exciting time."[3] Mexican gunnery, however, seldom scored hits, as an American newspaper correspondent noted, reporting that "shells of the heaviest kind have been thrown" but that "no one . . . has been killed so far."[4] Scott worried, however, that enough practice would improve Mexican marksmanship. Meanwhile, Mexican regular and irregular forces continually probed the rear of Scott's siege lines, threatening to break through to reinforce Veracruz, and rumors told of Santa Anna's assembling a major relief force. If this were true, and if that force were to combine with the Veracruz garrison and the plucky soldiers already harassing Scott's perimeter, it would outnumber Americans. A lengthy bombardment, like a prolonged siege, was out of the question.

Morales, nearing the end of his tether, contemplated surrendering. He turned command of Veracruz over to Gen. José Juan Landero during the night of March 25–26, possibly in a forlorn effort to avoid exclusive responsibility for the inevitable. The unfortunate Landero, a supporter of Santa Anna, would have the distasteful chore of surrendering to the Americans, which he did on March 29. Scott was generous, parolling the Mexican soldiers and their officers, mainly because he did not have the resources to guard and provision them in Veracruz. Morales and Landero might have wished he had, for Santa Anna was not nearly so generous. He had them both arrested and thrown into prison.

Scott placed Veracruz under martial law with General Worth as its military governor. About one hundred civilians had died in the siege, and the extended bombardment had left survivors shattered. As the American army began cleaning up the rubble and tending to the injured, Scott promised the return of order and the strict enforcement of laws to protect civilian lives and property. He was as good as his word. Unlike Zachary Taylor, Scott enforced strict military discipline and harshly punished anyone found guilty of abusing Mexican civilians. More than altruism and honor guided his actions, for Scott was a student of Napoleon's disastrous efforts during the Iberian war to control Spaniards with coercion and terror. The only result had been Spanish insurgency and vicious, irregular fighting by elusive guerrillas. Scott was about to head inland, and he needed tranquility in occupied Veracruz unless his march to Mexico City was to become a trap that isolated his army in an increasingly hostile countryside. He believed fair and kind treatment was the best way to pacify conquered people, and he applied the theory first in the coastal town and then wherever he marched in the interior. It worked. Though guerrillas would plague Scott's supply lines throughout the war, Veracruz was occupied without serious incident, and Mexico's population did not generally resist Scott's advance.

He had only to worry about Santa Anna's army, which was somewhere in front of him on the National Highway, and yellow fever, which threatened to be where he was right at the moment. In fact, he was more afraid of the fetid lowlands of Veracruz and the black vomit they mysteriously spawned than he was of any Mexican military force. The hot season was upon him, and he planned to race his army inland to the higher ground that promised a fight, but also a healthful climate.

Cerro Gordo

More than anger prompted Santa Anna to imprison Morales and Landero. He wanted to shift the blame for the fall of Veracruz. Although the government had known for weeks that Scott was preparing his expedition, Mexico City had done little to prepare Veracruz for the assault. Santa Anna not only deflected blame from himself to the generals who had unsuccessfully defended Veracruz, he used the crisis of Scott's invasion to get rid of the troublesome Gómez Farías while stirring patriotism to shield his regime from criticism and increase resources for his coming campaign. This new and looming American threat, in fact, had a magical effect on the Mexican polity. *Moderados* and *puros* suddenly found common ground as they prepared the capital to repel the invaders. The factions authorized new incentives for joining the army and activated the civic militia with hardly a cross word being uttered. They took comfort that these measures were merely precautions, of course, for Santa Anna was expected to stop Scott on the road to Mexico City.

On April 2, Santa Anna took his army east, confident that the terrain, yellow fever, and preparations being made at Jalapa would make easy work of stopping and possibly destroying the American army. He concentrated on mounting a crushing attack in the lowlands near a place called Cerro Gordo. If Scott could be stopped or even delayed there, Santa Anna hoped that yellow fever would begin its own attack on the Americans.

Scott delayed his march for the interior only long enough to equip his column with draught animals, but suddenly the vexing dispute between Twiggs and Worth that had previously bedeviled Zachary Taylor and the entire military establishment unexpectedly resurfaced. When Scott gave command of his army's vanguard to General Twiggs, he inadvertently renewed the feud between Twiggs and Worth over seniority. Worth was incensed, but his feelings were also hurt because he considered Scott a close friend. A true friend, he brooded, would not have slighted him by giving the advanced position to Twiggs. Scott assured Worth that "others shall have it in turn," but he stiffly added that he would "not do injustice to please my best friend."[5]

The disagreement festered, but for the moment, Scott had spoken and accordingly on April 8, 1847, Twiggs started west from Veracruz toward Jalapa with about three thousand regular infantry, artillery companies and guns, and some forty-five supply wagons. The march went quickly, unimpeded by the slightest Mexican presence. In fact, debris strewn for miles along the road suggested that Mexican military forces in the area had hurriedly fled, perhaps in panic. The American column made good time then and was barely able to pull up when it encountered the place where the Mexicans had stopped running, the place where Santa Anna had brought his army.

As Santa Anna had planned, that place was Cerro Gordo. On April 12, Twiggs was approaching Cerro Gordo. Santa Anna had arrayed his men on the hills that protected a pass, the path of the National Highway. Two large hills, El Telégrafo and Cerro Gordo, and a smaller one, La Atalaya, offered an extremely advantageous defensive position while providing the means to spring a trap on the unsuspecting Americans. Twiggs was dangerously unaware of the Mexican position and almost walked into Santa Anna's trap, but a few overeager Mexican troops fired prematurely and revealed that something hostile was dug in at Cerro Gordo. Startled, Twiggs immediately pulled back. He briefly considered launching a frontal assault but wisely decided to wait for Scott to come up with the rest of the army.

Scott did not like what he saw. The ground with its hills held a sinister potential, especially if it had been carefully fortified with defenders correctly deployed. He sent two engineers, Capt. Robert E. Lee and Lt. P.G.T. Beauregard, on a reconnaissance, and they discovered that some of the Mexican lines were not correctly placed at all. This had troubled a few Mexican officers as well: they knew that their left flank was exposed, but Santa Anna insisted on tending to other arrangements. Amazingly then, the defensive flaw went uncorrected for the several days it took Lee and Beauregard to discover a narrow path that ran around the Mexican left. Enlarging the trail allowed the American army to gain the Mexican Army's rear. Santa Anna's trap had become an American opportunity.

Scott's preliminary attack began on April 17 with Twiggs' division taking La Atalaya to plant a battery there. Under orders from their colorful general to "charge them to hell," Twiggs' men did just that to the defenders of La Atalaya.[6] They briefly tried to take El Telégrafo as well but decided to wait until they had more support. It came that night when Twiggs was reinforced. The following day his men charged up two sides of El Telégrafo to seize it, and once that task was accomplished, American cannon controlled the entire battlefield. As Captain Lee placed batteries atop El Telégrafo, Cerro Gordo threatened to become a slaughter pen for the Mexicans. Santa Anna's army began a spontaneous, wholesale retreat.

It could have ended there with the thorough destruction of the demoralized Mexican Army, but Twiggs' rapid success surprised the Americans as much as it did the Mexicans. Although American forces could have easily controlled it, the road to Jalapa remained open, and half of the Mexican Army streamed westward on it, escaping. Santa Anna, according to one Mexican source, was among them, dodging capture "by cutting through [his own men] with a column of 400 men . . . who protected him so that he could get away."[7] The rest fell prisoner, along with most of the entire army's equipment, too cumbersome to lug in flight, including much of Santa Anna's personal property. Picking through the Mexican baggage was a festive enterprise for the victorious Americans, and they would have been at it longer had Scott not been so mindful of the calendar.

The low terrain was as deadly as any Mexican gun, as Santa Anna knew, but the Mexican plan to stall Scott in the yellow fever regions had failed. The American army again began moving quickly toward the higher town of Jalapa where cooler temperatures would mean safety from sickness. Scott sent Worth's division even farther ahead to secure the town of Puebla, beyond Jalapa. The prickly Worth finally had his advanced position. Scott would soon have reason to question if Worth deserved it.

The March to Mexico City

After resting briefly in the cool mountain breezes of Jalapa, Scott moved the army to Puebla. There he found that Worth had taken Puebla without a fight, but was dismayed that he had done so by offering its civilian government extremely lenient terms. Worth planned to allow local courts to try Mexicans who had committed crimes against American soldiers, including murder. Like Scott, officers and the rank and file were equally dismayed that Worth had exposed them to random insurgent attacks that would likely go unpunished. Bandits and irregular Mexican forces had been viciously preying on American stragglers, and now Worth had virtually institutionalized the practice.

When Scott rescinded the arrangement, Worth went into a brooding pout and "demanded a court of Inquiry."[8] Scott consented to the hearing, and to Worth's chagrin, the court recommended that he be publicly reprimanded for his indefensible arrangement. Scott tried to soften the blow by limiting the reprimand's circulation to general officers, but Worth was irrevocably alienated. He never forgave his former friend for what he regarded as a betrayal.

For the moment, however, Worth was the least of Scott's problems. Delays had placed his army in jeopardy from yellow fever, but they had also exhausted his volunteers' terms of enlistment. As those enlistments were due to expire, Scott faced the prospect that a substantial portion of his force would return to Veracruz and sail for home, reducing the army to a mere seven thousand men. That number was simply insufficient to continue the march on Mexico City, let alone assail it. Lingering in Puebla while awaiting new volunteers was frustrating, but Scott could not risk being shorthanded in the middle of

Mexico with extended supply lines behind him and Santa Anna still somewhere to his west. He waited for fresh enlistments who would give him the men and the time to finish the job.

A Bogus Peace Offer

While waiting in Puebla, Scott unexpectedly received a message from someone in the Mexican government claiming to speak for Santa Anna. The content of the message certainly reeked of Santa Anna, for it proposed selling out Mexico for the right price, specifically $10,000 down and $1,000,000 after the war ended with a treaty favorable to the United States. The money would be used to pay off influential legislators to have them persuade their followers to make peace. Scott knew that Santa Anna had made similar promises before, but given the situation in Puebla, this was a tempting offer. Scott had discretionary cash— it was held in the cryptically named "secret service fund"—and had been paying small bribes to local bandits to keep them from ambushing American patrols, but paying out $10,000 would seriously deplete his reserves. He consulted his generals and a new civilian member of his entourage, Nicholas Trist, chief clerk of the State Department, who had recently arrived from Washington to facilitate negotiations with Mexican officials.

Only a few weeks before, Scott would not have sought Trist's counsel about anything because the diplomat's arrival had deeply offended him. President Polk sent Trist to Scott's army with the power to suspend hostilities if a truce would advance peace negotiations. As a matter of course, Scott bristled over anyone interfering with military decisions, but he especially disliked Trist. Scott was well aware of the president's tendency to suspect successful generals of having political ambitions, and he deduced that Trist was James Polk's spy, sent as much to keep tabs on Scott's aspirations as to conduct negotiations with Mexico. The perceived slight and suspicions over Trist's varied purposes caused Scott to treat the newest member of his official family with more than decided coolness. In fact, the two quarreled about everything as Scott resorted to his favorite method of carrying on a dispute, which was to write venomous letters. Trist gave as good (or as bad) as he got in these written exchanges, and soon the two were behaving far below the threshold of dignity, let alone ordinary civility.

Into this troubled setting, the message, purportedly from Santa

Anna, arrived. It seemed legitimate, though, because of Trist's activities, for he had been trying to fashion a peace settlement in any way he could. He had contacted Charles Bankhead, the British minister in Mexico City, asking him to act as an intermediary in preparing talks with the Mexican government. The British had been trying to broker a peace since early spring, and Bankhead promptly agreed to move Trist's overture forward. Santa Anna, however, balked at the risky move of opening negotiations without the support of Congress. The *puros* had been ousted from his government, but they were still strong in Congress and popular with the people. Santa Anna could not show a lack of resolve about the war unless he wanted to endanger his government.

Actually, his political troubles had become so snarled that they almost defied understanding. Buena Vista had been finally revealed as something other than a grand victory, and Cerro Gordo could not be disguised as anything but a defeat. These military setbacks and the advancing American army had invigorated his enemies, who were all the more vehement because Santa Anna had promised deliverance and had delivered only disaster. In a desperate gamble, he resigned the presidency, hoping that a public outcry would force his detractors in Congress to endorse him, but when the public remained gloomily silent about his departure, Santa Anna took back his resignation. He claimed it was his patriotic duty to remain in power until the Americans were defeated.

Such maneuvers only created additional problems by alienating his latest political allies. *Moderado* leaders were working with Bankhead to negotiate a settlement with the United States while Santa Anna withdrew his resignation by vowing to fight to the bitter end. By the late spring of 1847, he had tangled himself in such a snarled web of deceit that he had no choice but to twist back around to where he had started, which was with the *puros*. Leaders of that faction again entered the cabinet. Yet, Santa Anna was not finished with deceit. His bellicose statements and renewed *puro* alliance obscured the fact that like many *moderados* he too wanted peace, but the trick would be sustaining the appearance of his professed determination to destroy the Americans while surrendering to them. When he received word that Bankhead had offers from Trist in writing, Santa Anna tried to refer the matter to Congress, but *moderados* cleverly demurred. All diplomacy, they insisted, was clearly an executive concern.

Having exhausted the benefits of half-truths and opportunistic alliances, Santa Anna apparently turned to the final, basic, and basest of strategies, which was bribery. To persuade members of Congress to drink from the bitter cup of dealing with the Americans, he needed money. Evidently he asked for it through the intermediary to Scott at the end of June 1847—at least, that is what the Americans thought.

Trist endorsed the idea of making the down payment, certain that negotiations would shortly follow. As he and Scott's staff debated the matter, though, Trist fell ill with a fever and severe stomach complaint. Scott had a soldier's sympathy for anyone with such an ailment, even the quarrelsome Trist, so he sent to Trist's quarters a container of marmalade, which lore claimed was a remedy for diarrhea. Trist's rapid recovery indebted him to Scott, and his unvarnished gratitude convinced the general that Trist was not such a bad sort after all. Scott's new joviality, in turn, convinced Trist that he had misjudged the general. The two men became close friends, stopped exchanging letters, and instead met regularly to discuss the situation in Mexico. They decided to pay the $10,000 and hope for the best.

Trist could have at least claimed the naïve optimism of a new man on the scene, but Scott should have known better. As it was, nobody knew then nor has since ever discovered what happened to the $10,000 that was sent from Puebla to Mexico City. In retrospect, no one was quite certain that the request for the money actually came from Santa Anna in the first place. If it had, and if he received the money, he either stole it or spent it ineffectually, for congressional sentiment remained unchanged about dealing with the United States. Congress soon adjourned and left the entire conduct of the war to Santa Anna, including any blame for it.

While all this was unfolding, the U.S. Army received reinforcements as new volunteers under Gen. Franklin Pierce arrived in Puebla to boost Scott's numbers and make possible a renewed march on the Mexican capital. It had been exasperating sitting idle in Puebla, so perhaps Scott regarded the episode of the false peace philosophically. Even if it had been a costly amusement, it had given everyone something to do. As he drafted orders for the push to Mexico City, he could console himself that soon enough he would make whoever had cheated him pay.

On to Mexico City

Urging his men to let loose with "a Cerro Gordo Shout," David Twiggs led his division out of Puebla on August 7, 1847.[9] The next few days saw the rest of the army depart the town that had been home for two months, and a few more days out, the army again stopped, this time at Ayotla while Scott and his generals chose the best approach to Mexico City. (See Map 5.2.) All agreed it was best to approach the capital from the south. Yet Scott wanted it to appear that he would move due west along the base of the mountain El Peñón, hopeful that the Mexicans would prepare defenses there instead of on the southern approach. Accordingly, when the army moved out of Ayotla on August 15, part of it remained behind to mislead Mexican defenders into thinking that an attack toward El Peñón was being contemplated. Four days later, as Scott's army assembled near San Agustín, Mexico City's defenders were no longer in the dark. Clearly, the American advance would come from the south.

The southern line of attack presented its own set of problems. An ancient lava bed, the Pedregal, lay directly between Scott and Mexico City. The Pedregal's craggy lava formations were described as a stormy sea whose towering waves had been frozen in midtumult. Moving artillery and supplies across such a landscape was impossible. Two roads wound around the Pedregal, but the Mexican Army was sure to anchor its defenses on them. Scott needed a way around those defenses, and as they had at Cerro Gordo, his engineers found him one. A modest path ran along the southwest corner of the Pedregal, and Capt. Robert E. Lee suggested that enlarging it into a road would allow part of the American army to gain the rear of at least some Mexican forces. The Mexicans remembered Cerro Gordo too, however, and were intent on preventing another such tactical disaster. The Americans had a challenge in conducting their engineering operation under increased Mexican vigilance.

The job of widening the path and then moving on it to take San Angel fell to Gen. Gideon Pillow's volunteer division and David Twiggs' regulars. By seizing San Angel, they would gain control of the road that skirted the Pedregal to the north and then curved around its eastern side. From there they could attack heavily defended San Antonio from the west. The plan, however, hit a snag early and nearly foundered. When American forces began trekking through the Pedregal on August

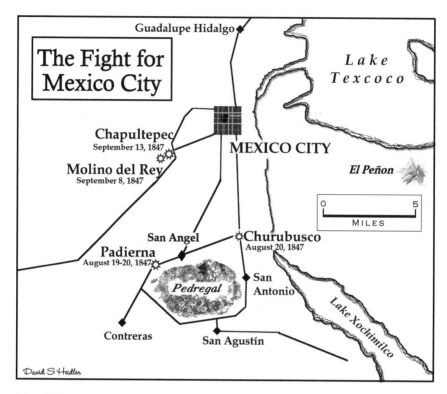

Map 5.2

19, their lead elements suddenly ran into a stiff Mexican defense under Gen. Gabriel Valencia. The Mexican general was in an advantageous position on two counts: first, he occupied high ground at Padierna, between San Angel and Contreras, and second, from that high ground he could attack the Americans before all their people had crossed the Pedregal. At first, everything went the Mexicans' way, and Valencia was in the process of isolating four American brigades when Santa Anna unwisely recalled crucial reinforcements that would have boosted Valencia's forces and ensured his victory. As it was, darkness saved the struggling Americans and gave their officers time to formulate a plan. During the night, in the midst of a raging thunderstorm, Pillow and Twiggs slowly felt their way across the Pedregal to Scott's headquarters at San Agustín where a coordinated effort was quickly cobbled together for the following day. In the morning, Twiggs and Pillow staged a diversion in front of Valencia while Gen. Persifor Smith used a ravine to conceal his march around the Mexican position. Smith's attack on the Mexican rear was so unexpected that it put Valencia's men in full retreat, sending many of them to the safety of San Antonio. Yet, the Americans were resolutely moving on that place as well, for as Twiggs and Pillow fought on the west side of the Pedregal, William Jenkins Worth led his men toward San Antonio. With Valencia out of the way, Twiggs and Pillow were also ready to move against the town and cut off a Mexican retreat into the relative security of Mexico City.

Scott had ordered Twiggs to take his division north of San Antonio, but Twiggs stumbled on a heavily fortified Mexican position at the convent of San Mateo at Churubusco. Churubusco proved impervious to assault, and the Americans soon resorted to their artillery. By then, Worth had fought his way through San Antonio and was ready to join the attack on the Mexican position at the convent. Escape was now hopeless for Mexican forces there, and as they gathered within the inner walls of the compound, some of these men considered the prospect of surrender just as impossible.

Gen. Manuel Rincón was in command of a motley military assortment that included a jumble of Mexican National Guard units and the San Patricio Battalion of the Mexican Army. The San Patricio Battalion was in part a Mexican foreign legion that contained American deserters from the U.S. Army. It did not matter that some of those deserters had been Irish immigrants to the United States who later claimed they joined the Mexican Army to fight alongside fellow Catholics. Their defense would have been no more compelling to American authorities than those of men who had deserted for the bald self-interest of earning claims to Mexican land bounties. Whatever their motives, they had deserted their army and had joined the one it was fighting, and either action was a hanging offense; the two of them together were indefensible to the warrior's code. As hopeless as resistance at Churubusco had become, these men faced the prospect of either dying in this battle or surviving it to die on gallows. It is little wonder then that when American forces finally stormed the convent, the San Patricios fought with extraordinarily fierce determination, many of them swinging empty muskets after their ammunition ran out. About seventy were finally captured and put on trial, and fifty of those were sentenced to hang. The rest were flogged and branded with a D (for deserter) on their cheeks, a permanent disfiguring mark of shame for a deed so universally condemned that many might have regarded those put to death as the lucky ones.

In retrospect, the battles of Padierna and Churubusco spelled the doom of Mexico City, leaving in doubt only the question of how much longer the capital could resist. Yet at the time, no such unclouded surety existed. American forces were so far victorious and had suffered far fewer casualties than the Mexican Army, but they were also exhausted, disorganized, and a long way from home. Years later Scott told of how the Duke of Wellington had read that the American army was nearly at the gates of Mexico City and had exclaimed, "Scott is lost. He has been carried away by successes. He can't take the city, and he can't fall back upon his base."[10] Most perceptive military observers probably shared the gloomy forecast by the man who had defeated Napoleon, and Scott himself was likely more than a bit worried about his prospects. Consequently, he was receptive to the idea of an armistice that would give the diplomats a chance to talk about peace. Discussions did ensue between Trist and Mexican commissioners, but they were disappointing. As it turned out, the commissioners—former president José Joaquín Herrera, Miguel Aristán, Ignacio Mora y Villamil, and José Bernardo Couto—had no authority and were actually only glorified couriers. In fluent Spanish, Trist laid out what the Mexicans already knew: Americans wanted the Texas boundary on the Rio Grande, wanted New Mexico, wanted Alta California, were willing to pay an undisclosed amount of money for the real estate, and would assume much of Mexico's foreign debt. The commissioners forlornly carried Trist's written proposals to Congress, which rejected the terms out of hand. Scott, fearing that he had again been duped by an empty Mexican gesture, immediately advised Santa Anna that hostilities would recommence on September 7, 1847. Scott had reason to be suspicious. Santa Anna had used the time bought by the armistice to strengthen the city's defenses.

Mexico City Falls

Mexico City was situated in a shallow depression, the remnant of what had been a huge inland lake. It was a walled city accessible by several gated causeways. To the city's southwest sat Chapultepec, an imposing hill, on top of which sat an old castle that housed the Colegio Militar, a military school. Santa Anna had strengthened defenses along the roads that led to Chapultepec to keep Americans from taking control of its commanding heights, something he regarded as unlikely in any event. Mexican infantry posted at Molino del Rey protected the western approach to Chapultepec, and posed such a daunting obstacle that they were best avoided. Yet, Americans believed that brass cannons were being cast at Molino del Rey, and that intelligence gave Scott a compelling reason to take it. Three Mexican brigades manned Molino del Rey's two stone buildings and outlying defenses, and though their numbers were fewer than four thousand, they could also count on about three thousand cavalry under Gen. Juan Álvarez to support them. William Jenkins Worth had the job of assailing this position. Hoping that a diversion by Twiggs and Pillow against Mexico City's southern defenses would prevent Santa Anna from reinforcing Álvarez, Worth sent his division of a little more than three thousand men toward the stone buildings on the morning of September 8. Their unbroken successes had lulled American commanders into misjudging all Mexican soldiers as indifferent warriors prone to run rather than fight. Molina del Rey educated them harshly as it immediately became a costly fight for the Americans.

Mexican artillery repaired its poor reputation from previous engagements by inflicting considerable punishment on the first wave of Americans. Successive attacks against the stone buildings also met determined and deadly resistance. Finally Worth's large guns allowed his infantrymen to fight their way into the buildings where the battle degenerated into vicious hand-to-hand fighting. As at Padierna, Mexican reinforcements failed to arrive, and Molina del Rey's defenders ultimately were forced to retreat, but not before both sides had suffered horrific casualties. The toll on American forces was especially sobering when no cannon foundry was found at Molino del Rey, emphasizing the pointlessness of the engagement. With many of Worth's people dead or mangled, Scott was no closer to taking Mexico City than he had been before.

Winfield Scott had to force a decision by assaulting the city's defenses. On September 11, he consulted with his senior officers and indispensable engineers about the best way to do that in a meeting later dubbed the Council of Piedad. It was an important conference, for decisions reached at it would decide the fate of many of the soldiers that Scott had led into the heart of the enemy's territory. Scott solicited everyone's opinion, but he clearly preferred to approach the city from the west, which would require securing the fortifications atop Chapultepec. Americans could then command the roads leading to the San Cosmé and Belén gates. Because Chapultepec protected those causeways, Scott presumed that they were lightly defended just as he surmised that Santa Anna's expectation about an American attack from the south would cause him to bolster defenses at the Niño Perdido and San Antonio gates there. In any case, the time for talk and planning was done. Scott told his officers that before they left the "meeting, *he was determined* the orders for the attack should be given."[11]

On September 12, American maneuvers south of the city confused the Mexican military. Scott seemed to be advancing from the south, as everyone had expected, but that same day most of his artillery rolled into position to bombard Chapultepec. With fewer than one thousand men and artillery inadequate for the task of resisting a concentrated American attack, Gen. Nicolás Bravo nervously watched the batteries deploy and begin pounding the hill's lower works. Clearly, something important was in motion, but it was unclear exactly what. Chapultepec was lightly defended because it was an unlikely target, imposing in its two-hundred-foot height and distant from the expected point of attack. Yet, American artillery was making it a target nonetheless. Even before full light on the 13th, the bombardment of Chapultepec and its lower defenses resumed. It had all happened so quickly and under such a cloak of tactical guile that Santa Anna never thought to shift men to shore Chapultepec's defenses. Even the impressive artillery barrages did not persuade him that the attack on Chapultepec was anything but a diversion to screen the real attack from the south. General Bravo, on the receiving end of American gunnery, had good reason to believe otherwise.

After the artillery had done its work, particularly that of softening up the defenses that guarded the approaches to the steep hill, the infantry began its assault, helped in part by U.S. Marines who had accompanied Scott's army from Veracruz.[12] The marines and American infantry moved up the hill toward the fortress defended by what was left of Bravo's small force, which now included a handful of cadets from the Colegio Militar. Six cadets, some merely children, died defending the castle that day and became for Mexicans "a symbol and image of this unrighteous war."[13] In only a short time, American forces gained the Colegio's walls. Bravo had sent a frantic call to Santa Anna for immediate reinforcements but received word none would be coming. He surrendered the fort about 9:30 A.M. on September 13, 1847. It was another unmitigated disaster for the Mexicans that could not be veiled with hedging euphemisms or cloudy statements about tactics and strategy. According to one report, Santa Anna could not hide his pent-up frustration when he saw the American flag fluttering over Chapultepec. "I believe if we were to plant our batteries in Hell," he shouted, "the damned Yankees would take them from us."[14]

Other men had more immediate cause to lament this latest American success. Thirty of the San Patricio deserters were scheduled to hang that morning. With nooses over their heads, they stood on wagons arranged to give them a view of Chapultepec. The raising of the flag there was the last thing they saw on this earth; the wagons jolted out from under the doomed men.

With control of Chapultepec, Scott's army could advance on the San Cosmé and Belén gates, and as John Quitman's and Worth's divisions began moving east toward the city, they removed all doubt about the direction of the main American attack. Santa Anna began rushing troops toward the San Cosmé and Belén gates, but the Mexican defenders at the Belén gate had already exhausted their ammunition and were conducting an orderly withdrawal. Santa Anna was dumbfounded when he arrived, and he lashed out verbally and physically, striking the commander of those troops, Gen. Andrés Terrés.

Defenders at the San Cosmé gate were better supplied and were able to stall the American attack there, but Worth's men passed through the deserted Belén gate. Twilight halted any additional advance into the city, giving everyone time to imagine the dangerous job of occupying the city, a prospect sure to feature building-to-building fighting and mounting casualties. Yet, it was not to be dangerous or deadly after all. That night, Santa Anna assembled those of his generals who could be rounded up and concluded that defending the city was a hopeless cause. He announced that he would immediately take what was left of the army out of the capital. During that night, he and his generals led about nine thousand soldiers to safety. Scott entered the city in triumph on September 14 and set up his headquarters at the National Palace.

Possession of the capital ended the major combat of the war, but it did not mean a complete end to fighting. In fact, Americans faced a thorny task in Mexico City. Many civilians were resentful of the American presence and secretly cheered the activities of irregular forces. Civilians were also enraged by the behavior of their own army and government. Being abandoned was bad enough, but the departing army had opened the city's jails and prisons, unleashing thousands of criminals on the city. Scott had to put these people back under lock and key to protect Mexico City's population as well as his own men. Snipers made patrolling the streets perilous, and Scott's long supply lines to Veracruz were easy prey for guerrillas.

Most exasperating, though, was the absence of a viable Mexican government to negotiate a meaningful peace. Shortly after leaving the capital, Santa Anna resigned the presidency and when he designated the *moderado* Manuel de la Peña y Peña as his successor, he closed the circle on the disaster. Peña y Peña had been foreign minister when all the trouble had started over Slidell.

Without consulting the man he ostensibly had put in charge, Santa Anna made Querétaro the temporary capital. Peña y Peña also took his time accepting the post of president, waiting more than a week to make an appearance. He could hardly be faulted for his reluctance, for anyone taking the reins of this wreck was sure to take the blame for its misfortunes. Yet Peña y Peña knew that if there were to be a peace treaty, there would have to be a government. He despondently filled his government with fellow *moderados* who had been maneuvering toward a negotiated settlement for months.

Negotiating a treaty was not uncomplicated in any case. The agreement of a politically divided and now physically scattered Congress was necessary. Peña y Peña also had to weigh the possibility that when Santa Anna gathered himself from his most recent calamity, he might again seize control of the government or that ambitious generals still in command of large bodies of troops might try to establish a dictatorship. And the chronic conflict between *moderados* and *puros* continued to hamper peace efforts as *puros* persisted in their calls for vigorous military resistance. When Congress finally gathered and elected *moderado* Pedro María Anaya interim president on November 11—he was to hold office until Peña y Peña was formally installed on January 8, 1848—Anaya immediately appointed Peña y Peña foreign minister to continue his efforts to form a workable peace with the United States. Trouble continued to rumble inside the Mexican government, though.

That *puros* wanted to continue a hopeless fight called into question their motives, and actually some evidence suggests that a few *puros* wished for the complete destruction of the Mexican Army and its leadership. Winfield Scott's soldiers were to be the instrument to sweep the corrupt army away. *Puros* could then establish a true federalist state under civilian control whose government would rely exclusively on the civic militia for national defense. Some *puros* apparently hoped for even more radical change, such as becoming an American protectorate or even being annexed by the United States, a situation that would place the Mexican people under a genuine republican government controlled by civilians. Either way Mexico would have the electoral and religious reforms that *puros* had been striving to attain for years. Such opinions, of course, represented a radical fringe among the *puros*. The core of the faction also wanted to continue the war, but like Gómez Farías, they loathed the United States for what it had done to their country. Firmly believing that any peace agreement would be dishonorable to Mexico, they resolutely worked to derail Peña y Peña's peacemaking initiatives.

Ultimately, they went even further. Leading *puros*, including Gómez Farías, soon were hatching a conspiracy to overthrow the government. The coup was set for January 12 and was to start with a rebellion in San Luis Potosí. The conspirators hoped to force Winfield Scott into defending the Peña y Peña government, a reasonable calculation since Nicholas Trist was deeply involved in talks with Peña y Peña's people. Scott's saving the government possibly would have tainted its *moderado* leaders in the eyes of the Mexican people, yet the rebellion never gathered steam, and the U.S. military consequently avoided this messy intrigue. Instead, Peña y Peña's people continued to negotiate with Nicholas Trist, trying to end the war with some honor intact, if not their country.

All Mexico?

Losing territory was a nightmare for Mexico. Ironically, the prospect of gaining territory became a nightmare for the United States. Warning signs cropped up everywhere on the political landscape. Opposition to the war, revealed most coherently by the Wilmot Proviso during the summer of 1846, had not dissipated, but neither had the expansionist fever known as Manifest Destiny. Many northerners still suspected that the war was a southern plot to add more slave territory to the United States, but the North was not completely immune to the lure of expansionism. Northern politicians heard their constituents lauding the advantages of territorial increase, as long as the new lands were to be marked off into small farms. Many Southerners, however, wanted the territory acquired from Mexico opened to slavery. They reasoned that slavery in the West would place new states carved from the Mexican cession in the southern congressional bloc, giving it the edge in sectional votes. For Northerners, even those who had not given much thought to the moral issues of spreading slavery, that was precisely the problem.

These were not the only points of division over this question. Some fretted that the country was large enough and already too difficult to govern as it was. For years, people in the Northeast had been anxious about their section's shrinking influence, and a sizable Mexican cession promised to worsen the trend. Northern abolitionists saw nothing good resulting from an expansion that would give slave owners the opportunity to spread their blighted institution to new places. In the House of Representatives, John Quincy Adams—for years since leaving the presidency, congressman for his neighbors in Quincy, Massachusetts—eloquently described the broadening of slavery as a moral outrage and labeled the war a wicked breach of international peace. John C. Calhoun's apprehensions about the conflict dredging up old sectional animosities and further dividing the country were all being realized.

In the end, opponents could not dampen expansionist enthusiasm, and President Polk exploited that fervor to check his critics. Just as military recruitment to prosecute the conflict had depended on popular support of the war, plucking the fruits of victory would depend on popular support for the peace. With help from congressional supporters, Polk had been able to obtain the resources he needed to prosecute the war, had defeated efforts to pass the Wilmot Proviso, and had succeeded in branding his critics as vaguely unpatriotic. Then in early 1847, some expansionists' eyes grew larger than America's political stomach to advocate annexing more of Mexico than originally planned. Although an indistinct sense of war weariness among the public muted that talk for a while, truly dedicated expansionists liked the idea so much they began peddling the cost of the war as a reason to widen territorial demands on Mexico. After Scott entered Mexico City and the Mexican government collapsed, a growing fever gripped ardent expansionists as they began urging what only months before would have been unthinkable: the annexation of the entire country. In fact, the cry for "all Mexico" had reached such volume by the late fall of 1847 that even highly placed officers of the U.S. government were entertaining it. For his part, Polk concluded that Mexico should at least turn over more land than Trist's instructions called for and for less money than he had been told to offer.

Such talk soon put the war's critics in full counter cry. Nothing could justify the wholesale annexation of a foreign country, they argued, and it was even more reprehensible that it would be accomplished at the point of a gun. Some critics were less principled in their objections. "All Mexico" advocates pointed out that annexation would bless Mexico with the benefits of enlightened American government, but opponents raised the ominous implications of establishing dominion over a large population they regarded as racially inferior. Many congressmen worried less about blood purity and more about the enormous military expenditures necessary to occupy and then control an immense expanse of potentially hostile territory.

Nevertheless, Polk remained committed to getting more of Mexico for less money. He abruptly recalled Trist because he believed his emissary was too eager to make a peace with overly generous terms. Trist received his recall in November, which amounted to awkward timing, for he was convinced that dealing with the interim Anaya government was his best chance to end the war. As a result, in direct defiance of the president's order, Trist did not leave Mexico. Instead, he told Mexican authorities about his being summoned home and advised them to begin rapid and serious negotiations unless they wanted to deal with his successor. Trist warned that if Polk were given time, he would levy harsher terms. Mulling over the hard terms that Trist had proposed and imagining a more severe set, the Mexicans felt their hearts sink. The *puros* were trying to rile the population at their backs, an American army occupied their erstwhile capital, and a sterner American envoy was evidently to be dispatched to exact a greater price for their defeat. Although negotiations proceeded with a new urgency, the Mexican government worked in the shadow of possible coups and certain disgrace.

Notes

1. William A. DePalo Jr., *The Mexican National Army, 1822–1852* (College Station: Texas A&M University Press, 1997), 111.

2. Yellow fever attacks the body's internal organs, including the liver, the failure of which gives skin a sickly yellow hue, hence the name. The final stages of the disease are accompanied by violent attacks of bloody vomiting, and it was thus sometimes called *el negro vomito*.

3. Theodore Laidley, *"Surrounded by Dangers of All Kinds": The Mexican War Letters of Lieutenant Theodore Laidley*, ed. James M. McCaffrey (Denton: University of North Texas Press, 1997), 50.

4. George Wilkins Kendall, *Dispatches from the Mexican War*, ed. Lawrence Delbert Cress (Norman: University of Oklahoma Press, 1999), 156.

5. Quoted in Lloyd Lewis, *Captain Sam Grant* (Boston: Little, Brown, 1950), 204.

6. Douglas Southall Freeman, vol. 1, *R. E. Lee: A Biography* (New York: Charles Scribner's Sons, 1934), 243.

7. José Fernando Ramírez to Francisco Elorriaga, April 21, 1847, in José Fernando Ramírez, *Mexico during the War with the United States*, ed. Walter V. Scholes, trans. Elliott B. Scherr (Columbia: University of Missouri, 1950), 118.

8. Charles Winslow Elliott, *Winfield Scott: The Soldier and the Man* (New York: Macmillan, 1937), 487.

9. Charles L. Dufour, *Gentle Tiger: The Gallant Life of Roberdeau Wheat* (Baton Rouge: Louisiana State University Press, 1957), 29.

10. Winfield Scott, vol. 2, *Memoirs of Lieut.-General Scott, LL.D Written by Himself* (New York: Sheldon, 1864), 466.

11. T. Harry Williams, ed., *With Beauregard in Mexico: The Mexican War Reminiscences of P.G.T. Beauregard* (Baton Rouge: Louisiana State University Press, 1956), 69.

12. The presence of marines with Scott's army led to the inclusion of the words "to the halls of Montezuma" in the "Marine Hymn."

13. Quoted in Rodolfo Acuña, "Treaty of Guadalupe Hidalgo," in *Mexico: From Independence to Revolution, 1810–1910*, ed. W. Dirk Raat (Lincoln: University of Nebraska Press, 1982), 100.

14. Bauer, *Mexican War*, 318.

CHAPTER 6

LEGACIES

The Treaty of Guadalupe Hidalgo

When Trist refused to obey Polk's orders, Scott agreed with the decision, as did the British legation in Mexico City, which was eagerly anticipating the resumption of trade with their hosts. Trist wrote a lengthy letter of more than sixty pages to Secretary of State James Buchanan justifying his actions.

The Mexican government was still hesitant, but realized by the end of 1847 that it was either Trist's terms or harsher ones to come with another envoy. Even after negotiations began in early January, fear of popular uprisings—especially those inspired by a San Luis Potosí rebellion—prevented Mexican commissioners from making concessions, and Trist threatened to break off talks. Finally, the commissioners bitterly sent Trist's proposed treaty to Peña y Peña. The new president, like a man facing a dose of foul medicine, resolved to swallow the treaty as quickly as he could. It was signed on February 2, 1848, at Guadalupe Hidalgo, a village north of Mexico City. The document was immediately dispatched to both governments for ratification.

The treaty ceded to the United States, Alta California and New Mexico, recognized American ownership of Texas with the Rio Grande boundary, and stipulated a U.S. payment of $15 million to Mexico as well as U.S. assumption of any Mexican debts to American citizens, a sum of more than $3 million. (See Map 6.1.) Yet, the territorial terms that transferred approximately half of Mexico to the United States were simply stunning and sure to be unpopular with the Mexican people. The *puros* hoped to exploit this unrest to regain control of the government. Yet the country was more tired of the hopeless war than indignant over the wages of defeat, and the *puros'* expectations for a

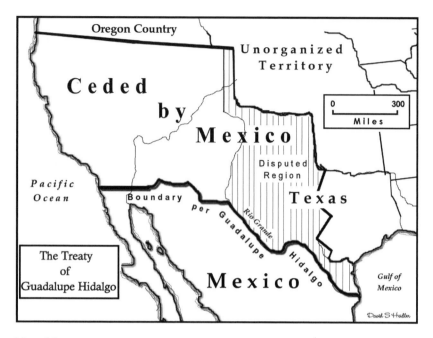

Map 6.1

groundswell of resentment carrying them to power were disappointed. In May, a new Congress ratified the treaty.

By then, the U.S. Senate had already ratified the Treaty of Guadalupe Hidalgo, although it very nearly was not submitted for a vote. Scott and the British legation might have seen the wisdom of Trist's defying his recall, but President Polk did not. When Trist's handiwork arrived in Washington on February 19, Polk was livid at Trist for disobeying orders, and the envoy's explanatory letter, which Polk described as "arrogant, impudent, and very insulting,"[1] had done nothing to mollify him. A close examination of the treaty, though, and the temperate counsel of his advisors made Polk realize that it contained everything he had originally wanted. Critics of the war were growing more voluble, and Polk wisely concluded to close the matter by submitting the treaty to the Senate. After omitting a section that recognized land grants made by the Mexican government in Texas after its independence, the Senate ratified the Treaty of Guadalupe Hidalgo on March 10, 1848 by 38–14, a mere three votes more than the required two-thirds majority. The sizable opposition to the treaty was a peculiar coalition of those who were disappointed over not acquiring all of Mexico and those who were outraged by acquiring any of it. Nevertheless, at the end of May, both governments exchanged ratifications. The war was over, and Polk had his Rio Grande border, his Pacific ports, and all the mountains and desert that lay between.

Manifest Destiny

In 1847, when Sam Houston remarked that the North American continent was an American birthright, he was not boasting. He was stating what many Americans of his generation perceived as simple fact. When they spoke of Manifest Destiny, they invoked a Divine Providence who had predestined their expansion to the Pacific, and they easily saw James K. Polk and the American armies he dispatched as agents to bring about this lofty, ordained result. In the realization of this purpose, many Americans did not regard stripping Mexicans of their territory as a necessary evil; in keeping with racial prejudices of that time, they considered Mexicans as inferior and consequently thought that taking their territory and making better use of it was a positive good.

By any measure, American expansion during the four years of James Polk's presidency was a startling achievement. The United States added Texas, the Oregon country, California, and New Mexico to its territorial expanse, additions that increased the size of the country by a third. The country's population was similarly increasing as immigrants from Europe began pouring into the United States, some to crowd into its eastern cities, but many to strike westward for the new lands recently brought into the national dominion. Newspapers describing America's Manifest Destiny and touting the opportunities afforded by new western lands encouraged these recent arrivals to become ardent supporters of expansion and eager devotees of the expansionist Democratic Party. As they escaped the economic hardships of overcrowded cities to cultivate small farms in the West, they seemed a way to fulfill the Jeffersonian vision of a nation composed of small farmers, a pastoral idyll that lionized self-sufficiency, economic independence, and political stability.

Ironically, some thought that expansion was a cure not only for the problems of urban tensions but for sectional divisions as well. The balance of weighing Oregon against Texas was only one aspect of that optimism, yet this winsome buoyancy was the most delusory of all, for the addition of the western territories aggravated sectional discord rather than allayed it, leading to arguments so charged and discordant that the broadly based political parties collapsed underneath them. The debates over the Wilmot Proviso were not the beginning of the slavery controversy, but they were the opening of its final chapter, the one that would end with the nation divided by secession and angry men leaving their homes to join armies and kill their brothers.

Quite soon after the Mexican War, in fact, the fragility of the American polity was revealed when gold was discovered in California early in 1848. While the rich California gold fields made a few prospectors fabulously wealthy and provided the capital for a generation of American enterprise, the lure of gold fever rapidly enlarged California's population and compelled the hasty formation of a government. California thus applied for admission to the Union in 1849, citing a population large enough to skip territorial status and merit immediate statehood. The problem was that the self-generated California convention drafted a constitution excluding slavery, and the subsequent debates over this and other issues surrounding the fate of the western territories deeply divided Congress and threatened the Union. The Compromise of 1850 was the difficult bargain that resolved this crisis and temporarily quieted the slavery debate, but nothing could permanently halt the consideration of the moral calamity slavery posed. The tumultuous discord of the 1850s stemmed directly from the consequences of the Mexican War, the breeding ground for the Civil War just as it was the training ground for the Civil War's most accomplished generals.

Mexico after the War

Mexicans never forgot nor forgave the United States for the war that tore away half of their country, and the events of 1846–1847 soured affairs between the United States and other Latin America countries as well. In the war's aftermath, the country that had served as an inspiration and example for Latin American independence movements became the "Colossus of the North," perceived as prone to meddlesome ways at best and possibly aiming to purloin additional territory from other Latin American countries at worst.

In the years following the Treaty of Guadalupe Hidalgo, Mexico faced a host of dire troubles. A running ulcer was a serious revolt in the Yucatán Peninsula that pitted the native Maya against whites and mestizos. Called the Caste War of the Yucatán, it began in 1847 even as Mexico struggled against the Yankee invader, a reaction to mistreatment of the Maya and the expropriation of their lands. It flared up intermittently for the next six years, and greatly altered the demographics of the Yucatán Peninsula as many Maya fled to isolated enclaves. The Yucatán's overall population fell some 30 percent through disease and violence. Sugar plantations were devastated, and survivors ran from the region en masse, which impaired Mexico's ability to regenerate a healthy economy in the years following the war.

Mexico's demolished economy was a symptom of its wrecked government, which struggled with the humiliation of losing the war with the United States. Santa Anna had been disgraced by the disaster, but his return to power in 1853 was a testament to the bankrupt Mexican polity as much as his puckish resiliency. As dictator, Santa Anna presided over the final territorial cession to the United States by selling a narrow sliver of northwestern Mexico on the New Mexico border to American envoy James Gadsden for $10 million. It was said that when Santa Anna gazed upon the map to fix the extent of the Gadsden Purchase, he burst into tears upon realizing how much territory he had lost to the United States. It is a doubtful story.

More grounded in truth was a mounting, and this time permanent, dissatisfaction with not only Santa Anna but also with what he represented, which were the worst impulses of *criollo* rule. In only a year after Santa Anna's return to power, plots were hatched to unseat him, their authors were youthful politicians who embraced the persistent *puro* philosophy of decentralization. The revolt that began in 1854 took longer than a year to achieve victory, but its final triumph in 1855 again exiled Santa Anna, this time for good, and installed a provisional government under the leadership of Juan Álvarez. For all appearances, these events were only another chapter in a cyclical chronicle that had pitted the federalists against the centralists, one to have the upper hand in this contest, the other to prevail in that one. Yet, the government that came to power in 1855 pursued the most meaningful agenda of reform up to that time in the life of the troubled Mexican republic. The program came to be called *La Reforma*, and its initial success in curbing the influence of the church and diminishing the role of the military was largely due to attempts to make changes at a measured pace, the work of President Ignacio Comonfort, who had succeeded provisional president Álvarez. Federalism was officially installed by a new constitution in 1857, which completely eliminated the military and clerical *fueros*.

The reforms, however, were inflexibly opposed by conservatives and bred a new revolt that removed Comonfort and threw Mexico into yet another round of violent domestic conflict, a three-year civil war called the War of the Reform (Three Years War). During the war, the charismatic Indian Benito Juárez emerged to become the leading figure in Mexican politics. Initially installed as Comonfort's provisional successor, Juárez was soon driven from the capital by conservative opposition; he fled to Veracruz and established a government there in opposition to the conservative regime in Mexico City. Three years of bitter fighting finally saw the Juárez administration gaining popular support in the country and final victory on the battlefield. In 1861, Juárez was elected president and took office in Mexico City.

Yet wounds over reform remained, for the Juárez administration's sweeping gestures were radical and unsettling. A sizable number of Mexicans were troubled by the expropriation of church property and the suppression of influential religious orders. Most ominous to overseas observers was Juárez's decision to suspend interest payments on foreign loans, an action compelled by Mexico's ruined economy. Spain, Britain, and France threatened intervention, and France under Napoleon III fashioned plans far beyond mere debt collection. Napoleon III regarded weakened Mexico as ripe for colonization and envisioned the restoration of a monarchy bolstered by the French military. In 1861, France persuaded Britain and Spain to join an intervention by occupying Veracruz, but the following year, France alone remained because neither London nor Madrid would support Napoleon III's colonial scheme. As it turned out, and to Napoleon III's surprise, most of Mexico would not support it either. A Mexican force soundly defeated the French at Puebla on May 5, 1862, and Mexico ever since has celebrated Cinco de Mayo as a national holiday.

The French were persistent, though, and Napoleon deployed a larger army that finally occupied Mexico City in June 1863, where conservatives satisfied their nostalgia for monarchical rule by turning the country over to an Austrian archduke, Maximilian, a European prince that Napoleon III had selected for the job. In only forty years, Mexico had come full circle from Iturbide's empire to Maximilian's. For a time, the new regime appeared secure as Juárez and his followers went into hiding and the Civil War in the United States prevented the enforcement of the Monroe Doctrine, the U.S. position announced in 1823 that opposed new European colonization in the Western Hemisphere. Yet, Maximilian's days were numbered, for he was never popular with Mexicans, and the end of the American Civil War in 1865 allowed the United States to warn France that it would not permit the continued occupation of Mexico. The French withdrew their support from Maximilian in 1867, and Juárez was able to reassert control with the help of Gen. Porfirio Díaz. That year, friendless Maximilian fell before a Mexican firing squad.

Governing Mexico proved no easier in the wake of these disruptive events, although Juárez weathered failed coups and internal dissent that labeled him an autocrat to remain president until his death in 1872. The routine of succession remained the barracks rebellion as much as the democratic ballot, and Porfirio Díaz staged a revolt in 1876 that made him president until 1880.

After a hiatus from power, Díaz returned to the presidency in 1884 and held the post until 1911, an era of personal rule commemorated by the title, the *Porfiriato*. During his long tenure, Díaz managed Mexico with a mixture of statesmanlike gravitas and shrewd political alliances. The former inspired confidence in foreign investors whose capital helped to modernize key aspects of the Mexican transportation system and infrastructure, but the latter too often catered to large landowners, who enhanced their holdings at the expense of Mexico's chronic poor. As the landless population accordingly grew, many fell into hopeless debt peonage, or debt servitude, a system in which indebted laborers depended upon employers for food and shelter while trying to pay off obligations with work. Such debts were almost impossible to retire and could be inherited, making debt peonage very much like slavery in practice if not name. The social and economic implications for the country were staggering as it is estimated that at the end of the *Porfiriato*, as much as nine-tenths of the population in certain regions were landless peasants. It was not a good way to start the twentieth century.

The Two Generals

In 1877, one year after Porfirio Díaz first came to power, the United States officially ended Reconstruction, the troubled government plan to reshape and readmit the formerly rebellious southern states, the last official remnant of the war that had nearly brought the Colossus of the North to its knees. At the end of that war, in April 1865, two men who had served in Mexico almost two decades before sat down in a modest house in southern Virginia at Appomattox Court House, one to dictate terms of surrender and the other compelled by necessity to accept them.

Here was a strange reversal of fortune indeed, for the victor, Ulysses S. Grant, had been a lowly lieutenant during the Mexican War, while the vanquished, Robert E. Lee, had been a lionized captain, one of Winfield Scott's indispensable engineers. Grant had met Lee only once before. During the Mexican War, Lee had briefly visited the brigade to which Grant was attached, and Grant always remembered the meeting vividly. When the two met a second time—the momentous meeting in the small parlor that April day many years later—Grant mentioned the first encounter, but Lee confessed he had no recollection of it, which was understandable, for Grant was habitually unkempt while Lee had the effortless ability to appear polished under the most trying circumstances. Grant's service had not been unmemorable (he was cited for bravery in combat), but it had not been particularly glamorous. Lee's record was the stuff of legend with his discovering the path at Cerro Gordo and crossing the impassable Pedregal to find a way through it with seeming ease. Winfield Scott was said to have thought, "God Almighty had to spit on his hands to make Bob Lee."[2] After the Mexican War, Grant's fortunes had fallen to such a low state that he was nearly indigent with a weakness for whiskey, while Lee's career had remained steady and constant as he scored significant engineering achievements and rose to the rank of colonel. Scott had wanted Lee to command the Union armies at the outset of the Civil War, but he had declined to bear arms against his native Virginia. Grant had been compelled to scramble for even a modest command, and his emergence as a talented general was gradual and marked by setbacks. Yet now the two men sat with their pasts completely irrelevant to their present circumstance. The impecunious and unprepossessing Grant at the head of the vast Army of the Potomac had won the war. The graceful and elegant Lee at the head of the dwindling Army of Northern Virginia had lost it.

For all their differences, though, their service in Mexico had struck them in a strangely similar way. In retrospect, both found that war troubling. Lee compared the American campaign to that of a bully browbeating a weakling, and Grant was later convinced that the entire episode was a direct cause of the Civil War. "Nations, like individuals," he said, "are punished for their transgressions. We got our punishment in the most sanguinary and expensive war of modern times."[3]

At the least, the conflict carried few of the trappings of honor, a quality that was equally important to the two men throughout their lives, one who desperately sought it and the other who wore it as a natural mantle. For soldiers, it might have seemed strange that their hard chores, the marching and fighting and killing, had brought such bounty at such little cost, until the actual bill finally came due. The campaigns in Mexico had not been much of a war, as war was to be measured by Americans a decade and a half later. The fight had cost the country about thirteen thousand dead, most of those from disease, and like all wars had been the setting for notable acts of heroism and villainy. But it was as nothing for those two men, their fellow officers, and the survivors in their ranks, who could count a staggering six hundred thousand dead in the contest for the Union. That contest had been foreordained by the one years before in Mexico, the occasion when the scruffy lieutenant met the dazzling captain in the middle of nowhere, on a road that ultimately led to Appomattox.

Notes

1. Polk, *The Diary of a President*, 296.
2. Douglas Southall Freeman, vol. 1, *R. E. Lee* (New York: Charles Scribner's Sons, 1947), 417.
3. U. S. Grant, *Personal Memoirs of U. S. Grant*, ed. E. B. Long (Cleveland: The World Publishing Company, 1952), 24.

BIOGRAPHIES OF NOTABLE PEOPLE

Pedro de Ampudia (1805–1868)

Pedro de Ampudia served as the commander of the Mexican Army of the North immediately preceding the advent of hostilities in the Mexican War. He was then second-in-command of that army and was finally returned to command to protect Monterrey from Zachary Taylor's army. He had the dubious distinction of surrendering that city to Taylor, but he saved his army to fight another day.

A native of Cuba, Ampudia joined the Spanish Army as a youth. He came to Mexico as a Spanish officer in 1821 where he changed sides and joined the Mexican Army. He served as an artillery officer under Antonio López de Santa Anna during the Texas war for independence and was present at the fall of the Alamo and Santa Anna's defeat at San Jacinto. After Texas achieved independence, he helped to guard the border against Texans and commanded the force that captured Texans at Mier in 1842. He carried out Santa Anna's orders to execute some of those prisoners.

Ampudia received the appointment as commander of the Army of the North in April 1846 after Zachary Taylor had moved his army to the Rio Grande. His own men at Matamoros received him coolly because of his reputation for cruelty and his outspoken conservative politics. Soon *moderado* Mariano Arista superseded him, and he served as Arista's second-in-command at Palo Alto and Resaca de la Palma during which he harshly criticized his superior, perhaps contributing to the defeats.

Arista's losses cost him his command, and Ampudia led the army's retreat to Monterrey. As Ampudia prepared the defenses of that fortified city, Santa Anna returned to power and instructed him to retreat from Monterrey rather than risk the army, but Ampudia believed that another retreat would hopelessly demoralize his already disheartened men. He chose to remain in the city.

On September 21, 1846, Zachary Taylor's army began its assault on Monterrey. Ampudia's men put up a stiff defense and were engaged in house-to-house fighting in the middle of the city when Ampudia proposed an armistice. In the negotiations that followed, he agreed to surrender the city if his army could march south. Although President James Polk later renounced the armistice of Monterrey and the war in northern Mexico resumed, Ampudia had managed to extricate his army.

He remained active for the remainder of the war, but the disgrace of the surrender at Monterrey and Santa Anna's assuming personal command of the army prevented Ampudia from again holding a major command. Instead, he was in charge of artillery at the battles of Buena Vista and Cerro Gordo.

After the war, Ampudia remained active in Mexican politics and fought against the French puppet government of the Emperor Maximilian. He never fully recovered from the wounds he received in that conflict and died in 1868.

Valentín Gómez Farías (1781–1858)

Mexico's leading *puro* federalist, Gómez Farías fought for years to reduce the power of the Catholic Church and Mexican military in the political affairs of the nation. He and his supporters believed that individual states could best deal with their own domestic issues and hence a decentralized state best suited Mexican needs.

Born to a wealthy Guadalajara family, Gómez Farías was educated as a physician. The Mexican independence movement brought him into politics. His political work on the local level convinced him of the need for a decentralized approach to Mexico's problems. As acting president from 1833 to 1834, he tried to put his views into practice, but his attempts to reduce the power of the church caused President Antonio López de Santa Anna to banish him.

Goméz Farías was not idle during his exile. In constant communication with friends and potential allies back home, he planned for a return to power and a chance to implement the reforms he believed necessary for the nation. In 1846 during the early months of the war with the United States, he again joined forces with Santa Anna to bring down the government of Mariano Paredes y Arrillaga. As before, Santa Anna assumed the presidency with Gómez Farías as his vice president, meaning that during Santa Anna's absence with the army, Gómez Farías acted as president.

To fund a government perennially strapped for cash, Gómez Farías tried to negotiate church loans to fight the United States, but persuasion failed and Gómez Farías moved to confiscate church property. The policy frightened not only church leaders but also wealthy citizens, and these powerful forces precipitated the *Polkos* Revolt in February 1847. Santa Anna restored order by muscling Gómez Farías out of the government.

As the war wound down to its dismal conclusion, Gómez Farías and the *puros* continued to resist making peace with the United States, but their arguments were unavailing because the government was determined to cut its losses. Gómez Farías died in retirement a decade after the war.

José Joaquín de Herrera (1792–1854)

As president of Mexico the year before the outbreak of the Mexican-American War, Herrera adopted a moderate line to avoid war with the more powerful United States.

Like so many Mexican politicians, Herrera began his adult life in the army and was part of the revolutionary movement for Mexican independence. After independence, however, he spent most of his time in civilian government service where he held a variety of positions. As a leading member of the *moderados*, he helped to overthrow Santa Anna in 1844 and served as interim president until he was elected to the post in August 1845.

Herrera was all too aware of the country's precarious financial and social conditions. He knew that Mexico was incapable of retaking Texas and at one point considered recognition of Texas independence in exchange for Texan renunciation of annexation by the United States. This effort not only failed, it also infuriated the *puro* faction. Herrera's enemies used his apparent weakness to stir up opposition to his presidency.

American emissary John Slidell's arrival in the fall of 1845 spelled Herrera's doom. By then, U.S. annexation of Texas had been accomplished, and *puros* were joining with other administration enemies to demand that Mexico go to war over the matter. Herrera knew that a war would be disaster, but he also knew that negotiating with Slidell would be perceived as weakness. His hesitancy spurred his enemies to action, and in December 1845 Gen. Mariano Paredes y Arrillaga marched on Mexico City, forcing Herrera to resign the presidency and flee.

During the war, Herrera mostly remained out of sight. Yet, he emerged during the peace negotiations as one of the Mexican commissioners and was a party to the Treaty of Guadalupe Hidalgo. After the war he again served as Mexico's president, though with little more success than during his first administration. He died in retirement at Tacubaya.

Sam Houston (1793–1863)

The military commander who defeated Santa Anna at San Jacinto, winning Texas its independence, Sam Houston subsequently served as president of Texas. During his presidency he worked hard to secure the annexation of Texas by the United States. During the Mexican-American War he served as U.S. Senator from Texas.

Houston was born in Virginia but moved to Tennessee as a youth where he lived with Cherokee Indians for about three years. After leaving the Cherokees, Houston briefly taught school, but the outbreak of the War of 1812 convinced him to join the Tennessee militia. He was recognized for bravery at the battle of Horseshoe Bend where he was severely wounded. For a short time after the war, Houston served as subagent to the Cherokee but left that position to study law, and as a protégé of his former commander, Andrew Jackson, he entered politics. He served two terms in Congress before successfully running for governor of Tennessee.

In the early part of his second term, Houston married but the union ended after only a few weeks. Neither Houston nor his wife ever revealed the reason for their separation. Perhaps to avoid scandal, he resigned as governor and moved to live among the Cherokees who had immigrated to Arkansas Territory.

Houston moved to Texas in 1832 and practiced law. He also became involved in the growing movement for Texas independence and commanded Texas troops during the Texas Revolution. After his victory at San Jacinto, he was elected the first president of Texas. One of the main objectives of his presidency was to persuade the United States to annex Texas, but all he could obtain was recognition of Texas as an independent nation. When elected again to the presidency in 1841, Houston renewed his efforts to secure annexation, finally achieving his goal in 1845.

During the Mexican War, Houston served in the U.S. Senate and staunchly supported President Polk's conduct of the war. Aware of the Rio Grande boundary's importance to Texas' future, Houston was pleased that the final treaty established that border, but he criticized the Treaty of Guadalupe Hidalgo for not annexing more Mexican lands.

During the crises of the 1850s, Houston took a strong unionist stand that alienated many Texans. Yet, he was still able to win the governorship in 1859. He resolutely but unsuccessfully opposed Texas' secession in 1861. He left office in March 1861 and remained in Texas until his death in 1863.

Stephen Watts Kearny (1794–1848)

As commander of the Army of the West, Stephen Watts Kearny secured New Mexico for the United States and participated in the subjugation of Alta California.

A career army officer, Kearny entered the service during the War of 1812. At the beginning of the Mexican War, he commanded the 1st Dragoons headquartered at Fort Leavenworth. Upon the outbreak of hostilities, the War Department ordered him to raise a volunteer force in Missouri to augment his dragoons and march what was dubbed the Army of the West to New Mexico.

The first leg of his trip took him over largely uninhabited lands to the trading post of Bent's Fort where Kearny rested his men and gathered intelligence for the final push into New Mexico. Fortunately for the Army of the West, the governor of New Mexico decided not to put up resistance to the invading force, and Kearny occupied Santa Fe without firing a shot.

During his brief stay in New Mexico, Kearny set up a civilian U.S. government, established a legal system compatible with that of the United States, and attempted to make peace with Indians. Leaving part of his army behind to continue the occupation and sending part of his Missouri volunteers to Chihuahua to cooperate with U.S. forces there, Kearny set out with several hundred dragoons to join American naval forces in California to take that region for the United States.

Traveling over mountain passes and through desert with the help of legendary mountain man Kit Carson, Kearny and his men reached the outskirts of Mexican settlement in California in early December 1846. En route to San Diego, Kearny attacked a Mexican military force at San Pascual on December 6. He was seriously wounded in the engagement but recovered after arriving in San Diego.

Kearny worked in concert with Commodore Robert Stockton despite their dispute over who was in supreme command of the campaign against Los Angeles, which was secured in January 1847. Kearny's orders clearly placed him in command of any operations in California, but Stockton argued that having preceded him there rendered those orders invalid. To make matters worse for Kearny, Capt. John C. Frémont, army explorer and son-in-law of powerful Missouri senator Thomas Hart Benton, refused to recognize Kearny's authority and insisted on taking his instructions from Stockton. When new orders arrived confirming Kearny's authority, Stockton departed leaving Frémont no choice but to return east with Kearny. Kearny proffered charges of disobedience of orders and insubordination against Frémont who was found guilty and eventually resigned from the army.

The war not yet over, and Kearny was sent to Mexico to serve as military governor of Veracruz, a duty that probably resulted in his contracting malaria. Shortly after his return to the United States to take command of Jefferson Barracks in St. Louis, Kearny died from the disease.

Mariano Paredes y Arrillaga (1797–1849)

Mariano Paredes y Arrillaga, general and aspiring president, was a firm believer that only a monarchy could restore Mexican stability, especially with him on the throne.

Paredes y Arrillaga became an officer in the Spanish Army while still a teenager. After realizing that Mexico's fight for independence would succeed, he changed sides to become an officer in the Mexican Army. He rose quickly in the army and opportunistically participated in the overthrow of Augustín de Iturbide, Anastasio Bustamante, José Joaquín de Herrera, and Antonio López de Santa Anna, usually after initially supporting them.

The toppling of Herrera's government brought Paredes y Arrillaga to power in early 1846 as the crisis with the United States was nearing the breaking point, and in fact, Paredes y Arrillaga's belligerent attitude toward the United States was a key factor in his garnering broad political support. He had been a vocal critic of the Herrera government's ostensible impotence in the face of Texas annexation and had pledged to protect all Mexican territory (including Texas) from American aggression. After he had assumed the reins of power, however, Paredes y Arrillaga realized that Mexico's economic disarray would make a war against the United States a likely disaster.

Paredes y Arrillaga also faced the violation of Mexican territory when Zachary Taylor brought his army across the Nueces River to the Rio Grande. Lacking the resources to mount a major campaign against Taylor, he swore to fight a defensive war against the Americans. Even that proved impossible as Mexican defeats at Palo Alto and Resaca de la Palma led to Taylor's occupation of Matamoros.

The setbacks were not altogether Paredes y Arrillaga's fault for he received little help from the Mexican Congress. Yet, suspicions about his intention to establish a monarchy with himself wearing the crown were his undoing, and they prompted numerous conspiracies against his government. Finally in August 1846, one of those plots brought Santa Anna back to power.

Paredes y Arrillaga spent the next year and a half in exile in Europe where he tried but failed to find a monarch willing to conquer Mexico on his behalf. He returned to Mexico at war's end and argued against the Treaty of Guadalupe Hidalgo while trying to sustain resistance with guerrilla warfare. He died in hiding a year after the war ended.

James Knox Polk (1795–1849)

As president of the United States from 1845 to 1849, James Knox Polk worked diligently to expand the country's territory. He was accused of instigating the Mexican War in that quest. In that war, the United States fixed the Rio Grande as the boundary between Mexico and Texas and secured the vast territorial expanse comprising New Mexico and Alta California.

Polk began his political career in Tennessee as a protégé of Andrew Jackson. He served in Congress, was Speaker of the House, and served one term as governor of Tennessee. Although he was not nameless in American politics, he did not become a serious candidate for the 1844 Democratic presidential nomination until front-runner Martin Van Buren publicly opposed the annexation of Texas. Polk's strong record on territorial expansion and the backing of many Jacksonian Democrats, including Jackson himself, gained Polk the nomination.

Polk campaigned on an expansionist platform to eke out a victory over Whig candidate Henry Clay. In addition to keeping Texas—Congress approved annexation before Polk took office—he upheld American claims against the British for the Oregon Territory and proposed to purchase California and New Mexico from Mexico. The American claim that Oregon's boundary should be 54°40' seemed unreasonable to London, however, and negotiations broke down.

When President Polk sent John Slidell to Mexico to purchase New Mexico and California, Mexico was even less inclined to negotiate than Great Britain. Polk dispatched Zachary Taylor's army to the Rio Grande to guard American claims to the territory, a move Mexico viewed as an invasion of its territory. Meanwhile, Mexico's rebuff of Slidell angered Polk, and he was considering asking Congress to declare war over the diplomatic insult when the Mexican military attacked an American patrol along the Rio Grande.

The attack won Polk his declaration of war, making him the second American president to preside over a declared war. Handling his duties with a characteristically meticulous attention to detail, he personally supervised all major decisions in the war, an attentiveness that the military frequently found meddlesome. Polk often quarreled with his generals and frequently critiqued from hindsight their strategic decisions. Overall, however, the president managed matters with remarkable skill. American victory meant he realized almost all of his original goals, including the acquisition of New Mexico and Alta California and the establishment of the Rio Grande boundary. At the same time, acquiring the western territories revived debates over the expansion of slavery that greatly troubled the nation over the next decade. Polk did not live to see the political strife that was the most terrible legacy of his dramatic accomplishment. Shortly after leaving office, he died, possibly from the exhausting toll of his busy presidency.

Antonio López de Santa Anna (1794–1876)

Before, during, and after the Mexican War, Antonio López de Santa Anna commanded the Mexican Army and served as president of

Mexico. Born into a middle-class *criollo* family in Jalapa, Santa Anna began his adult life as an army *caballero cadete* in the Spanish Army. Like many other *criollo* officers, however, he joined the independence movement, and upon the success of the revolution, he became a twenty-seven-year-old brigadier general in the Mexican Army.

Also like many Mexican officers, Santa Anna was always keenly interested in the nation's political affairs and used his military activities to gain political influence. His victory against the Spanish invasion in 1829 won him the presidency in 1833, and though his alliance with the *puro* federalists under Valentín Gómez Farías, who served as Santa Anna's vice president, aided his rise to power, Santa Anna joined rival *moderados* and ousted the *puros* from his government in 1834.

As dictator of Mexico over the next two years, Santa Anna strengthened the central government by virtually eliminating the states' autonomy. His centralizing policies provoked rebellions in several states, including one in Texas that quickly turned into a fight for independence. Santa Anna assumed overall command of the Mexican armies to suppress this revolt and personally directed the siege and attack on Texans' makeshift fort at the Alamo. He ordered no quarter be given the Alamo's defenders, and their deaths along with those of the Texans captured near Goliad enraged the entire province. On April 21, 1836, Texans under Sam Houston defeated Santa Anna at San Jacinto. Santa Anna was captured and forced to sign a treaty recognizing Texas independence. In disgrace with the Mexican political establishment, the erstwhile dictator retired from public affairs.

In the so-called Pastry War of 1838, Santa Anna on his own fought against a French invasion at Veracruz and suffered a nasty wound that cost him his left leg. Yet his audacious exploits again won the hearts of his countrymen and gave him new political life. With the help of the military he became president again in 1843, but political divisions over whether to retake Texas and the fiscal excesses of his government brought about his overthrow in 1844. Suspected of plotting a return to power, he was exiled in 1845.

Those suspicious of Santa Anna's unrelenting ambition were confirmed in their judgment by the schemes that brought Santa Anna back to power in September 1846 with his occasional *puro* ally Valentín Gómez Farías. The United States helped Santa Anna return to power when he promised to end the war that had broken out between the two countries in May 1846. Accordingly, the U.S. Navy allowed Santa Anna to move through the blockade to Veracruz.

Making peace as Santa Anna had promised was probably impossible politically, but he did not even try. Instead, he enlarged the Mexican military and in early 1847 tried to destroy Zachary Taylor's army at Buena Vista. Yet, everything went to ashes for Santa Anna. Taylor repulsed him, Gen. Winfield Scott invaded Veracruz as a prelude to his march on Mexico City, and the internal rebellion called the *Polkos* Revolt broke out in the capital. Santa Anna calmed the *Polkos* by ousting Gómez Farías as vice president, but Scott soundly defeated him at Cerro Gordo and forced his retreat toward Mexico City.

A series of battles outside Mexico City in August 1847 forced Santa Anna's army into the capital, and when the Americans marched into the city in September, Santa Anna withdrew with the army and government. Shortly thereafter he resigned the presidency.

After the war, Santa Anna spent several years in exile in Venezuela but returned to the Mexican presidency in 1853. This time in office, he sold a strip of northwestern Mexico to the United States that would be known as the Gadsden Purchase. Again overthrown by coup in 1855, Santa Anna spent the next nineteen years in Cuba. Only near the end of his life did he return to Mexico.

Winfield Scott (1786–1866)

As commanding general of the U.S. Army, Winfield Scott presided over the early phases of the Mexican War from Washington. In late 1846, President Polk gave Scott command of the expedition that landed at Veracruz and marched inland to Mexico City.

Born in Virginia to a middle-class family, Winfield Scott read law and was an attorney before accepting a commission in the army in 1808. Scott chaffed at the boredom of the peacetime army and resented superiors he deemed incompetent and corrupt. The War of 1812 allowed him to demonstrate his abilities, and he emerged from that conflict a hero with the rank of brevet major general.

Scott believed the War of 1812 proved the need for a professional army, and he traveled extensively to study European military establishments. Yet, his abrasive personality frequently caused quarrels with fellow officers, and many years passed before he had the support and seniority to implement some of his reforms.

Before the Mexican War, Scott's combat experience was limited. He missed the Black Hawk War because of a cholera epidemic among his men. Other than the War of 1812, he tried to suppress the Seminoles in the Second Seminole War, which was a failed and dismal undertaking. Otherwise, he was given the disagreeable chore of commanding the expedition that escorted the Cherokees on the Trail of Tears to the Indian Territory.

At the beginning of the Mexican War, Scott handled many of the conflict's administrative details from Washington. When it became increasingly apparent that the war would consist of more than a couple of battles in northern Mexico, Scott was eager to take to the field. His ties to the Whig Party, however, made him a questionable figure for Democrat president Polk, always a suspicious partisan. Talk that Whigs intended to make Zachary Taylor their 1848 presidential nominee made Polk wary about creating another Whig military hero in Winfield Scott.

By the fall of 1846, it was apparent that Taylor's victories in northern Mexico had left the government in Mexico City unfazed. The solution was to launch another campaign against Mexico City, starting with an amphibious landing at Veracruz. Polk did not want to give Taylor any additional military glory, and though he was equally suspicious of Scott, the president ultimately felt he had no choice but to give Scott the assignment.

Scott engrossed himself with planning the landing at Veracruz and the subsequent march into the interior. He cadged most of Taylor's regulars for the campaign, incurring Taylor's lasting hatred in the process. In spite of a desire for even more thorough planning, Scott was in a hurry. He had to make his landing early in the year to reach higher ground before yellow fever season began in the late spring.

Scott landed unopposed on March 9, 1847, and quickly besieged Veracruz, forcing its surrender by the end of the month. He then marched inland and won a major battle against Santa Anna at Cerro Gordo. Despite these successes, many of Scott's volunteers were nearing the end of their enlistments, and he had to stop the campaign to await reinforcements. Supplied with fresh troops, he began the final push to Mexico City. Several bloody engagements outside the city preceded the American capture of Chapultepec, a commanding hill that gave entrée to Mexico City and forced Mexican military forces to evacuate the city.

Following these signal accomplishments, Scott and his generals immediately fell to squabbling with one another, revisiting old grudges and inventing new causes for disagreement. The anti-Scott generals included Gideon Pillow, a personal friend of President Polk, and the president summoned Scott home to answer charges. The court of inquiry cleared Scott, but the dispute tarnished his reputation.

The Whigs nominated Scott for the presidency in 1852, but Franklin Pierce, who had served under Scott in the Mexican War, soundly defeated him. Scott remained the commander of the army and was in that post as the Civil War loomed. Physically incapable of taking the field, he nonetheless directed many army movements during the early months of the war. He retired to West Point in November 1861 and died there in 1866.

Zachary Taylor (1784–1850)

As commander of the Army of Occupation, Zachary Taylor invaded northern Mexico in 1846. His victories at Palo Alto, Resaca de la Palma, Monterrey, and Buena Vista made him a national hero and gained him the Whig nomination to the presidency in 1848.

Taylor was born in Virginia but spent most of his childhood in Kentucky. He entered the army as a first lieutenant in 1808 and before the outbreak of the War of 1812 had attained the rank of captain. He commanded Fort Harrison in the Northwest Territory in the early months of the war and protected it from an Anglo-Indian attack.

Taylor served on the frontier for the duration of the war but army reductions afterward convinced him to leave the service rather than accept a demotion in rank. In 1816 he returned to the army as a major and spent two decades on the western frontier. Summoned east in 1837, he took command of U.S. troops in Florida fighting the Second Seminole War. His methodical approach to capturing Seminoles yielded significant results, but frustrated over not receiving enough men and adequate supplies for his mission, he requested a transfer. He was serving in the Southwest when the United States annexed Texas in 1845 and was dispatched to the Nueces River to guard against an angry Mexican response.

When negotiations between the United States and Mexico broke down, Polk ordered Taylor to take his army to the Rio Grande. In April 1846 Mexican Army forces attacked an American patrol belonging to Taylor's command, an incident that brought a declaration of war from Congress.

Before learning that war had been declared, Taylor moved to secure his supply lines to the coast. As he tried to return to the Rio Grande, he fought battles at Palo Alto and Resaca de la Palma, both American victories. With war now official, the War Department instructed Taylor to cross the Rio Grande, and after receiving supplies and reinforcements, he moved on the large city of Monterrey where he fought a major battle in September 1846. Taylor accepted the surrender of the city by concluding an armistice with Mexican forces.

President Polk rejected the armistice because it did nothing to further his aims of acquiring New Mexico and California. Insulted by the president's action, Taylor was soon even angrier when he learned that Gen. Winfield Scott would command a campaign against Veracruz that included most of Taylor's regulars. Taylor refused to remain idle at Monterrey, and though lacking his regulars, he moved to take possession of more territory. Antonio López de Santa Anna learned of Taylor's vulnerability and marched north to destroy him, but Taylor defeated Santa Anna at the battle of Buena Vista on February 22 and 23, 1847.

Buena Vista was Taylor's last major engagement of the war, but it added to an already formidable reputation. The Whig Party saw this military hero as a perfect nominee to defeat the Democrats in the 1848 presidential contest. Taylor won the election, but he was soon confronted by growing sectional divisions over the territory acquired from Mexico, and he refused to support attempts to settle the argument with compromises that he regarded as expedient and unprincipled. As the controversy raged, Taylor grew ill and died on July 9, 1850, after serving only a little more than a year as president.

PRIMARY DOCUMENTS OF THE PERIOD

The Crisis over Texas

The fall of Emperor Agustín de Iturbide ushered in the era of republican government in independent Mexico. The first manifestation of that government was embodied in the Constitution of 1824, which inclined markedly toward the Federalist program of decentralization. Consequently, state autonomy was quite generously bestowed with constitutional restrictions that were designed to protect citizens from even overreaching local authority. The following excerpt from the Constitution of 1824 stipulates state responsibilities and limitations in the new Mexican union. It was this document and its protections that were nullified by the advent of the caudillo state under Santa Anna in the mid-1830s. The establishment of a strong central government under the Constitution of 1836 made the states military departments administered by the Mexican president's handpicked governors. This radical change provoked a revolt in the Mexican state of Texas, a fact emphasized by the flag over the Alamo, which had emblazoned on it "1824" to venerate what Texans regarded as inalienable rights under the constitution of that year.

Document 1
Excerpt from the Constitution of 1824

SECTION 7th—General Rules to which all the States and Territories in the Federation shall conform in the administration of Justice.
145. In each one of the States of the Federation, full faith and credit shall be given to the acts, registers, and proceedings; of the judges and other authorities of the other States. The general Congress shall regu-

late the laws by which said acts, registers, and proceedings shall be authenticated.

146. The sentence of infamy shall not extend beyond the criminal that may have merited it according to law.

147. There is forever prohibited the penalty of confiscation of estates.

148. There is forever prohibited all judgements by commission and all retroactive laws.

149. No authority shall apply any form of torture, whatever may be the nature or state of the prosecution.

150. No one shall be imprisoned, unless there is reasonable ground to suppose him criminal.

151. No one shall be imprisoned on suspicion for more than seventy hours.

152. No authority shall give an order for the search of any houses, papers, and other effects of the inhabitants of the Republic, except in the cases expressly provided for by law, and in the form which it designates.

153. No inhabitant of the Republic shall be compelled to take an oath relative to his own acts in criminal affairs.

154. The military and ecclesiastics will remain subject to the authority under which they actually are, according to the existing laws.

155. No suit can be instituted, neither in civil or criminal cases, for injuries, without being able to prove, having legally attempted, the means of conciliation.

156. None can be deprived of the right of terminating his differences by means of arbitrators appointed by each party, whatever may be the situation of the controversy.

TITLE 6th.

SECTION 1st—Of the individual government of the States.

157. The government of each State shall be divided for its exercise in three powers, Legislative, Executive, and Judicial, and never can be united two or more of these in one corporation or person, nor the Legislative deposited in one individual.

158. The legislative power of each State shall reside in one Legislature, composed of the number of individuals which their respective constitutions may determine, to be elected popularly, and removable in the time and manner which said constitutions may designate.

159. The person or persons to whom the States confide their executive power, cannot exercise it except for a definite time, which shall be fixed by their respective constitutions.

160. The judicial power of each state shall be exercised by the Tribunals that the Constitution may establish or designate, and all cases, civil or criminal, which appertain to the cognizance of those Tribunals, shall be conducted in them to final judgment and execution.

SECTION 2nd—Of the obligations of the States.

161. Each one of the States is obliged-First, to organize its interior government and administration, without opposing this Constitution nor the constitutional act. Second, to publish by means of their Governors, their respective Constitutions, laws and decrees. Third, to obey, and cause to be obeyed, the Constitution and general laws of the Union, and treaties made and those that henceforward may be made, by the supreme authority of the Federation with any foreign Power. Fourth, to protect its inhabitants in the free use and liberty which they have to write, print, and publish their political ideas, without the necessity of license, revision, or approbation previous to publication, always taking care to observe the general laws on the subject. Fifth, to deliver immediately, the criminals of other states, to the authority which reclaims them. Sixth, to deliver the fugitives of other states, to the person that justly reclaims them, or compel them in some other mode to satisfy the interested party. Seventh, to contribute for the consolidation and extinguishment of the debts acknowledged by the general Congress. Eighth, to remit annually to each one of the Houses of Congress, a general, circumstantial, and comprehensive note, of the ingress and egress in all the treasuries they may have in their respective districts, with a relation of the origin of one and the other, of the situation in which are found the branches of industry, agriculture, commerce and manufactures, of the new branches of industry which they can introduce and extend, designating the means by which it can be obtained, and of their respective population and means of protecting and augmenting it. Ninth, to remit to both Houses, and in their recess, to the Council of Government, and likewise to the Supreme Executive Power, authorized copies of the constitutions, laws and decrees.

SECTION 3rd—Restrictions of the Powers of the State.

162. None of the States can—First, establish, without the consent of the General Congress, any tonnage duty, nor other port duty. Second, impose, without the consent of the general Congress, contributions or duties on importations or exportations, whilst the law does not regulate it as it must do. Third, hold, at no time, a permanent troop nor vessels of war, without the consent of the general Congress. Fourth, enter into no agreement or compact with any foreign power, nor declare war against them, resisting in case of actual invasion, or in such danger as will not admit of delay, giving immediate notice thereof to the President of the Republic. Fifth, enter into no agreement or compact with other States of the Federation, without the previous consent of the general Congress or its posterior approbation, if the transaction were upon the regulation of limits.

Source: David B. Edward, *The History of Texas; or the Emigrant's Farmer's, and Politician's Guide to the Character, Climate, Soil and Productions of that Country: Arranged Geographically from Personal Observation and Experience.* With a new introduction by Margaret S. Henson (Cincinnati: J. A. James, 1836; reprint, Austin: Texas State Historical Association, 1990), 334–35.

After more than a decade of American immigration into Texas, the burgeoning size of the Anglo population troubled Mexican authorities who tried to curb Texas privileges and enforce Mexican law. Their efforts, however, were either fruitless or provoked stiff resistance. Finally in 1836, American transplants and native Tejanos revolted against the centralized Mexican regime of Antonio López de Santa Anna. Santa Anna's army assailed the Alamo in San Antonio while Texans met at Washington-on-the-Brazos. At the convention, a drafting committee produced a declaration of independence, a near replica of the United States Declaration of Independence of 1776, which was approved after only one day of deliberation. The assertion of independence seemed quixotic at best in March, especially when the fall of the Alamo and the advance of Santa Anna's armies put Texas revolutionaries to flight. But the Texan victory at San Jacinto in April secured sovereignty and set the stage for Texas to become a major point of contention between the United States and Mexico.

Document 2
The Texas Declaration of Independence
March 2, 1836

THE DECLARATION OF INDEPENDENCE Made by the Delegates of The People of Texas in General Convention, at Washington, ON MARCH 2nd, 1836.

When a government has ceased to protect the lives, liberty and property of the people, from whom its legitimate powers are derived, and for the advancement of whose happiness it was instituted; and so far from being a guarantee for their inestimable and inalienable rights, becomes an instrument in the hands of evil rulers for their suppression.

When the federal republican Constitution of their country, which they have sworn to support, no longer has a substantial existence, and the whole nature of their government has been forcibly changed, without their consent, from a restricted federative republic, composed of sovereign states, to a consolidated central military despotism, in which every interest is disregarded but that of the army and the priesthood, both the eternal enemies of civil liberty, the ever ready minions of power, and the usual instruments of tyrants.

When, long after the spirit of the constitution has departed, moderation is at length so far lost by those in power, that even the semblance of freedom is removed, and the forms themselves of the constitution discontinued, and so far from their petitions and remonstrances being regarded, the agents who bear them are thrown into dungeons, and mercenary armies sent forth to force a new government upon them at the point of the bayonet.

When, in consequence of such acts of malfeasance and abduction on the part of the government, anarchy prevails, and civil society is dissolved into its original elements, in such a crisis, the first law of nature, the right of self-preservation, the inherent and inalienable right of the people to appeal to first principles, and take their political affairs into their own hands in extreme cases, enjoins it as a right towards themselves, and a sacred obligation to their posterity, to abolish such government, and create another in its stead, calculated to rescue them from impending dangers, and to secure their welfare and happiness.

Nations, as well as individuals, are amenable for their acts to the public opinion of mankind. A statement of a part of our grievances is therefore submitted to an impartial world, in justification of the hazardous but unavoidable step now taken, of severing our political connection with the Mexican people, and assuming an independent attitude among the nations of the earth.

The Mexican government, by its colonization laws, invited and induced the Anglo–American population of Texas to colonize its wilderness under the pledged faith of a written constitution, that they should continue to enjoy that constitutional liberty and republican government to which they had been habituated in the land of their birth, the United States of America.

In this expectation they have been cruelly disappointed, inasmuch as the Mexican nation has acquiesced to the late changes made in the government by Gen. Antonio Lopez de Santa Anna, who, having overturned the constitution of his country, now offers, as the cruel alternative, either to abandon our homes, acquired by so many privations, or submit to the most intolerable of all tryanny, the combined despotism of the sword and the priesthood.

It has sacrificed our welfare to the state of Coahuila by which our interests have been continually depressed through a jealous and partial course of legislation, carried on at a far distant seat of government, by a hostile majority, in an unknown tongue, and this too, notwithstanding we have petitioned in the humblest terms for the establishment of a separate state government, and have, in accordance with the provisions of the national constitution, presented to the general Congress a republican constitution, which was, without a just cause, contemptuously rejected.

It incarcerated in a dungeon, for a long time, one of our citizens, for no other cause but a zealous endeavor to procure the acceptance of our constitution, and the establishment of a state government.

It has failed and refused to secure, on a firm basis, the right of trial by jury, that palladium of civil liberty, and only safe guarantee for the life, liberty, and property of the citizen.

It has failed to establish any public system of education, although possessed of almost boundless resources, (the public domain,) and although it is an axiom in political science, that unless a people are educated and enlightened, it is idle to expect the continuance of civil liberty, or the capacity for self government.

It has suffered the military commandants, stationed among us, to exercise arbitrary acts of oppression and tyranny, thus trampling upon the most sacred rights of the citizens, and rendering the military superior to the civil power.

It has dissolved, by force of arms, the state Congress of Coahuila and Texas, and obliged our representatives to fly for their lives from the seat of government, thus depriving us of the fundamental political right of representation.

It has demanded the surrender of a number of our citizens, and ordered military detachments to seize and carry them into the Interior for trial, in contempt of the civil authorities, and in defiance of the laws and the constitution.

It has made piratical attacks upon our commerce, by commissioning foreign desperadoes, and authorizing them to seize our vessels, and convey the property of our citizens to far distant parts for confiscation.

It denies us the right of worshipping the Almighty according to the dictates of our own conscience, by the support of a national religion, calculated to promote the temporal interest of its human functionaries, rather than the glory of the true and living God.

It has demanded us to deliver up our arms, which are essential to our defence, the rightful property of freemen, and formidable only to tyrannical governments.

It has invaded our country both by sea and by land, with the intent to lay waste our territory, and drive us from our homes; and has now a large mercenary army advancing, to carry on against us a war of extermination.

It has, through its emissaries, incited the merciless savage, with the tomahawk and scalping knife, to massacre the inhabitants of our defenceless frontiers.

It has been, during the whole time of our connection with it, the contemptible sport and victim of successive military revolutions, and hath continually exhibited every characteristic of a weak, corrupt, and tyrannical government.

These, and other grievances, were patiently borne by the people of Texas, until they reached that point at which forbearance ceases to be a virtue. We then took up arms in defence of the national constitution. We appealed to our Mexican brethren for assistance. Our appeal has been made in vain. Though months have elapsed, no sympathetic response has yet been heard from the Interior. We are, therefore, forced to the melancholy conclusion, that the Mexican people have acquiesced in the destruction of their liberty, and the substitution therefor of a military government; that they are unfit to be free, and incapable of self government.

The necessity of self-preservation, therefore, now decrees our eternal political separation.

We, therefore, the delegates, with plenary powers, of the people of Texas, in solemn convention assembled, appealing to a candid world for the necessities of our condition, do hereby resolve and declare, that our political connection with the Mexican nation has forever ended, and that the people of Texas do now constitute a FREE, SOVEREIGN, and INDEPENDENT REPUBLIC, and are fully invested with all the rights and attributes which properly belong to independent nations; and, conscious of the rectitude of our intentions, we fearlessly and confidently commit the issue to the supreme Arbiter of the destinies of nations.

In witness whereof we have hereunto subscribed our names.

RICHARD ELLIS,
President and Delegate from Red River.

Source: *Laws of the Republic of Texas*, vol. 1 (Houston: Secretary of State, 1838), 3–7.

Mexico insisted that Texas was still a state within that nation, but it actually remained a separate republic for almost ten years before U.S. annexation finally sealed the region's fate and set Mexico and the United States on the path to war. During those years, American reluctance to annex Texas stemmed from arguments over slavery, but by the mid-1840s persuasive advocates of America's Manifest Destiny were gradually subsuming those disputes and were on the verge of carrying the day for expansion at any cost. The presidential election of 1844 was carried out in this heated context and expansionist Democrat James K. Polk's victory was interpreted by many as revealing the country's will to annex Texas. Because opponents, though, still commanded enough votes in the Senate to prevent ratification of an annexation treaty with the Texas Republic, the departing Tyler administration resorted to a joint resolution that would require only simple majorities in both houses of Congress. Although the resolution stirred robust opposition in the Senate, it was adopted on February 28, 1845, and was signed by Tyler the next day. Texas accepted it on July 4.

Document 3
The Resolution Annexing Texas to the United States
March 1, 1845

Resolved by the Senate and House of Representatives of the United States in Congress assembled, That Congress doth consent that the territory properly included within, and rightfully belonging to the Republic of Texas, may be erected into a new State, to be called the State of Texas, with a republican form of government, to be adopted by the people of said republic, by deputies in convention assembled, with the consent of the existing government, in order that the same may be admitted as one of the States of this Union.

2. *And be it further resolved*, That the foregoing consent of Congress is given upon the following conditions, and with the following guarantees, to wit: *First*, Said State to be formed, subject to the adjustment by this government of all questions of boundary that may arise with other governments; and the constitution thereof, with the proper evidence of its adoption by the people of said Republic of Texas, shall be transmitted to the President of the United States, to be laid before Congress for its final action, on or before the first day of January, one thousand eight hundred and forty-six. *Second*, Said State, when admitted into the Union, after ceding to the United States, all public edifices, fortifications, barracks, ports and harbors, navy and navy-yards, docks, magazines, arms, armaments, and all other property and means pertaining to the public defense belonging to said Republic of Texas, shall retain all the public funds, debts, taxes, and dues of every kind, which may belong to or be due and owning said republic; and shall also retain all the vacant and unappropriated lands lying within its limits, to be applied to the payment of the debts and liabilities of said Republic of Texas, and the residue of said lands, after discharging said debts and liabilities, to be disposed of as said State may direct; but in no event are said debts and liabilities to become a charge upon the Gov-

ernment of the United States. *Third*, New States, of convenient size, not exceeding four in number, in addition to said State of Texas, and having sufficient population, may hereafter, by the consent of said State, be formed out of the territory thereof, which shall be entitled to admission under the provisions of the federal constitution. And such States as may be formed out of that portion of said territory lying south of thirty-six degrees thirty minutes north latitude, commonly known as the Missouri compromise line, shall be admitted into the Union with or without slavery, as the people of each State asking admission may desire. And in such State or States as shall be formed out of said territory north of said Missouri compromise line, slavery, or involuntary servitude, (except for crime,) shall be prohibited.

3. *And be it further resolved*, That if the President of the United States shall in his judgment and discretion deem it most advisable, instead of proceeding to submit the foregoing resolution of the Republic of Texas, as an overture on the part of the United States for admission, to negotiate with the Republic; then,

Be it resolved, That a State, to be formed out of the present Republic of Texas, with suitable extent and boundaries, and with two representatives in Congress, until the next appointment of representation, shall be admitted into the Union, by virtue of this act, on an equal footing with the existing States, as soon as the terms and conditions of such admission, and the cession of the remaining Texian territory to the United States shall be agreed upon by the Governments of Texas and the United States: And that the sum of one hundred thousand dollars be, and the same is hereby, appropriated to defray the expenses of missions and negotiations, to agree upon the terms of said admission and cession, either by treaty to be submitted to the Senate, or by articles to be submitted to the two houses of Congress, as the President may direct.

Approved, March 1, 1845.

Source: *U.S. Statutes at Large*, 5:797–98.

The annexation of Texas caused a major diplomatic crisis between the United States and Mexico. For years, Mexico had warned that incorporating Texas into the American Union would be regarded as an act of war, a sentiment that is articulately set forth in the following proclamation, which ends with the Mexican government rattling as best it could its military saber.

Document 4
Proclamation Protesting Texas Annexation

The minister of foreign affairs has communicated to me the following decree: José Joaquín de Herrera, general of division and president ad interim of the Mexican Republic, to the citizens thereof.

Be it known: That the general congress has decreed, and the executive sanctioned, the following:

The national congress of the Mexican Republic, considering:

That the congress of the United States of the North has, by a decree, which its executive sanctioned, resolved to incorporate the territory of Texas with the American union;

That this manner of appropriating to itself territories upon which other nations have rights, introduces a monstrous novelty, endangering the peace of the world, and violating the sovereignty of nations;

That this usurpation, now consummated to the prejudice of Mexico, has been in insidious preparation for a long time; at the same time that the most cordial friendship was proclaimed, and that on the part of this republic, the existing treaties between it and those states were respected scrupulously and legally;

That the said annexation of Texas to the U. States tramples on the conservative principles of society, attacks all the rights that Mexico has to that territory, is an insult to her dignity as a sovereign nation, and threatens her independence and political existence;

That the law of the United States, in reference to the annexation of Texas to the United States, does in nowise destroy the rights that Mexico has, and will enforce, upon that department;

That the United States, having trampled on the principles which served as a basis to the treaties of friendship, commerce and navigation, and more especially to those of boundaries fixed with precision, even previous to 1832, they are considered as inviolate by that nation.

And, finally, that the unjust spoilation of which they wish to make the Mexican nation the victim, gives her the clear right to use all her resources and power to resist, to the last moment, said annexation;

IT IS DECREED

1st. The Mexican nation calls upon all her children to the defence of her national independence, threatened by the usurpation of Texas, which is intended to be realized by the decree of annexation passed by the congress, and sanctioned by the president, of the United States of the north.

2nd. In consequence, the government will call to arms all the forces of the army, according to the authority granted it by the existing laws; and for the preservation of public order, for the support of her institutions, and in case of necessity, to serve as the reserve to the army, the government, according to the powers given to it on the 9th December 1844, will raise the corps specified by said decree, under the name of "Defenders of the Independence and of the Laws."

MIGUEL ARTISTAN,
President of the Deputies

FRANCISCO CALDERON,
President of the Senate

Approved, and ordered to be printed and published.

JOSÉ JOAQUÍN DE HERRERA
A. D. LUIS G. CUEVAS

Palace of the National Government, City of Mexico, June 4, 1845.

Source: Steven R. Butler, ed., *A Documentary History of the Mexican War* (Richardson, TX: Descendants of Mexican War Veterans, 1995), 5.

The War

James K. Polk became president in March 1845 with already troubled Mexican relations becoming even more discordant. Mexico had broken off diplomatic relations over Texas annexation just when Polk was eager to negotiate the purchase of California, and his efforts to restore relations only met with Mexican refusals. Polk then dispatched

Zachary Taylor's oddly labeled "Army of Observation" to the Rio Grande, a provocative move that forcefully supported the Texan claim that the Rio Grande, not the Nueces River, was the border with Mexico. Ultimately, Mexican forces attacked a portion of Taylor's command, and he promptly sent a report of the engagement, which Polk used to assert that war with Mexico was already in progress, a sentiment that a majority of Congress endorsed.

Document 5
Polk's War Message, 1846

The existing state of the relations between the United States and Mexico renders it proper that I should bring the subject to the consideration of Congress. . . .

The strong desire to establish peace with Mexico on liberal and honorable terms, and the readiness of this Government to regulate and adjust our boundary and other causes of difference with that power on such fair and equitable principles as would lead to permanent relations of the most friendly nature, induced me in September last to seek the reopening of diplomatic relations between the two countries. . . . An envoy of the United States repaired to Mexico with full powers to adjust every existing difference. But though present on the Mexican soil by agreement between the two Governments, invested with full powers, and bearing evidence of the most friendly dispositions, his mission has been unavailing. The Mexican Government not only refused to receive him or listen to his propositions, but after a long-continued series of menaces have at last invaded our territory and shed the blood of our fellow-citizens on our own soil. . . .

In my message at the commencement of the present session I informed you that upon the earnest appeal both of the Congress and convention of Texas I had ordered an efficient military force to take a position "between the Nueces and the Del Norte." This had become necessary to meet a threatened invasion of Texas by the Mexican forces, for which extensive military preparations had been made. The invasion was threatened solely because Texas had determined, in accordance with a solemn resolution of the Congress of the United States, to annex herself to our Union, and under these circumstances it was plainly our duty to extend our protection over her citizens and soil. . . .

The Army moved from Corpus Christi on the 11th of March, and on the 28th of that month arrived on the left bank of the Del Norte opposite to Matamoras, where it encamped on a commanding position, which has since been strengthened by the erection of fieldworks. A depot has also been established at Point Isabel, near the Brazos Santiago, 30 miles in the rear of the encampment. The selection of his position was necessarily confided to the judgment of the general in command.

The Mexican forces at Matamoras assumed a belligerent attitude, and on the 12th of April General Ampudia, then in command, notified General Taylor to break up his camp within twenty-four hours and to retire beyond the Nueces River, and in the event of his failure to comply with these demands announced that arms, and arms alone, must decide the question. But no open act of hostility was committed until the 24th of April. On that day General Arista, who had succeeded to the command of the Mexican forces, communicated to General Taylor that "he considered hostilities commenced and should prosecute them." A party of dragoons of 63 men and officers were on the same day dispatched from the American camp up the Rio del Norte, on its left bank, to ascertain whether the Mexican troops had crossed or were preparing to cross the river, "became engaged with a large body of these troops, and after a short affair, in which some 16 were killed and wounded, appear to have been surrounded and compelled to surrender."

. . . The cup of forbearance had been exhausted even before the recent information from the frontier of the Del Norte. But now, after reiterated menaces, Mexico has passed the boundary of the United States, has invaded our territory and shed American blood upon the American soil. She has proclaimed that hostilities have commenced, and that the two nations are now at war.

As war exists, and, notwithstanding all our efforts to avoid it, exists by the act of Mexico herself, we are called upon by every consideration of duty and patriotism to vindicate with decision the honor, the rights, and the interests of our country.

Source: James D. Richardson, ed., *A Compilations of the Messages and Papers of the President, 1789–1908* (Washington: Bureau of National Literature and Art, 1908), 4:437–43.

South Carolinian John C. Calhoun was one Southerner who had warned that war with Mexico would reinvigorate the divisive debate over slavery, and when Pennsylvania Democrat David Wilmot proposed the following provisional amendment to an administration request for money to negotiate peace with Mexico, Calhoun's fears were revealed as prophetic. The Wilmot Proviso twice passed the House of Representatives, but southern resolve in the Senate defeated the measure. Yet, a growing animus against slavery could be traced to these debates, and Southerners were on edge ever afterwards. The Mexican cession, which was the crux of Wilmot's failed initiative, nevertheless became fertile ground for angry arguments over the extension of slavery that set the tone of political discourse during the 1850s. At the end of that decade, the country would be divided and again going to war, this time with itself.

Document 6
The Wilmot Proviso, 1846

Provided, That, as an express and fundamental condition to the acquisition of any the Republic of Mexico by the United States, by virtue of any treaty which may be negotiated between them, and to the use by the Executive of the moneys herein appropriated, neither slavery nor involuntary servitude shall ever exist in any part of said territory, except for crime, whereof the party shall first be duly convicted.

Source: *Congressional Globe*, 29th Cong., 1st sess., 1217.

Aging commodore John Sloat arrived off the coast of California after the outbreak of war in Mexico and found the province already well along the path toward independence. At Monterey, he impetuously issued the following proclamation, which exceeded his orders but even so had the effect of accomplishing the Polk administration's aims. Sloat would later reassess his haste, especially after he met with John C. Frémont, whose rash actions in fomenting a California rebellion against Mexican authority had been undertaken without official sanction.

Document 7
John D. Sloat's Proclamation

To the Inhabitants of California:

The central government of Mexico having commenced hostilities against the United States of America, by invading its territory and attacking the troops of the United States stationed on the north side of the Rio Grande, and with a force of seven thousand men, under the command of General Arista, which army was totally destroyed and all their artillery, baggage, &c., captured on the 8th and 9th of May last, by a force of two thousand three hundred men, under the command of General Taylor, and the city of Matamoras taken and occupied by the forces of the United States; and the two nations being actually at war by this transaction, I shall hoist the standard of the United States at Monterey immediately, and shall carry it throughout California.

I declare to the inhabitants of California, that although I come in arms with a powerful force, I do not come among them as an enemy to California; on the contrary, I come as their best friend—as henceforward California will be a portion of the United States, and its peaceable inhabitants will enjoy the same rights and privileges they now enjoy; together with the privileges of choosing their own magistrates and other officers for the administration of justice among themselves, and the same protection will be extended to them as to any other State in the Union. They will also enjoy a permanent government under which life, property and the constitutional right and lawful security to worship the Creator in the way most congenial to each one's sense of duty will be secured, which unfortunately the central government of Mexico cannot afford them, destroyed as her resources are by internal factions and corrupt officers, who create constant revolutions to promote their own interests and to oppress the people. Under the flag of the United States California will be free from all such troubles and expense, consequently the country will rapidly advance and improve both in agriculture and commerce; as of course the revenue laws will be the same in California as in all other parts of the United States, affording them all manufactures and produce of the United States, free of any duty, and all foreign goods at one quarter of the duty they now pay, a great increase in the value of real estate and the products of California may also be anticipated.

With the great interest and kind feelings I know the government and people of the United States possess towards the citizens of California, the country cannot but improve more rapidly than any other on the continent of America. Such of the inhabitants of California, whether natives or foreigners, as may not be disposed to accept the high privileges of citizenship, and to live peaceably under the government of the United States, will be allowed time to dispose of their property and to remove out of the country, if they choose, without any restriction, or remain in it, observing strict neutrality.

With full confidence in the honor and integrity of the inhabitants of the country, I invite the judges, alcaldes, and other civil officers, to retain their offices and to execute their functions as heretofore, that the public tranquility may not be disturbed; at least, until the government of the territory can be more definitely arranged.

All persons holding titles to real estate, or in quiet possession of lands under a color of right, shall have those titles and rights guarantied to them.

All churches, and the property they contain, in possession of the clergy of California, shall continue in the same rights and possessions they now enjoy.

All provisions and supplies of every kind, furnished by the inhabitants for the use of United States ships and soldiers, will be paid for at fair rates, and no private property will be taken for public use without just compensation at the moment.

JOHN D. SLOAT,
Commander-in-chief of the United States naval forces in the Pacific Ocean
United States Flagship *Savannah*, Harbor of Monterey, July 7, 1846

Source: Steven R. Butler, ed., *A Documentary History of the Mexican War* (Richardson, TX: Descendants of Mexican War Veterans, 1995), 146.

Freshman Illinois congressman Abraham Lincoln was a resolute opponent of the war. He early presented resolutions (to which he al-

ludes in the opening section of the following speech) demanding that
Polk prove that Zachary Taylor's army was not in Mexico when it was
attacked, but his efforts left most Whigs unmoved and brought considerable ridicule from Democrats. In this speech, Lincoln also reproaches
the administration for its apparent plan to enlarge territorial claims on
a defeated Mexico.

Document 8
Lincoln Objects to "All Mexico"

I introduced a preamble, resolution and interrogatories, intended
to draw the President out, if possible, on this hitherto untrodden
ground. To show their relevancy, I propose to state my understanding
of the true rule for ascertaining the boundary between Texas and Mexico. It is, that *wherever* Texas was *exercising* jurisdiction was hers; and
wherever Mexico was exercising jurisdiction was hers; and that *whatever*
separated the actual exercise of jurisdiction of the one from that of the
other, was the true boundary between them. If, as is probably true,
Texas was exercising jurisdiction along the western bank of the Nueces, and Mexico was exercising it along the eastern bank of the Rio
Grande, then *neither* river was the boundary, but the uninhabited country between the two was. The extent of our territory in that region depended not on any *treaty-fixed* boundary, (for no treaty had attempted
it,) but on revolution. Any people anywhere, being inclined and having the power, have the *right* to rise up and shake off the existing government, and form a new one that suits them better. This is a most
valuable, a most sacred right—a right which, we hope and believe, is
to liberate the world. Nor is this right confined to cases in which the
whole people of an existing government may choose to exercise it. Any
portion of such people that *can may* revolutionize, and make their own
of so much of the territory as they inhabit. More than this, a *majority*
of any portion of such people may revolutionize, putting down a *minority*, intermingled with, or near about them, who may oppose their
movements. Such minority was precisely the case of the Tories of our
own Revolution. It is a quality of revolutions not to go by *old* lines, or
old laws; but to break up both, and make new ones. As to the country
now in question, we bought it of France in 1803, and sold it to Spain
in 1819, according to the President's statement. After this, all Mexico,
including Texas, revolutionized against Spain; and still later, Texas rev-

olutionized against Mexico. In my view, just so far as she carried her revolution, by obtaining the *actual*, willing or unwilling, submission of the people, *so far* the country was hers, and no farther.

Now, sir, for the purpose of obtaining the very best evidence as to whether Texas had actually carried her revolution to the place where the hostilities of the present war commenced, let the President answer the interrogatories I proposed, as before mentioned, or some other similar ones. Let him answer fully, fairly, and candidly. Let him answer with *facts*, and not with arguments. Let him remember he sits where Washington sat; and, so remembering, let him answer as Washington would answer. As a nation *should* not, and the Almighty *will* not, be evaded, so let him attempt no evasion, no equivocation. And if, so answering, he can show that the soil was ours where the first blood of the war was shed—that it was not within an inhabited country, or, if within such, that the inhabitants had submitted themselves to the civil authority of Texas, or of the United States, and that the same is true of the site of Fort Brown—then I am with him for his justification. In that case, I shall be most happy to reverse the vote I gave the other day. I have a selfish motive for desiring that the President may do this; I expect to give some votes, in connection with the war, which, without his so doing, will be of doubtful propriety, in may own judgment, but which will be free from the doubt, if he does so. But if he cannot or will not do this—if, on any pretence, or no pretence, he shall refuse or omit it—then I shall be fully convinced of what I more than suspect already, that he is deeply conscious of being in the wrong, that he feels the blood of this war, like the blood of Abel, is crying to Heaven against him; that he ordered General Taylor into the midst of a peaceful Mexican settlement, purposely to bring on a war; that originally having some strong motive—what I will not stop now to give my opinion concerning—to involve the two countries in a war, and trusting to escape scrutiny by fixing the public gaze upon the exceeding brightness of military glory—that attractive rainbow that rises in showers of blood— that serpent's eye that charms to destroy—he plunged into it, and has swept *on and on*, till, disappointed in his calculation of the ease with which Mexico might be subdued, he now finds himself he knows not where. How like the half insane mumbling of a fever dream is the whole war part of the late message! At one time telling us that Mexico has nothing whatever that we can get but territory; at another, showing us how we can support the war by levying contributions on Mexico. At one time urging the national honor, the security of the future, the prevention of foreign interference, and even the good of Mexico herself, as among the objects of the war; at another, telling us that, "to reject indemnity by refusing to accept a cession of territory, would be to abandon all our just demands, and to wage the war, bearing all its expenses, without a *purpose or definite object*." So, then, the national honor, security of the future, and everything but territorial indemnity, may be considered the *no-purposes* and *indefinite* objects of the war! But, having it now settled that territorial indemnity is the only object, we are urged to seize, by legislation here, all that he was content to take a few months ago, and the whole province of Lower California to boot, and to still carry on the war—to take *all* we are fighting for, and *still* fight on. Again, the President is resolved, under all circumstances, to have full territorial indemnity for the expenses of the war; but he forgets to tell us how we are to get the *excess* after those expenses shall have surpassed the value of the *whole* of the Mexican territory. So, again, he insists that the separate national existence of Mexico shall be maintained; but he does not tell us *how* this can be done after we shall have taken *all* her territory.

Source: *Congressional Globe*, Appendix, 30th Cong., 1st sess., 94–95.

Santa Anna never lost his ability to spin tales with just enough threads of truth to make them plausible to the uninformed. Almost forty years after the war, his habit of self-aggrandizement and vilifying his enemies persisted. In this passage from his memoirs, he depicts his return to Mexico in a highly favorable light, artfully skirting the issue of his disreputable dealings with the United States in effecting that return. He exaggerates his reception by Mexicans at Veracruz, castigates fellow officers for their incompetence, blandly misrepresents the proceedings at Monterrey, and falsely claims that Zachary Taylor (Zacarias in Santa Anna's account) intended to advance on Mexico City. Yet, his descriptions of the state of Mexican finances and of the army on the eve of the Battle of Buena Vista were not altogether inaccurate, nor was his pronouncement, no matter its grandiose verbosity, that a battlefield victory was the only way to resolve Mexico's predicament. Santa Anna, however, proved incapable of providing that victory.

Document 9
Santa Anna Describes His Return to Mexico

While I was there [Havana, Cuba], the government of the United States, having annexed the province of Texas, coveted the rich and vast territories of Alta California and New Mexico. The United States government was well prepared to acquire the territories and swooped down on her sister and neighbor, Mexico, already torn by civil wars. The scandal and injustice of such a move did not matter. The United States had the forces, and that was all that was needed. General Zacarias Taylor moved against the Mexican troops along the frontier, defeating them at Palo Alto and Resaca de la Palma, owing to the bungling of the incompetent General Arista. When war was declared, faithful Mexicans recalled me to head the army.

No veteran of the War for Independence could refuse a call to arms for his beloved country. No matter how humble my services might be, I answered the call. I chartered a ship—paying all expenses from my own purse—and sailed to Vera Cruz, defying the blockade. We sailed into the port on September 12, 1846, causing a sensation. What a change from my last look at Vera Cruz. The applause of the people let me know they had forgotten that fatal December 6. I journeyed to the capital amidst a continuous ovation, and my heart was overjoyed.

However, the affairs of the state were sad indeed! The Treasury was completely depleted, and the amount coming in could not even cover the necessary expenses. There was not even an army to meet the enemy. Our best men had been defeated on the frontier, and another regiment, under orders from General Pedro Ampudia, had surrendered in Monterey. The sad remainder of the army was scattered over the countryside. The mere handful of troops in the capital could not move for lack of equipment. And through all of this deplorable state of affairs, General Taylor triumphantly advanced toward the capital. But my faith held firm, and I renounced all hope of personal gain for the task at hand.

I felt that San Luis Potosi was a strategic point in the campaign, and I immediately marched there and set up my headquarters. Quickly we began to prepare for the battle. Only one thing bothered me. I was constantly puzzled as to how to meet the necessary expenses.

Previously, the General Treasury of the nation had supplied the commissary of the army with the basic necessities for each soldier. Now there was no money to supply these needed essentials, and each day our needs increased. The government answered my entreaties with false hopes and evasions. The soldiers grew more anxious with each passing day. "No one wants to send even bread and meat to the army," they grumbled.

To put the crowning touch to the situation and to try my patience to the end, a traitorous faction began circulating ugly rumors. "General Santa Anna is conspiring with the enemy! The enemy allowed him to enter the country! Santa Anna is a traitor to Mexico!" With its usual good sense and feeling for justice, the army ignored such ridiculous rumors.

Harassed on every side, I racked my brain searching for a way out. Victory was the only answer. I knew that if we did not move, we were dead. Victory was the only way out.

Source: Antonio López de Santa Anna, *The Eagle: The Autobiography of Santa Anna*. Ann Fears Crawford, ed. (Austin, TX: The Pemberton Press, 1967), 88–90.

Lawyer and politician José Fernando Ramírez was an astute observer of political and military affairs in Mexico during the war. From Mexico City, he provided a running commentary of events in a series of letters to his friend Don Francisco Elorriaga. A passage from his letter of April 25, 1847, describes the attitude of defeated Mexican soldiers returning from the rout at Cerro Gordo. Ramírez is also gloomy about the likelihood of Mexico's losing the war and its consequences, especially when he considers the policy advocated by the *puros*, whom he labels the "ultra-democratic party."

Document 10
A Mexican Assesses
The Military and Political Situation

The troops have come back very much depressed. The leaders and officers declare that the Yankees are *invincible*, and the soldiers are telling terrible tales that bring to mind the Conquest. Some say that the enemy soldiers are such huge, strong men that they can cut an opponent in two with a single sweep of their swords. It is also said that their horses are gigantic and very fast and that their muskets discharge shots which, once they leave the gun, divide into fifty pieces, each one fatal and well-aimed. Let us say nothing about their artillery, which has inspired fear and terror in all our troops and is undeniable proof of our backwardness in military art.

The question of the war has assumed a frightening aspect. If we go on fighting we shall surely be conquered, and if we sue for peace we cannot expect any good from the people of the interior of the country from whence come the destructive elements that are gnawing at the vitals of the nation. What are we going to do with the numerous, filthy remnants of the army? What shall we do with this host of leaders and officers? And what shall we do about the anarchy and disorder now enthroned and masked beneath the mantle of the federation? The states are now in a position to disregard orders without fear of reprisals, and they are making a great ado about it. Even a fifteen-year-old girl is not as precise in matters of honor as those states are in respect to their inflated sovereignty. The ultra-democratic party is proclaiming that the war is one way that should lead us to conquest, fancying that in this manner we can go on to obtain perfect freedom. This is their program.

Source: José Fernando Ramírez, *Mexico During the War with the United States.* Walter V. Scholer, ed. Elliot B. Scherr, trans. The University of Missouri Studies, vol. 23, no. 1 (Columbia: University of Missouri, 1950), 135–36.

In 1847, Mexico was not only militarily defeated, it was politically incoherent. Gen. Winfield Scott and U.S. diplomatic envoy Nicholas Trist tried to cope with this problem by agreeing to an armistice to allow Mexican authorities to sue for peace, but an angry President Polk began to doubt Trist's judgment. The president accordingly recalled Trist and thus revoked his authority to negotiate any settlement, but Trist remained in Mexico and continued his efforts to end the war, efforts which resulted in a treaty being signed in the village of Guadalupe Hidalgo. Although Polk was still angry, he reluctantly had to acknowledge that the treaty satisfied every stipulation the United

States had originally lodged. Trist nevertheless remained out of favor, and his career was ruined when he was abruptly discharged from government service.

Document 11
The Treaty of Guadalupe Hidalgo

ARTICLE V

The boundary line between the two Republics shall commence in the Gulf of Mexico, three leagues from land, opposite the mouth of the Rio Grande, otherwise called Rio Bravo del Norte, or Opposite the mouth of its deepest branch, if it should have more than one branch emptying directly into the sea; from thence up the middle of that river, following the deepest channel, where it has more than one, to the point where it strikes the southern boundary of New Mexico; thence, westwardly, along the whole southern boundary of New Mexico (which runs north of the town called Paso) to its western termination; thence, northward, along the western line of New Mexico, until it intersects the first branch of the river Gila; (or if it should not intersect any branch of that river, then to the point on the said line nearest to such branch, and thence in a direct line to the same); thence down the middle of the said branch and of the said river, until it empties into the Rio Colorado; thence across the Rio Colorado, following the division line between Upper and Lower California, to the Pacific Ocean. . . .

The boundary line established by this article shall be religiously respected by each of the two republics, and no change shall ever be made therein, except by the express and free consent of both nations, lawfully given by the General Government of each, in conformity with its own constitution. . . .

ARTICLE XII

In consideration of the extension acquired by the boundaries of the United States, as defined in the fifth article of the present treaty, the Government of the United States engages to pay to that of the Mexican Republic the sum of fifteen millions of dollars. . . .

ARTICLE XIV

The United States do furthermore discharge the Mexican Republic from all claims of citizens of the United States, not heretofore decided against the Mexican Government, which may have arisen previously to the date of the signature of this treaty; which discharge shall be final and perpetual, whether the said claims be rejected or be allowed by the board of commissioners provided for in the following article, and whatever shall be the total amount of those allowed.

ARTICLE XV

The United States, exonerating Mexico from all demands on account of the claims of their citizens mentioned in the preceding article, and considering them entirely and forever canceled, whatever their amount may be, undertake to make satisfaction for the same, to an amount not exceeding three and one-quarter millions of dollars. . . .

ARTICLE XVI

Each of the contracting parties reserves to itself the entire right to fortify whatever point within its territory it may judge proper so to fortify for its security.

Source: Hunter Miller, ed., vol. 5, *Treaties and Other International Acts of the United States of America* (Washington, DC: GPO, 1931–1938), 207–36.

ANNOTATED BIBLIOGRAPHY

Armies, Units

Biggs, Donald C. *Conquer and Colonize: Stevenson's Regiment and California*. San Rafael, CA: Presidio Press, 1977. Attempt to rehabilitate the reputation of New York volunteers in California during the war.

Caruso, A. Brooke. *The Mexican Spy Company: United States Covert Operations in Mexico, 1845–1848*. Jefferson, NC: McFarland, 1991. A look at how effectively the U.S. Army used espionage during the war.

Chance, Joseph E. *Jefferson Davis's Mexican War Regiment*. Jackson: University Press of Mississippi, 1991. Examines the role of the Mississippi Rifles in the war.

Dawson, Joseph G., III. *Doniphan's Epic March: The 1st Missouri Volunteers in the Mexican War*. Lawrence: University Press of Kansas, 1999. Well-written and researched look at the importance of the 1st Missouri's march into Mexico.

DePalo, William A., Jr. *The Mexican National Army, 1822–1852*. College Station: Texas A&M University Press, 1997. Explains how politics and the revolutionary tradition hampered professionalism in the Mexican Army.

Dillon, Lester R., Jr. *American Artillery in the Mexican War, 1846–1847*. Austin, TX: Presidial Press, 1975. Demonstrates importance of artillery in most Mexican-American War battles.

Gudde, Erwin G., ed. *Chronicle of the West: The Conquest of California, Discovery of Gold, and Mormon Settlement, as Reflected in Henry Bigler's Diaries*. Berkeley: University of California Press, 1962. Biography and diary of member of the Mormon Battalion.

Hackenburg, Randy W. *Pennsylvania in the War with Mexico: The Volunteer Regiments*. Shippensburg, PA: White Mane Publishing, 1992. Good social and military history of the impact of the war on volunteer units and their communities.

Illinois. Adjutant General's Office. *Record of the Services of Illinois Soldiers in the Black Hawk War, 1831–32, and in the Mexican War, 1846–8, Containing a Complete Roster of Commissioned Officers and Enlisted Men of Both Wars, Taken from the Official Rolls on File in the War Department. . . .* Springfield, IL: H. W. Rokker, State Printer, 1882. Short section on Mexican-American War with complete lists of Illinois participants.

McCaffrey, James M. *Army of Manifest Destiny: The American Soldier in the Mexican War, 1846–1848*. New York: New York University Press, 1992. Social history of American soldiers in the war.

Ricketts, Norma B. *The Mormon Battalion: U.S. Army of the West, 1846–1848*. Logan: Utah State University Press, 1996. Comprehensive account of this unit's trek to California during the Mexican-American War.

Santelli, Gabrielle M. N., and Charles R. Smith. *Marines in the Mexican War*. Washington, DC: History & Museums Div., HQ, USMC, 1991. A very brief examination of the importance of marine operations during the war.

Tyler, Daniel. *A Concise History of the Mormon Battalion in the Mexican War, 1846–1848*. Waynesboro, VA: M&R Books, 1964. A combination of narrative and letters by a member of the battalion.

Bibliographies

Fehrenbacher, Don Edward, ed. *Manifest Destiny and the Coming of the Civil War*. New York: Appleton, 1970. Bibliography of sources on expansion (including the Mexican-American War) as a cause of the Civil War.

Garrett, Jenkins, and Katherine R. Goodwin, eds. *The Mexican-American War of 1846–1848: A Bibliography of the Holdings of the Libraries, the University of Texas at Arlington*. College Station: Texas A&M, 1995. Good look at available unpublished sources.

Snoke, Elizabeth R. *The Mexican War: A Bibliography of MHRC Holdings for the Period 1835–1850*. Carlisle Barracks, PA: U.S. Army Military History Research Collection, 1973. Excellent guide to manuscripts on the war at the Military History Research Collection.

Tutorow, Norman E. *The Mexican-American War: An Annotated Bibliography*. Westport, CT: Greenwood Press, 1981. Dated but still excellent guide to published sources.

Biographies

Ambrose, Stephen. *Halleck: Lincoln's Chief of Staff.* Baton Rouge: Louisiana State University Press, 1962. Reprint, 1990. Straightforward biography with interesting information on the Mexican-American War but with an emphasis on the Civil War.

Baker, Jean H. *James Buchanan.* New York: Henry Holt, 2004. Short biography in the American President series.

Barker, Eugene Campbell. *The Life of Stephen Austin: Founder of Texas, 1793–1836.* New York: Da Capo, 1968. Massive account of Austin's efforts to establish the colony and Republic of Texas.

Barrows, Edward M. *The Great Commodore: The Exploits of Matthew Calbraith Perry.* Indianapolis, IN: Bobbs-Merrill, 1935. Dated but still good biography of Perry.

Bauer, K. Jack. *Zachary Taylor: Soldier; Planter, Statesman of the Old Southwest.* Baton Rouge: Louisiana State University Press, 1985. Excellent biography that analyzes Taylor's military career and short, though pivotal, presidency.

Bemis, Samuel Flagg. *John Quincy Adams and the Union.* New York: Alfred A. Knopf, 1970. Good examination of Adams' opposition to the Mexican-American War.

Bergeron, Paul H. *The Presidency of James K. Polk.* Lawrence: University of Kansas Press, 1987. Well-researched look at Polk's eventful presidency.

Callcott, Wilfrid H. *Santa Anna: The Story of an Enigma Who Once Was Mexico.* Norman: University of Oklahoma Press, 1936. Places Santa Anna's life amid the turbulence of Mexican politics during its first half century after independence. Sees him as having little or no principles.

Campbell, Randolph, and Oscar Handlin. *Sam Houston and the American Southwest.* New York: HarperCollins, 1993. New York: Longman, 2002. Part of Library of American Biography series that examines Sam Houston's life in the light of American expansion.

Cantrell, Gregg. *Stephen F. Austin: Impresario of Texas.* New Haven: Yale University Press, 1999. Scholarly examination of Austin's mission to colonize Texas and to protect his creation.

Capers, Gerald M. *John C. Calhoun: Opportunist, A Reappraisal.* Gainesville: University of Florida Press, 1960. Generally negative look at Calhoun's political career.

Chitwood, Oliver Perry. *John Tyler: Champion of the Old South.* New York: D. Appleton-Century, 1939. Largely focuses on Tyler's presidency with a good discussion of the efforts to annex Texas.

Claiborne, J.F.H. *Life and Correspondence of John A. Quitman.* New York: Harper & Brothers, 1960. Older look at a colorful expansionist.

Clarke, Dwight L. *Stephen Watts Kearny: Soldier of the West.* Norman: University of Oklahoma Press, 1961. Excellent biography of this agent of American expansion.

Cleaves, Freeman. *Meade of Gettysburg.* Norman: University of Oklahoma Press, 1960. Dated but still definitive biography of Meade.

Coit, Margaret L. *John C. Calhoun: American Portrait.* Boston: Houghton Mifflin Company, 1950. Laudatory, but well-researched biography of Calhoun.

Cutrer, Thomas W. *Ben McCulloch and the Frontier Military Tradition.* Chapel Hill: University of North Carolina Press, 1993. Solid biography of a colorful frontier figure who fought in the Texas War for Independence, the Mexican-American War, and the Civil War.

Cuttings, Elizabeth. *Jefferson Davis: Political Soldier.* New York: Dodd, Mead, 1930. Examination of how Davis' political career was tied to his military service.

De Bruhl, Marshall. *Sword of San Jacinto: A Life of Sam Houston.* New York: Random House, 1993. Highly readable, laudatory account of Houston's life.

Donald, David. *Lincoln.* New York: Simon & Schuster, 1995. Definitive one-volume biography of Lincoln.

Drexler, R. W. *Guilty of Making Peace: A Biography of Nicholas P. Trist.* Lanham, MD: University Press of America, 1991. Brief biography of U.S. government's peace commissioner.

Duncan, Robert L. *Reluctant General: The Life and Times of Albert Pike.* New York: Dutton, 1961. Interesting biography about a pioneer entrepreneur who fought in Mexican-American War and Civil War.

Dyer, Brainerd. *Zachary Taylor.* New York: Barnes and Noble, 1946. Standard biography of Old Rough and Ready.

Egan, Ferol. *Frémont: Explorer for a Restless Nation.* New York: Doubleday, 1977. Detailed biography of Frémont with an emphasis on his explorations.

Eisenhower, John S. D. *Agent of Destiny: The Life and Times of General Winfield Scott.* Reprint, Norman: University of Oklahoma Press, 1999. Engagingly written biography of the early nineteenth century's greatest soldier.

Elliott, Charles W. *Winfield Scott: The Soldier and the Man.* New York: Macmillan, 1937. Detailed biography of Scott.

Fowler, Will. *Tornel and Santa Anna: The Writer and the Caudillo, Mexico, 1795–1853.* Westport, CT: Greenwood Press, 2000. Discusses how the lives of these men were intertwined and analyzes the importance of José María Tornel y Mendívil's influence on Mexican development.

Freeman, Douglas Southall. *R. E. Lee.* 4 vols. New York: Charles Scribner's Sons, 1934. Laudatory though extremely detailed biography of Lee.

Fuentes Mares, José. *Santa Anna: El Hombre.* 6th ed. Mexico: Grijalbo, 1982. Solid, Spanish language biography of Santa Anna.

Fuess, Claude M. *The Life of Caleb Cushing.* 2 vols. New York: Harcourt Brace, 1923. Detailed look at the political and military career of this political general. Volume 2 discusses his role in Mexico.

Gambrell, Herbert. *Anson Jones: The Last President of Texas.* Austin: University of Texas Press, 1964. Solid examination of one of the men who brought Texas into the United States.

Going, Charles B. *David Wilmot: Free Soiler.* New York: D. Appleton-Century, 1924. Older biography of the congressman who tried to prohibit slavery in territories acquired from Mexico.

Govan, Gilbert E. *A Different Valor: The Story of General Joseph E. Johnston.* Indianapolis, IN: Bobbs-Merrill, 1956. Older biography that details Johnston's role in the Mexico City campaign.

Guild, Thelma S., and Harvey L. Carter. *Kit Carson: A Pattern for Heroes.* Lincoln: University of Nebraska Press, 1984. Exciting, balanced biography of the great mountain man.

Hague, Harlan, and David J. Langum. *Thomas O. Larkin: A Life of Patriotism and Profit in Old California.* Norman: University of Oklahoma Press, 1990. Interesting biography of the American consul and agent in California.

Haley, James L. *Sam Houston.* Norman: University of Oklahoma Press, 2002. Intimate look at Houston's entire life.

Hamilton, Holman. *Zachary Taylor.* 2 vols. Indianapolis, IN: Bobbs-Merrill, 1941–1951. Detailed look at Taylor's life with good sections on military career.

Handlin, Lilian. *George Bancroft: The Intellectual as Democrat.* New York: Harper & Row, 1984. Interesting look at Bancroft's role as secretary of the navy.

Hanighen, Frank C. *Santa Anna: The Napoleon of the West.* New York: Coward-McCann, 1934. Dated but very detailed biography of Santa Anna. For popular audiences.

Hartje, Robert G. *Van Dorn: The Life and Times of a Confederate General.* Nashville: Vanderbilt University Press, 1967. Lively look at the life of this Jefferson Davis protégé.

Haynes, Sam W. *James K. Polk and the Expansionist Impulse.* New York: Longman, 1997. Places Polk in the context of Manifest Destiny.

Hebert, Walter H. *Fighting Joe Hooker.* Indianapolis, IN: Bobbs-Merrill, 1944. Still the best biography of Hooker.

Hughes, Nathaniel C., Jr. *General William J. Hardee: Old Reliable.* Baton Rouge: Louisiana State University Press, 1965. Definitive biography of Hardee.

Good coverage of Hardee's experiences in Mexico including his time as a prisoner of war.

Hughes, Nathaniel C., Jr., and Roy P. Stonesifer Jr. *The Life and Wars of Gideon J. Pillow*. Chapel Hill: University of North Carolina Press, 1993. Interesting account of Pillow's battles with Winfield Scott.

Hughes, William J. *Rebellious Ranger: Rip Ford and the Old Southwest*. Norman: University of Oklahoma Press, 1964. Biography of an early Texan who came from Tennessee to fight in the Texas Revolution and became one of Texas' most adventurous pioneers.

James, Marquis. *Andrew Jackson: Portrait of a President*. New York: Grosset & Dunlap, 1937. Positive look at Jackson's presidency, including his dealings with Texas.

———. *The Raven: A Biography of Sam Houston*. Indianapolis, IN: Bobbs-Merrill, 1929. Excellent, though somewhat dated, biography of the hero of the Texas Revolution.

Johnson, Timothy D. *Winfield Scott: The Quest for Military Glory*. Lawrence: University Press of Kansas, 1998. A thorough analysis of Scott's military career and his impact on the U.S. military.

Jones, Oakah L., Jr. *Santa Anna*. New York: Twayne Publishers, 1968. Straightforward biography in Rulers and Statesmen of the World series.

Kiefer, Charles L. *Maligned General: The Biography of Thomas Sidney Jesup*. San Rafael, CA: Presidio Press, 1979. Positive appraisal of Jesup's career.

Klein, Philip S. *President James Buchanan: A Biography*. University Park: Pennsylvania State University Press, 1962. Largely positive biography of Buchanan, who served as Polk's secretary of state.

Launius, Roger D. *Alexander William Doniphan: Portrait of a Missouri Moderate*. Columbia: University of Missouri Press, 1997. Comprehensive biography of Doniphan's career.

Lewis, Lloyd. *Captain Sam Grant*. Boston: Little, Brown, 1950. Looks at Grant's life up to the Civil War with good coverage of his service in the Mexican-American War.

Lewis, Paul. *Yankee Admiral: A Biography of David Dixon Porter*. New York: D. McKay Company, 1968. Biography of the naval officer who commanded the landing party that secured Fort Tabasco.

May, Robert E. *John A. Quitman: Old South Crusader*. Baton Rouge: Louisiana State University Press, 1985. Standard biography of Mexican-American War general and proponent of national expansion.

McKinley, Silas Bent. *Old Rough and Ready: The Life and Times of Zachary Taylor*. New York: Vanguard Press, 1946. Standard biography with good description of his Mexican-American War experience.

McKinney, Francis F. *Education in Violence: The Life of George H. Thomas and the Army of the Cumberland.* Detroit: Wayne State University Press, 1961. Comprehensive biography of Thomas with short section on his Mexican-American War activities.

Morgan, Robert J. *A Whig Embattled: The Presidency Under John Tyler.* Lincoln: University of Nebraska Press, 1954. Old but interesting look at Tyler's conflict-ridden presidency.

Morison, Samuel Eliot. *"Old Bruin": Commodore Matthew Calbraith Perry.* Boston: Little, Brown, 1967. Good coverage of Perry's time as commander of the Gulf Squadron during the Mexican-American War.

Nevins, Allan. *Frémont: Pathmarker of the West.* New York: Harper & Brothers, 1928. Reprint, Lincoln: University of Nebraska Press, 1992. Admiring but well-researched and well-written biography.

Nichols, Roy Franklin. *Franklin Pierce: Young Hickory of the Granite Hills.* Philadelphia: University of Pennsylvania Press, 1958. Definitive biography of New England expansionist and Mexican-American War volunteer general.

Niven, John. *John C. Calhoun and the Price of Union.* Baton Rouge: Louisiana State University Press, 1988. Balanced biography that explores the seeming conflict in Calhoun's political life.

Nye, Russell B. *George Bancroft: Brahmin Rebel.* New York: Alfred A. Knopf, 1944. Short section on Bancroft's role as secretary of the navy during the war.

Ohrt, Wallace. *Defiant Peacemaker: Nicholas Trist in the Mexican War.* College Station: Texas A&M University Press, 1997. Full biography of Trist with a focus on his peacemaking activities during the war.

Olivera, Ruth R., and Liliane Crété. *Life in Mexico Under Santa Anna, 1822–1855.* Norman: University of Oklahoma Press, 1991. The ups and mostly downs of Santa Anna's impact on Mexico.

Parks, Joseph H. *General Edmund Kirby Smith, C.S.A.* Baton Rouge: Louisiana State University Press, 1954. Contains short section on Kirby Smith's Mexican War experiences.

Patrick, Rembert W. *Aristocrat in Uniform: General Duncan L. Clinch.* Gainesville: University of Florida Press, 1963. Definitive biography of Clinch.

Peterson, Norma Lois. *The Presidencies of William Henry Harrison and John Tyler.* Lawrence: University Press of Kansas, 1989. Revisionist look at importance of Tyler's presidency.

Porte, Joel. *Representative Man: Ralph Waldo Emerson in His Time.* New York: Oxford University Press, 1979. Good analysis of Emerson's importance in American society.

Rea, Ralph R. *Sterling Price: The Lee of the West.* Little Rock, AR: Pioneer Press, 1959. Biography of Missouri Volunteer officer with emphasis on his Civil War career.

Remini, Robert V. *Andrew Jackson and the Course of American Democracy, 1833–1845.* New York: Harper & Row, 1984. Laudatory look at Jackson's latter years and his role in American expansion.

Richards, Leonard L. *The Life and Times of Congressman John Quincy Adams.* New York: Oxford University Press, 1986. Interesting study of Adams' congressional career and opposition to the Mexican-American War.

Roberts, David. *A New World: Kit Carson, John C. Frémont, and the Claiming of the American West.* New York: Simon & Schuster, 2000. Holds that these two explorers were responsible for United States gaining the Southwest and California.

Robertson, James I. *Stonewall Jackson: The Man, the Soldier, the Legend.* New York: Macmillan, 1997. Definitive biography of Jackson.

Roland, Charles P. *Albert Sidney Johnston.* Austin: University of Texas Press, 1964. Excellent biography of man who fought for three republics.

Scheina, Robert L. *Santa Anna: A Curse Upon Mexico.* Washington, DC: Brassey's, 2002. Short, uneven look at Santa Anna's career.

Sears, Louis Martin. *John Slidell.* Durham: Duke University Press, 1925. Dated but good biography of U.S. diplomat.

Sears, Stephen. *George B. McClellan: The Young Napoleon.* New York: Ticknor & Fields, 1988. Balanced portrait of McClellan with good section on his Mexican-American War career.

Sellers, Charles Grier. *James K. Polk: Continentalist, 1843–1846.* Princeton: Princeton University Press, 1966. Examination of Polk's political career with an emphasis on his run for the presidency to the outbreak of the Mexican-American War.

Shalhope, Robert E. *Sterling Price: Portrait of a Southerner.* Columbia: University of Missouri Press, 1971. Details how Price's military life was influenced by Missouri politics.

Shenton, James P. *Robert John Walker: A Politician from Jackson to Lincoln.* New York: Columbia University Press, 1961. Good biography of Polk's secretary of the treasury.

Smiley, David L. *Lion of White Hall: The Life of Cassius M. Clay.* Madison: University of Wisconsin Press, 1962. Looks at role of a Mexican-American War volunteer officer.

Smith, Elbert B. *The Magnificent Missourian: The Life of Thomas Hart Benton.* Philadelphia: J. B. Lippincott, 1958. Good biography of one of Polk's important Democratic allies in Congress.

Spencer, Ivor D. *The Victor and the Spoils: A Life of William L. Marcy.* Providence: Brown University Press, 1959. Solid biography of Polk's secretary of war.

Thomas, Emory. *Robert E. Lee: A Biography*. New York: W. W. Norton, 1995. Excellent one-volume biography of Lee.

Wallace, Edward S. *General William Jenkins Worth: Monterey's Forgotten Hero*. Dallas: Southern Methodist University Press, 1953. Very positive biography of Scott's difficult subordinate.

Wessels, William L. *Born to Be a Soldier: The Military Career of William Wing Loring of St. Augustine, Florida*. Fort Worth: Texas Christian University Press, 1971. Entire chapter on Loring's Mexican War adventures.

West, Richard S., Jr. *The Second Admiral: A Life of David Dixon Porter, 1813–1891*. New York: Coward-McCann, 1937. Short section on Porter's exploits in the Mexican-American War.

Williams, John Hoyt. *Sam Houston: The Life and Times of the Liberator of Texas, an Authentic American Hero*. New York: Simon & Schuster, 1993. Flattering portrait of Sam Houston.

Williams, T. Harry. *P.G.T. Beauregard: Napoleon in Gray*. Baton Rouge: Louisiana State University Press, 1954. Excellent biography of one of Scott's engineering officers and later Confederate general.

Wiltse, Charles M. *John C. Calhoun: Sectionalist, 1840–1850*. New York: Bobbs-Merrill, 1951. Deals briefly with Calhoun's opposition to the war.

Young, Otis E. *The West of Philip St. George Cooke, 1809–1895*. Glendale, CA: Arthur H. Clark, 1955. Three chapters on Cooke's involvement with the Army of the West.

Zollinger, James P. *Sutter: The Man and His Empire*. Gloucester, MA: P. Smith, 1967. A look at the importance of American settlement in California in securing the territory for the United States.

Campaigns and Battles

Dawson, Joseph G., III. *Doniphan's Epic March: The 1st Missouri Volunteers in the Mexican War*. Lawrence: University Press of Kansas, 1999. Looks at how Doniphan's leadership style brought success to the 1st Missouri.

Frost, John. *The Mexican War and Its Warriors: Comprising a Complete History of All the Operations of the American Armies in Mexico, with Biographical Sketches and Anecdotes of the Most Distinguished Officers in the Regular Army and Volunteer Force*. Bowie, MD: Heritage Books, 1989. Facsimile of 1850 ed. An effort to combine many of the postwar accounts of the conflict.

Haecker, Charles M., and Jeffrey G. Mauck. *On the Prairie of Palo Alto*. College Station: Texas A&M University Press, 1997. A detailed look at the historical archaeology of the battlefield.

Lavender, David S. *Climax at Buena Vista: The American Campaigns in Northeastern Mexico, 1846–47*. Philadelphia: J. B. Lippincott, 1966. Brief, popular account of the battle.

Nichols, Edward J. *Zach Taylor's Little Army*. Garden City, NY: Doubleday, 1963. Good account of Taylor's campaigns with useful maps.

Oliva, Leo E. *Soldiers on the Santa Fe Trail*. Norman: University of Oklahoma Press, 1967. Impact of the war on commerce along the Santa Fe Trail.

Twitchell, Ralph E. *The Conquest of Santa Fe, 1846*. Edited by Bill Tate. Truchas, NM: Tate Gallery, 1967. Comprehensive account of Kearny's Santa Fe campaign.

———. *The History of the Military Occupation of the Territory of New Mexico from 1846 to 1851*. Chicago: Rio Grande Press, 1963. Very detailed look at the campaign to take Santa Fe and the subsequent occupation and pacification.

Walker, Dale L. *Bear Flag Rising: The Conquest of California, 1846*. New York: Forge, 1999. Comprehensive look at the complex social dynamic that produced the Bear Flag Revolt.

Waugh, John C. *The Class of 1846: From West Point to Appomattox, Stonewall Jackson, George McClellan, and Their Brothers*. New York: Warner Books, 1994. Parallel biographies of the men from this outstanding class who saw their first combat in the Mexican-American War.

Causes

Brack, Gene M. *Mexico Views Manifest Destiny, 1821–1846: An Essay on the Origins of the Mexican War*. Albuquerque: University of New Mexico Press, 1975. Examines how Mexico was forced into war to protect its territory.

McAfee, Ward, and J. Cordell Robinson, comp. *Origins of the Mexican War: A Documentary Source Book*. 2 vols. Salisbury, NC: Documentary Publications, 1982. Good collection of primary sources on the causes of the war.

Price, Glenn W. *Origins of the War with Mexico: The Polk-Stockton Intrigue*. Austin: University of Texas Press, 1967. Seeks to prove that Polk conspired to persuade Texas to make war on Mexico before annexation so that when annexation occurred, Polk could use the war as a pretext to take California.

Ruiz, Ramon E. *The Mexican War: Was It Manifest Destiny?* New York: Holt, Rinehart and Winston, 1963. Anthology of writings on the war that largely blames the United States for the conflict.

Diplomacy

Callahan, James M. *American Foreign Policy in Mexican Relations.* New York: Macmillan, 1932. Straightforward look at U.S. State Department relations with Mexico.

Griswold del Castillo, Richard. *The Treaty of Guadalupe Hidalgo: A Legacy of Conflict.* Norman: University of Oklahoma Press, 1990. Examination of impact of treaty on Mexico and the United States.

Grivas, Theodore. *Military Governments in California, 1846–1850, with a Chapter on Their Prior Use in Louisiana, Florida, and New Mexico.* Glendale, CA: Arthur H. Clark, 1963. Sees American military governments as successful and beneficial to California.

Pletcher, David. *The Diplomacy of Annexation: Texas, Oregon, and the Mexican War.* Columbia: University of Missouri Press, 1975. Examines United States–British–Mexican relations.

Expansion

Billington, Ray Allen. *The Far Western Frontier, 1830–1860.* Albuquerque: University of New Mexico Press, 1956. A classic account of U.S. settlement of the far West.

Binkley, William C. *The Expansionist Movement in Texas.* Berkeley: University of California Press, 1925. Good look at the importance of Texas in the conflict with Texas.

Heidler, David S., and Jeanne T. Heidler. *Manifest Destiny.* Westport, CT: Greenwood Press, 2003. Overview through essays on stages of U.S. expansion through the Mexican-American War.

Hyslop, Stephen G. *Bound for Santa Fe: The Road to New Mexico and the American Conquest, 1806–1848.* Norman: University of Oklahoma Press, 2002. Vivid account of how Americans came to dominate the region.

Merk, Frederick. *Manifest Destiny and Mission in American History: A Reinterpretation.* New York: Alfred A. Knopf, 1963. Examines public expressions, primarily newspapers and pamphlets, of the spirit of Manifest Destiny.

Films

American Adventure. Television series. Produced by Dallas County Community College District. 1998; Austin, TX: Public Broadcasting System. Episode 15 examines Manifest Destiny in the United States.

The Battle of the Alamo. Videocassette. Produced by Arthur Drooker. 1992; United States: Arts and Entertainment Network. Contemporary pictures and interviews with scholars about the importance of the Alamo in American history.

Expansionism. Videocassette. Produced by William Hewitt. 1996; Bala Cynwyd, PA: Schlessinger Video Productions. Examination of American expansionism from the early nineteenth century through the Mexican-American War.

Manifest Destiny. Videocassette. Produced by Paul Bosner. 1987; Mesquite, TX: RMI Media Productions. Looks at westward expansion as a cause of the war.

The San Patricios. Videocassette. Produced by Mark R. Day. 1996; Vista, CA: San Patricio Productions. Looks at role of U.S. Army deserters who fought for Mexico.

Texas and the Mexican Cession. Videocassette. 1990; Chicago: Encyclopaedia Britannica Educational Corporation. Short video on role of Texas in provoking the war.

The U.S.-Mexican War (1846–1848). Videocassette. Robert Tranchin. 1998; Dallas, TX: KERA and Public Broadcasting System. Views war as one of aggression on the part of the United States.

General

Bauer, K. Jack. *The Mexican War, 1846–1848.* Lincoln: University of Nebraska Press, 1974. Standard history that compares opposition to the Mexican War to opposition during Vietnam.

Bill, Alfred H. *Rehearsal for Conflict: The War with Mexico, 1846–1848.* New York: Alfred A. Knopf, 1947. Popular account for general readers.

Chalfant, William Y. *Dangerous Passage: The Santa Fe Trail and the Mexican War.* Norman: University of Oklahoma Press, 1994. Looks at the trail as the path for Manifest Destiny.

Chidsey, Donald B. *The War with Mexico.* New York: Crown, 1968. Short overview of the war.

Clendenen, Clarence C. *Blood on the Border: The United States Army and the Mexican Irregulars.* New York: Macmillan, 1969. How Mexican guerrillas attempted to disrupt American military operations.

Cline, Howard F. *The United States and Mexico.* Cambridge: Cambridge University Press, 1953. Good section on Mexican-American relations before and during the war.

Coffman, Edward M. *The Old Army: A Portrait of the American Army in Peace Time, 1784–1898.* New York: Oxford University Press, 1986. Excellent social history of the nineteenth-century U.S. Army.

Connor, Seymour V., and Odie B. Faulk. *North America Divided: The Mexican War, 1846–1848.* New York: Oxford University Press, 1971. Attempts to look at both sides of the war and blames both Mexico and the United States for starting the conflict.

Cuncliffe, Marcus. *Soldiers & Civilians: The Martial Spirit in America, 1775–1865*. Boston: Little, Brown, 1968. Small section on how Mexican-American War influenced American military developments.

DeVoto, Bernard. *The Year of Decision, 1846*. Boston: Little, Brown, 1943. Fascinating look at U.S. activities in the Southwest in the first year of the war.

Eisenhower, John S. D. *So Far from God: The U.S. War with Mexico, 1846–1848*. New York: Random House, 1989. Sweeping narrative history of the war.

Faulk, Odie B., and Joseph A. Stout, eds. *The Mexican War: Changing Interpretations*. Chicago: Sage Press, 1973. Collection of the journal articles that take different approaches to the war.

Francaviglia, Richard V., and Douglas Richmond. *Dueling Eagles: A Reinterpretation of the Mexican-American War, 1846–1848*. Fort Worth: Texas Christian University Press, 2000. Essays by leading American and Mexican historians on different aspects of the war.

Harlow, Neal. *California Conquered: War and Peace on the Pacific, 1846–1850*. Berkeley: University of California Press, 1982. Detailed look at U.S. conquest of California.

Johannsen, Robert W. *To the Halls of Montezuma: The Mexican War in the American Imagination*. New York: Oxford University Press, 1985. Examination of American perceptions of the Mexican-American War.

Mahin, Dean B. *Olive Branch and Sword: The United States and Mexico, 1845–1848*. Jefferson, NC: McFarland & Company, 1997. Diplomatic history of the war.

Nevin, David, and the Editors of Time-Life Books. *The Mexican War*. Alexandria, VA: Time-Life Books, 1978. Well-illustrated popular account of the war.

Peterson, Charles J. *Peterson's American Wars: A History of the Wars of the United States Containing a History of the Revolution and of the Wars of 1812 and Mexico, with Biographical Sketches of All the Prominent American Military Heroes Engaged in Those Wars*. Philadelphia: J. B. Smith, 1854. Section on Mexican-American War very anti-Mexican in interpretation.

Richmond, Douglas W., ed. *Essays on the Mexican War*. College Station: Texas A&M University Press, 1986. Good collection of essays on several aspects of the war by some of the best historians of the conflict from the Walter Prescott Webb Memorial Lectures.

Ripley, Roswell S. *The War with Mexico*. 2 vols. New York: Harper & Brothers, 1849. Good contemporary history of the war by man who served as a major during the conflict.

Rives, George L. *The United States and Mexico, 1821–1848: A History of the Relations between the Two Countries from the Independence of Mexico to the Close of the War with the United States.* 2 vols. New York: Charles Scribner's Sons, 1913. Dated but still excellent look at diplomacy between the United States and Mexico.

Selby, John M. *The Eagle and the Serpent: The Spanish and American Invasions of Mexico, 1519 and 1846.* New York: Hippocrene Books, 1978. A comparison of Cortes' invasion of Mexico with the Mexican-American War.

Singletary, Otis A. *The Mexican War.* Chicago: University of Chicago Press, 1960. Short, straightforward narrative of the war.

Skelton, William B. *An American Profession of Arms: The Army Officer Corps, 1784–1861.* Lawrence: University Press of Kansas, 1992. A comprehensive look at the development of the American officer corps.

Smith, Justin H. *The War with Mexico.* 2 vols. New York: Macmillan, 1919. The most comprehensive treatment of the war.

Stephanson, Anders. *Manifest Destiny: American Expansionism and the Empire of Right.* New York: Hill and Wang, 1995. Short, provocative look at American expansionism through the twentieth century.

Stephenson, Nathaniel W. *Texas and the Mexican War: A Chronicle of the Winning of the Southwest.* New Haven: Yale University Press, 1921. Nice overview in older Chronicles of America series.

Weems, John Edward. *To Conquer a Peace: The War between the United States and Mexico.* College Station: Texas A&M University Press, 1974. Colorful account of the war that sees the conflict as leading to the Civil War.

Weinberg, Albert Katz. *Manifest Destiny: A Study of Nationalist Expansionism in American History.* Gloucester, MA: P. Smith, 1958. Dated but excellent overview of the movement.

Winders, Richard B. *Mr. Polk's Army: The American Military Experience in the Mexican War.* College Station: Texas A&M University Press, 1997. Examines the social and cultural origins of the American army in Mexico.

Home Front

Fuller, John D. P. *The Movement for the Acquisition of All Mexico, 1846–1848.* Baltimore: Johns Hopkins Press, 1936. Looks at how actions of Nicholas Trist prevented the movement to acquire all of Mexico from being successful.

Lander, Ernest M., Jr. *Reluctant Imperialists: Calhoun, the South Carolinians, and the Mexican War.* Baton Rouge: Louisiana State University Press, 1980. Examines difficulties in South Carolina occasioned by the state's general support of the war and the opposition of its favorite son, John C. Calhoun, to the war.

Schroeder, John H. *Mr. Polk's War: American Opposition and Dissent, 1846–1848.* Madison: University of Wisconsin Press, 1973. Examination of peace movements during Mexican-American War.

Mexico

Anna, Timothy E. *Forging Mexico: 1821–1835.* Lincoln: University of Nebraska Press, 1998. A well-informed examination of the pivotal struggle between federalism and centralism in the formative years of the Mexican Republic.

Bazant, Jan. *A Concise History of Mexico from Hidalgo to Cárdenas, 1805–1940.* New York: Cambridge University Press, 1977. Short section of the war from the Mexican viewpoint.

Bethell, Leslie, ed. *Spanish America After Independence, c. 1820–c. 1870.* New York: Cambridge University Press, 1987. A region-by-region look at the impact of independence throughout Latin America.

Brack, Gene M. *Mexico Views Manifest Destiny, 1821–1846: An Essay on the Origins of the Mexican War.* Albuquerque: University of New Mexico Press, 1975. Evolution of Mexican hostility toward the United States.

Costeloe, Michael P. *The Central Republic in Mexico, 1835–1846: Hombres de Bien in the Age of Santa Anna.* New York: Cambridge University Press, 1993. Explanation of why centralism failed in the Mexican government.

Lynch, John. *Caudillos in Spanish America, 1800–1850.* New York: Oxford University Press, 1992. Case studies of four important military/political leaders in Latin America, including Antonio López de Santa Anna.

Pitt, Leonard. *The Decline of the Californios.* Berkeley: University of California Press, 1971. One chapter looks at impact of the war on the Californios.

Robinson, Cecil, ed. *The View from Chapultepec: Mexican Writers on the Mexican-American War.* Tucson: University of Arizona Press, 1989. A collection of contemporary Mexican writings on the war as well analyses of shifting interpretations of the conflict.

Santoni, Pedro. *Mexicans at Arms: Puro Federalists and the Politics of War, 1845–1848.* Fort Worth: Texas Christian University Press, 1996. Analyzes the complicated political situation in Mexico during the Mexican-American War.

Van Young, Eric. *The Other Rebellion: Popular Violence, Ideology, and the Mexican Struggle for Independence, 1810–1821.* Stanford: Stanford University Press, 2001. Attempt to explain Mexican independence movement in the context of world events and the internal dynamic in Mexico.

Weber, David. *The Mexican Frontier, 1821–1846: The American Southwest Under Mexico.* Albuquerque: University of New Mexico Press, 1982. A look at those territories acquired by the United States in the Mexican-American War in the years preceding the war.

Naval Operations

Bauer, K. Jack. *Surfboats and Horse Marines: U.S. Naval Operations in the Mexican War*. Annapolis: U.S. Naval Institute Press, 1969. Comprehensive naval history of the war.

Slagle, Jay. *Ironclad Captain: Seth Ledyard Phelps & the U.S. Navy, 1841–1864*. Kent, OH: Kent State University Press, 1996. Look at the naval war through actions of a junior officer.

Personal Narratives, Letters, Documents

Adams, John Quincy. *Memoirs of John Quincy Adams: Comprising Portions of His Diary from 1795 to 1848*. 12 vols. Edited by Worthington Chauncey Ford. Philadelphia: J. B. Lippincott, 1874–1877. Intimate look at Adams' views on a wide range of political subjects, including expansion and the conflict with Mexico.

Alcaraz, Ramon. *The Other Side: Notes for the History of the War between Mexico and the United States*. Translated and edited by Albert C. Ramsey. New York: John Wiley, 1850. Contemporary Mexican view of the war that sees the United States as the aggressor.

Anderson, Robert. *An Artillery Officer in the Mexican War, 1846–1847: Letters of Robert Anderson*. Edited by E. A. Lawton. New York: G. P. Putnam's Sons, 1911. Standard source from perspective of artillery officer who would go on to surrender Fort Sumter to the Confederacy.

Ballentine, George. *Autobiography of an English Soldier in the United States Army*. New York: Stringer and Townsend, 1853. Well-educated British immigrant who joined the U.S. Army and participated in Scott's Mexico City campaign.

Beauregard, P.G.T. *With Beauregard in Mexico: The Mexican War Reminiscences of P.G.T. Beauregard*. Edited by T. Harry Williams. Baton Rouge: Louisiana State University Press, 1956. Recollections of one of Scott's top engineers.

Benton, Thomas H. *Thirty Years' View: Or, A History of the Working of the American Government for Thirty Years, from 1820 to 1850*. 2 vols. New York: D. Appleton-Century, 1956. Memoirs by one of the most important politicians of the day.

Brewerton, G. D. *Overland with Kit Carson: A Narrative of the Old Spanish Trail in '48*. Lincoln: University of Nebraska Press, 1993. Good firsthand accounts of adventures in the Southwest.

Carter, Harvey L., ed. *"Dear Old Kit": The Historical Christopher Carson.* Norman: University of Oklahoma Press, 1990. Newer edition of Carson's memoirs.

Castaneda, Carlos Eduardo, ed. *The Mexican Side of the Texan Revolution (1836) by the Chief Mexican Participants, General Antonio Lopez de Santa-Anna, D. Ramon Martinez Caro . . . General Vicente Filisola, General Jose Urrea, General Jose Maria Tornel.* Dallas, TX: Turner, 1928. Collection of firsthand accounts from Mexican perspective.

Chamberlain, Samuel E. *My Confession: The Recollections of a Rogue.* New York: Harper, 1956; reprint edition. Lincoln: University of Nebraska Press, 1987. Exciting adventures of one of U.S. Army's most colorful characters.

Cooke, Philip St. George. *The Conquest of New Mexico and California: An Historical & Personal Narrative.* Oakland, CA: Biobooks, 1952. Firsthand look at these events through the eyes of the commander of the Mormon Battalion.

Coulter, Richard. *Volunteers: The Mexican War Journals of Private Richard Coulter and Sergeant Thomas Barclay, Company E, Second Pennsylvania Infantry.* Edited by Allan Peskin. Kent, OH: Kent State University Press, 1991. Two young attorneys' personal accounts of Scott's Mexico City campaign.

Craven, Tunis A. M. *A Naval Campaign in the Californias, 1846–1849: The Journal of Lieutenant Tunis Augustus Macdonough Craven, U.S.N. United States Sloop of War.* San Francisco: Book Club of California, 1973. Very personal journal, intended only for the eyes of the writer's wife, by a young naval officer in the California theater.

Curtis, Samuel R. *Mexico Under Fire: Being the Diary of Samuel Ryan Curtis, 3rd Ohio Volunteer Regiment, during the American Military Occupation of Northern Mexico, 1846–1847.* Edited by Joseph E. Chance. Fort Worth: Texas Christian University Press, 1994. Regular officer's impressions of the chaos of American camps along the Rio Grande.

Cutts, James M. *The Conquest of California and New Mexico, by the Forces of the United States, in the Years 1846 & 1847.* Albuquerque: Horn & Wallace, 1965. Reprint of the 1847 ed. published by Carey & Hart, Philadelphia. Collection of official letters and speeches.

Dana, Napoleon J. T. *Monterrey is Ours! The Mexican War Letters of Lieutenant Dana, 1845–1847.* Edited by Robert H. Ferrell. Lexington: University Press of Kentucky, 1990. Candid impressions of a young officer in letters home.

Doubleday, Abner. *My Life in the Old Army: The Reminiscences of Abner Doubleday, From the Collections of the New York Historical Society.* Edited by Joseph E. Chance. Fort Worth: Texas Christian University Press, 1998. Large section on Doubleday's activities in the Mexican-American War.

Doubleday, Rhoda van Bibber Tanner, ed. *Journals of the Late Brevet Major Philip Norbourne Barbour, Captain in the 3rd Regiment, United States Infantry, and His Wife, Martha Isabella Hopkins Barbour, Written during the War with Mexico, 1846.* New York, London: G. P. Putnam's Sons, 1936. Interesting account of the first months of the war before Captain Barbour's death in the battle for Monterrey.

Downey, Joseph T. *The Cruise of the Portsmouth, 1845–1847: A Sailor's View of the Naval Conquest of California.* Edited by Howard Lamar. New Haven: Yale University Press, 1958. Excellent firsthand account of the California theater from the perspective of an enlisted sailor.

Edwards, Frank S. *A Campaign in New Mexico.* Ann Arbor: University Microfilms, 1966. Exciting account of soldier's trek on the Santa Fe Trail and as part of Doniphan's march.

Elliott, Richard S. *The Mexican War Correspondence of Richard Smith Elliott.* Edited by Mark L. Gardner and Marc Simmons. Norman: University of Oklahoma Press, 1997. Informative collection of letters written for newspaper publication by one of Kearny's Missouri volunteers.

Ford, John Salmon. *Rip Ford's Texas.* Austin: University of Texas Press, 1963. Reminiscence of a Texas Ranger during the Republic and Texas statehood.

General Scott and His Staff: Comprising Memoirs of Generals Scott, Twiggs, Smith, Quitman, Shields, Pillow, Lane, Cadwalader, Patterson and Pierce; Colonels Childs, Riley, Harney, and Butler, and Other Distinguished Officers Attached to General Scott's Army. Philadelphia: Grigg, Elliot & Company, 1848. Good collection of primary sources.

Gibson, George R. *Over the Chihuahua and Santa Fe Trails, 1847–1848: George Rutledge Gibson's Journal.* Edited by Robert W. Frazer. Albuquerque: University of New Mexico Press, 1981. Very good journal of these expeditions by an officer who had been a journalist before the war.

Glasgow, Edward J., and William H. Glasgow. *Brothers on the Santa Fe and Chihuahua Trails.* Edited by Mark L. Gardner. Niwot: University Press of Colorado, 1993. Start of the war in the Southwest from the viewpoint of two traders.

Grant, Ulysses S. *Personal Memoirs of U. S. Grant.* 2 vols. New York: Charles L. Webster & Company, 1885–1886. One of the best presidential memoirs with an interesting perspective on the Mexican-American War.

Halleck, Henry W. *The Mexican War in Baja California: The Memorandum of Captain Henry W. Halleck Concerning His Expeditions in Lower California, 1846–1848.* Edited by Doyce B. Nunis Jr. Los Angeles: Dawson's Book Shop, 1977. Halleck's diary and commentary on his experiences in California during the Mexican-American War.

Henry, William S. *Campaign Sketches of the War with Mexico.* New York: Arno Press, 1973. Good firsthand account of the campaigns in northern Mexico.

Hitchcock, Ethan Allen. *Fifty Years in Camp and Field: Diary of Major General Ethan Allen Hitchcock, U.S.A.* Edited by W. A. Cruffut. Freeport, NY: Books for Libraries, 1971. Insightful memoir by one of the army's most observant officers.

Houston, Sam. *The Autobiography of Sam Houston.* Edited by Donald Day and Harry Herbert Ullom. Norman: University of Oklahoma Press, 1954. Reprint, Westport, CT: Greenwood, 1980. Interesting editorial job of arranging Houston's writings into an autobiography.

————. *The Personal Correspondence of Sam Houston.* 4 vols. Edited by Madge Thornal Roberts. Denton: University of North Texas Press, 1996–2001. Much of Houston's surviving correspondence up to his death in 1863 and some family letters after 1863.

Hughes, John T. *Doniphan's Expedition: An Account of the U.S. Army Operations in the Great Southwest.* Chicago: Rio Grande Press, 1962. Memoir of one of the participants of the Kearny and Doniphan expeditions in the Southwest.

Jenkins, John H. *The Papers of the Texas Revolution, 1835–1836.* 10 vols. Austin, TX: Presidial Press, 1973. Excellent collection of official papers of the revolution.

Johnston, Abraham R., Marcellus B. Edwards, and Philip G. Ferguson. *Marching with the Army of the West, 1846–1848.* Edited by Ralph P. Bieber. Glendale, CA: Arthur H. Clark, 1936. Three excellent journals by soldiers who marched with Kearny.

Jones, Anson. *Memoranda and Official Correspondence Relating to the Republic of Texas, Its History and Annexation; Including a Brief Autobiography of the Author.* Chicago: Rio Grande Press, 1966. Deals primarily with annexation concerns.

Kendall, George W. *Dispatches from the Mexican War.* Edited by Lawrence D. Cress. Norman: University of Oklahoma Press, 1999. Kendall's filings with the *New Orleans Picayune* about the progress of the war from the vantage of a newspaper correspondent.

Kirkham, Ralph W. *The Mexican War Journal and Letters of Ralph W. Kirkham.* Edited by Robert Ryal Miller. College Station: Texas A&M University Press, 1991. Excellent account by young officer of Mexico City campaign.

Laidley, Theodore. *Surrounded by Dangers of All Kinds: The Mexican War Letters of Lieutenant Theodore Laidley.* Edited by James M. McCaffrey. Denton: University of North Texas Press, 1997. Young officer's letters to his father while on the Mexico City campaign.

Magoffin, Susan S. *Down the Santa Fe Trail and into Mexico: The Diary of Susan Shelby Magoffin, 1846–1847.* Edited by Stella M. Drumm. New Haven: Yale University Press, 1962. Life on the trail for a trader's bride.

Manigault, Arthur M. *A Carolinian Goes to War: The Civil War Narrative of Arthur Middleton Manigault, Brigadier General, C.S.A . . . and with His Mexican War Narrative.* Edited by R. Lockwood Tower. Columbia: University of South Carolina Press, 1983. Good look by a junior officer at Scott's Mexico City campaign.

Parker, William H. *Recollections of a Naval Officer, 1841–1865.* Annapolis: U.S.: Naval Institute Press, 1985. Young midshipman's look at the naval war in the Gulf of Mexico.

Peck, John J. *The Sign of the Eagle: A View of Mexico, 1830 to 1855.* San Diego: Union-Tribune Publishing Company, 1970. Well-illustrated look at the situation in Mexico by a young American junior officer.

Peña, Jose Enrique de la. *With Santa Anna in Texas: A Personal Narrative of the Revolution.* Edited by Carmen Perry. College Station: Texas A&M University Press, 1975. Mexican officer's account of the fall of the Alamo. Interesting account of the death of Davy Crockett.

Polk, James K. *Correspondence of James K. Polk.* 9 vols. Edited by Herbert Weaver, Wayne Cutler, and Paul Bergeron. Nashville: Vanderbilt University Press, 1969–1996. Comprehensive collection of Polk letters.

————. *The Diary of James K. Polk during His Presidency, 1845–1849.* 4 vols. Chicago: McClurg, 1910. Comprehensive diary kept by Polk during his presidency.

————. *Polk: The Diary of a President, 1845–1849, Covering the Mexican War, the Acquistion of Oregon, and the Conquest of California and the Southwest.* Edited by Allan Nevins. London: Longmans, Green, 1952. Condensed and more usable version of Polk's diary.

Raat, W. Dirk, ed. *Mexico: From Independence to Revolution, 1810–1910.* Lincoln: University of Nebraska Press, 1982. Collection of primary documents from each period of Mexico's development.

Ramírez, José Fernando. *Mexico during the War with the United States.* Edited by Walter V. Scholes. Translated by Elliott B. Scherr. Columbia: University of Missouri Press, 1950. Account of the war by a member of the Mexican government.

Santa Anna, Antonio López de. *The Eagle: The Autobiography of Santa Anna.* Edited by Ann Fears Crawford. Austin, TX: Pemberton, 1967. Interesting view of American expansion through the eyes of Santa Anna.

Sargent, Chauncey F. *Gathering Laurels in Mexico: The Diary of an American Soldier in the Mexican American War.* Edited by Ann B. Janes. Lincoln, MA: Cottage Press, 1990. A look at the actions of a Pennsylvania volunteer in Mexico.

Scott, Winfield. *Memoirs of Lieut.-General Scott, LL.D. Written by Himself.* 2 vols. New York: Sheldon, 1864. Somewhat self-serving, but interesting, perspective on the nation, with informative views on war.

Smith, Franklin. *The Mexican War Journal of Captain Franklin Smith*. Edited by Joseph E. Chance. Jackson: University of Mississippi Press, 1991. Unusual firsthand account of the war in northern Mexico in that, rather than glorifying the war, it attempts to paint an accurate picture of American excesses.

Smith, George W., and Charles Judah, eds. *Chronicles of the Gringos: The U.S. Army in the Mexican War, 1846–1848, Accounts of Eyewitnesses & Combatants*. Albuquerque: University of New Mexico Press, 1968. American soldiers' accounts of the war.

Smith, Gustavus Woodson. *Company 'A' Corps of Engineers, U.S.A., 1846–1848, in the Mexican War*. Edited by Leonne M. Hudson. Kent, OH: Kent State University Press, 2001. Memoir by commander of Winfield Scott's most elite engineer unit.

Watson, Henry B. *The Journals of Marine Second Lieutenant Henry Bulls Watson, 1845–1848*. Edited by Charles R. Smith. Washington, DC: History & Museums Div., HQ, USMC, 1990. A look at the important role of the marines in Mexico.

Williams, Amelia W., and Eugene C. Barker. *The Writings of Sam Houston, 1813–1863*. 8 vols. Austin: University of Texas, 1938–1943. Large collection of Houston's writings.

Wise, Henry A. *Los Gringos: Or, An Inside View of Mexico and California*. New York: Baker and Scribner, 1849. A naval lieutenant's recollections of the war along the California and Mexican coasts.

Wortham, Thomas, ed. *James Russell Lowell's Bigelow Papers: A Critical Edition*. DeKalb: Northern Illinois University Press, 1977. Collections of major critic of the war with commentary.

Zeh, Frederick. *An Immigrant Soldier in the Mexican War*. Edited by William J. Orr and Robert Ryal Miller. Translated by William J. Orr. College Station: Texas A&M University Press, 1995. Recent American immigrant's perspective on the Mexico City campaign.

Pictorial Works

Goetzmann, William H. *Sam Chamberlain's Mexican War: The San Jacinto Museum of History Paintings*. Austin: Texas State Historical Association, 1993. The war through the eyes of a private who painted striking scenes of the war.

Kendall, George W., and Carl Nebel. *The War Between the United States and Mexico, Illustrated*. Austin: Texas State Historical Association, 1994. Reprint of beautifully illustrated nineteenth-century history of the war.

Sandweiss, Martha A., Rick Stewart, and Ben W. Huseman. *Eyewitness to War: Prints and Daguerreotypes of the Mexican War, 1846–1848*. Fort Worth, TX: Amon Carter Museum of Western Art. Washington, DC: Smithsonian Institution Press, 1989. Definitive work on the contemporary illustrations of the war.

Reference Works

Beck, Warren. *Historical Atlas of the American West*. Norman: University of Oklahoma Press, 1989. Excellent resource for maps and text explaining the historical geography of the American West.

Byrnes, Mark E. *James K. Polk: A Biographical Companion*. Santa Barbara, CA: ABC-CLIO, 2001. Contains documents and selection of encyclopedia-like entries related to Polk's life.

Crawford, Mark., ed. *Encyclopedia of the Mexican-American War*. David S. Heidler and Jeanne T. Heidler, consulting editors. Santa Barbara: ABC-CLIO, 1999. Good, short reference.

Frazier, Donald S., ed. *The United States and Mexico at War: Nineteenth-Century Expansionism and Conflict*. New York: Macmillan Reference USA, 1998. Reference that puts Mexican-American War in perspective of American expansion.

Hatch, Thom, ed. *Encyclopedia of the Alamo and the Texas Revolution*. Jefferson, NC: McFarland, 1999. Good reference on some of the causes of the Mexican-American War.

Heitman, Francis B., comp. *Historical Register and Dictionary of the United States Army*. 2 vols. Washington, DC: GPO, 1903. Most complete source on U.S. officers who served in the Mexican-American War.

Moseley, Edward H. *Historical Dictionary of the United States-Mexican War*. Lanham, MD: Scarecrow Press, 1997. Good reference to begin research on the war.

Shrader, Charles R., ed. *Reference Guide to United States Military History*. 5 vols. New York: Facts on File, 1993. Volume 2 looks at Mexican-American War.

Wexler, Alan, ed. *Atlas of Westward Expansion*. New York: Facts on File, 1995. Looks at western expansion through maps from colonial period through the nineteenth century.

Results

Griswold del Castillo, Richard. *The Treaty of Guadalupe Hidalgo: A Legacy of Conflict*. Norman: University of Oklahoma Press, 1990. Analyzes the treaty's impact on Hispanic Americans.

Morrison, Michael A. *Slavery and the American West: The Eclipse of Manifest Destiny and the Coming of the Civil War.* Chapel Hill: University of North Carolina, 1997. Examines the evolution of political debate on western expansion over the issue of slavery.

Nevins, Allan. *Ordeal of the Union: Fruits of Manifest Destiny, 1847–1852.* New York: Charles Scribner's Sons, 1975. Readable look at the results of American expansion in the first half of the nineteenth century.

St. Patrick's Battalion

Hogan, Michael. *Irish Soldiers of Mexico.* Guadalajara, Mexico: Fondo Editorial Universitario, 1997. Points to anti-Catholicism as motivation for many deserters and demonstrates that many soldiers fought bravely.

Miller, Robert R. *Shamrock and Sword: The Saint Patrick's Battalion in the U.S.-Mexican War.* Norman: University of Oklahoma Press, 1989. Solid look at motivations and actions of American deserters.

Stevens, Peter F. *The Rogue's March: John Riley and the St. Patrick's Battalion.* Washington, DC: Brassey's, 1999. Argues that nativism pushed Irish Americans to desert the U.S. Army.

Texas

Adams, Ephraim Douglass. *British Interests and Activities in Texas, 1838–1846.* Gloucester, MA: P. Smith, 1963. Lectures given in early twentieth century on this topic.

Bannon, John Francis. *The Spanish Borderlands Frontier, 1513–1821.* Albuquerque: University of New Mexico Press, 1974. Emphasis on development of Mexico through its independence.

Barr, Alwyn. *Black Texans: A History of African Americans in Texas, 1528–1995.* Norman: University of Oklahoma Press, 1996. Traces black experience in Texas from colonial exploration to American frontier settlement.

Chipman, Donald E. *Spanish Texas, 1519–1821.* Austin: University of Texas Press, 1992. Comprehensive look at Spanish dominion over Texas.

Fehrenbach, T. R. *Lone Star: A History of Texas and the Texans.* New York: Macmillan, 1968. Well-written narrative of Texas history.

Hardin, Stephen L. *Texian Iliad: A Military History of the Texas Revolution, 1835–1836.* Austin: University of Texas Press, 1994. Exhaustively researched analysis of the military events of the Texas Revolution.

Keating, Bern. *An Illustrated History of the Texas Rangers.* Chicago: Rand McNally, 1975. As title would indicate, well-illustrated but also well-written history of the Rangers.

Lack, Paul D. *The Texas Revolutionary Experience: A Political and Social History, 1835–1836*. College Station: Texas A&M University Press, 1992. Looks at the background of the revolution and then analyzes the different groups involved.

Merk, Frederick. *Slavery and the Annexation of Texas*. New York: Alfred A. Knopf, 1972. Puts race at the center of annexation debates.

Nackman, Mark E. *A Nation Within a Nation: The Rise of Texas Nationalism*. Port Washington, NY: Kennikat, 1975. Author emphasizes its leaders in this look at Texas history from Mexican independence to the Civil War.

Nance, Joseph Milton. *After San Jacinto: The Texas-Mexican Frontier, 1836–1841*. Austin: University of Texas Press, 1963. Account of border difficulties between the Republic of Texas and Mexico.

———. *Attack and Counter Attack: The Texas-Mexican Frontier, 1842*. Austin: University of Texas Press, 1964. Texas-Mexico relations on the eve of statehood.

Nofi, Albert A. *The Alamo and the Texas War of Independence, September 30, 1835 to April 21, 1836: Heroes, Myths, and History*. Conshohocken, PA: 1992. Objective look at the war with an emphasis on the Alamo and the myths surrounding it.

Richardson, Rupert Noval. *Texas: The Lone Star State*. Englewood Cliffs, NJ: Prentice-Hall, 1981. Revised edition, 2000. Comprehensive textbook of the history of Texas.

Siegel, Stanley. *A Political History of the Texas Republic, 1836–1845*. Austin: University of Texas Press, 1956. An intimate look at the personal differences within the Texas government.

Tijerina, Andres. *Tejanos and Texas Under the Mexican Flag, 1821–1836*. College Station: Texas A&M University Press, 1994. An examination of the diversity of views of Mexican Texans before independence.

Tinkle, Lon. *13 Days to Glory: The Siege of the Alamo*. College Station: Texas A&M University Press, 1996. Fast-paced account of the siege.

Utley, Robert M. *The First Century of the Texas Rangers*. New York: Oxford University Press, 2002. Balanced look at this controversial group.

Vigness, David M. *The Revolutionary Decades: The Saga of Texas, 1810–1836*. Austin, TX: Steck-Vaughn, 1965. Background to American settlement of Texas and account of the revolution.

Web Sites

http://www.pbs.org/kera/usmexicanwar
Site dedicated to providing materials to supplement the PBS documentary on the war.

http://www.army.mil/cmh-pg/
Good source for information on army's participation, maintained by the U.S. Army Center for Military History.

http://cdl.library.cornell.edu/moa/
Cornell University's Making of America site. Great place to locate sources for research and view digitized sources.

http://www.sfmuseum.org/hist6/muzzey.html
Sources on the war in California.

http://www.tsha.utexas.edu/handbook/online/articles/view/MM/qdm2.html
Good overview of the war.

http://www.militarymuseum.org/History%20Mex%wpWar.html
Primary sources on the war in California.

http://www.dmwv.org/mexwar/mexwar1.htm
Good collection of documents on site maintained by the Descendents of Mexican War Veterans.

http://www.library.ci.corpus-christi.tx.us/MexicanWar/indexmexwar.htm
Good collection of pictures, biographies, newspaper articles, and letters.

INDEX

About the Authors

DAVID S. HEIDLER is a renowned award-winning historian on the faculty of Colorado State University, Pueblo. He is co-author with Jeanne T. Heidler of *Encyclopedia of the American Civil War: A Political, Social and Military History*; *Encyclopedia of the War of 1812*; *Encyclopedia of the Mexican-American War*; *Manifest Destiny*; *The War of 1812*; *Daily Life in the Early American Republic, 1790–1820*; and *Old Hickory's War: Andrew Jackson and the Quest for Empire*.

JEANNE T. HEIDLER is Professor of History at the United States Air Force Academy. Along with David S. Heidler she is the co-author of *Encyclopedia of the American Civil War: A Political, Social and Military History*; *Encyclopedia of the Mexican-American War*; *Encyclopedia of the War of 1812*; *Manifest Destiny*; *The War of 1812*; and *Old Hickory's War: Andrew Jackson and the Quest for Empire*.